# UNDER WATER

# UNDER WATER

## HOW OUR AMERICAN DREAM OF HOMEOWNERSHIP BECAME A NIGHTMARE

RYAN DEZEMBER

THOMAS DUNNE BOOKS
NEW YORK

First published in the United States by Thomas Dunne Books, an imprint of St. Martin's Publishing Group



www.thomasdunnebooks.com
www.stmartins.com

Designed by Devan Norman

Library of Congress Cataloging-in-Publication Data

Names: Dezember, Ryan, author.
Title: Underwater : how our American dream of homeownership became a nightmare / Ryan Dezember.
Description: First edition. | New York : Thomas Dunne Books, 2020. | Includes bibliographical references and index.
Identifiers: LCCN 2020010745 | ISBN 9781250241801 (hardcover) | ISBN 9781250241818 (ebook)
Subjects: LCSH: Homeowners—United States. | Homeowners—Alabama. | Housing—United States—Finance. | Mortgage loans—United States. | Housing—Prices—United States. | Real estate investment—United States.
Classification: LCC HD7287.82.U6 D49 2020 | DDC 333.33/80973—dc23
LC record available at https://lccn.loc.gov/2020010745



First Edition: 2020

10 9 8 7 6 5 4 3 2 1

*To Mom, Dad, Ashley, Justine, Grandma and Grandpa, Grandma and Grandpa, and the Grandpa that I never got to meet.*

# CONTENTS

## PART I

1. THIS IS THE ONE 3
2. THE CONDO GAME 9
3. "THEY NEVER SING SONGS ABOUT A PILE OF RENT RECEIPTS" 23
4. SWIM WITH THE DOLPHINS 33
5. THE BEACH PAC 40
6. TROUBLE ON MONKEY ISLAND 52
7. "LIKE WORKING AT WENDY'S" 60
8. FLIPPED 65
9. WANNA BUY A BRIDGE? 75
10. "THERE'S A MILLION DOLLARS TO BE MADE HERE" 81

## PART II

11. INTERESTONLY™ 95
12. OVER THE HEDGE 101
13. "WE'VE HAD QUITE A FEW PEOPLE WALK AWAY" 107
14. SYSTEM ERROR 112
15. "THE WHOLE CAPER WAS OVER" 117
16. STREETS WHERE NOBODY LIVES 126
17. BUYER'S REMORSE 136
18. THE SPILL 144

## PART III

19. FOR RENT 155
20. MEET YOUR NEW LANDLORD 166
21. JOANIE 175
22. FOR SALE 183
23. WALKING AWAY 190
24. FROM THREE HOUSES TO FOUR 200
25. COMPANY TOWN 206
26. CUT DOWN 226
27. EPILOGUE 234

NOTES 241
INDEX 265

# PART I

# 1

## THIS IS THE ONE

After looking at several houses along Alabama's Gulf Coast, my new wife and I decided the sunny cottage on Audubon Drive in Foley was the one—so long as the seller came down a little on the $145,000 asking price.

There were two bedrooms, two bathrooms, an attached garage, a tidy shed that was painted picnic-table red, and a pair of towering longleaf pines. It sat in an oval subdivision of cookie-cutter homes on a lot roughly the size of a basketball court. There was just enough room for the dog to run in the backyard without trampling the vegetable garden that we envisioned. It was convenient to my newspaper office in Foley's antique downtown and to the elementary school in Gulf Shores where my wife taught kindergarten in a trailer parked outside of the overcrowded elementary school.

The beaches along the Gulf of Mexico were a short drive from the house but far enough away that we didn't have to buy flood insurance. Just built and bland as an egg inside and out, it offered a blank canvas with years to go before we could expect major repairs such as a new furnace or roof. I replaced the tacky ceiling fans and planted bushes in my head as we looked around. The real estate agent walked us over to see the neighborhood playground.

A week before Thanksgiving in 2005, we signed papers to buy the house for $137,500. We painted the walls and hung blinds in time to have friends over for the holiday.

Twelve years later, little about my life remained the same. I'd left the Mobile newspaper to take a job at *The Wall Street Journal*. I was no longer married. Pierre, the dog, had died of old age. But I was still sending mortgage payments each month to a bank in Alabama.

I would have sold the house long ago, and in fact I tried. But when the U.S. housing market collapsed in 2007, the property's value fell far below the amount I had borrowed to buy it. Walking away was never an option. I'd signed papers promising to pay the money back and I intended to do so one way or another. In case my moral compass ever needed a shake, laws in Alabama, as in many states, allow lenders to pursue the difference between the mortgage debt on a property and what it fetches in a foreclosure sale. For much of the next decade, that number kept growing. At one point, it would have been nearly $70,000. That was more than half of what we'd borrowed to buy the place.

When I bought the house, I was a newlywed three years out of college who believed I had achieved a signature goal of most young Americans. Instead, I set myself up to pursue an inverted version of the American dream. Most young people aspire to buy their first home. I spent a decade trying to get rid of mine.

Looking back, I find it bemusing that I was ensnared despite being a newspaper reporter who had made a career writing about the frenzied and doomed real estate market along Alabama's beaches. I knew in the moment that the speculative paroxysm was superlative, even in the context of the national mania for real estate. I never doubted that it would end poorly. I thought I was at the zoo, though, watching some wild behavior from behind a barricade. As it happened, I was standing in the middle of the jungle.

In 2007, the worst economic disaster since the Great Depression roared to life. The collapse of the U.S. housing market wiped out some $11 trillion in household wealth and wreaked havoc on Wall Street. It sank household-name financial institutions Lehman Brothers, Bear Stearns, and Merrill Lynch. The mortgage industry became a ward of the state, and an unprecedented taxpayer bailout was needed to stop the nation's banks from bleeding out. Almost eight million people would lose homes to foreclosure. At its depths, more than twelve million Americans were "underwater," meaning their homes were worth less than the balances remaining on their mortgages. Some estimates put the number north of fifteen million.

The collapse pounded Alabama's Gulf Coast, where an anything-goes building boom gave way to an economic malaise prolonged by hurricanes, the Deepwater Horizon oil spill, and the opioid epidemic. In Audubon Place, my subdivision of starter homes, close to a third of the 109 houses were foreclosed. One of them twice.

Among underwater homeowners, I was fortunate. The house was modest and so was the mortgage. I was in the early stages of my career, with greater earnings potential ahead. And I was single again, not yet thirty, and had no children to support. Millions of homeowners moored to underwater properties had it worse, suffering in ways more subtle than those who lost houses. Many of these homeowners couldn't relocate for better jobs, move growing families into bigger houses, or enroll their children in better schools—or at least do so without draining savings. They couldn't tap home equity to pay for their children's college tuition or cover emergency health expenses. They probably couldn't refinance their homes to take advantage of interest rates that were kept historically low in response to the collapse.

People my age and a few years older were hit especially hard. We started off strong when it came to homeownership. By our tenth high school reunion, people born in the 1970s, of which I was at the tail end, owned homes at a rate of 42 percent, according to a demographic study by John Burns Real Estate Consulting. We were comfortably ahead of our predecessors at the same age. When their ten-year reunions rolled around, people born in the 1950s and 1960s owned homes at rates of 37 and 35 percent, respectively. But by our twentieth class reunions, once the dust had settled from the housing collapse, we had fallen way behind. Our homeownership rate at age thirty-eight was 52 percent, compared with 61 percent for Americans born in the 1950s and 63 percent among those born in the 1960s. I'm right on trend. A homeowner at twenty-eight, a renter (without qualm) at thirty-eight.

John Burns, whose eponymous consultancy advises home builders, Wall Street investors, and Fortune 500 companies on matters demographic and housing related, calls our cohort neither Gen X nor millennial. We are the Foreclosure Generation.

Regardless of whether we actually had our homes repossessed, the crisis and the forces that delivered it have shaped our approach and strained our access to homeownership. The dislocation has been a drag on builders, brokers, and even tree farmers, not to mention the aging baby boomers who are counting on us to come along and buy them out of their big suburban houses. Yet for some plucky entrepreneurs and deep-pocketed investors, the housing crash presented a once-in-a-lifetime opportunity to stake a claim to the world's largest asset class: U.S. single-family homes.

Some of the newer clients that Burns counsels are companies that own and manage tens of thousands of tidy suburban rental homes. Such businesses didn't exist a decade ago. Their conception required two tectonic forces: the foreclosure crisis, which gave them the chance to gain critical mass on the cheap; and a leap in cloud computing and mobile technology that enabled them to orchestrate one of history's great land grabs and efficiently manage the far-flung properties thereafter.

Today these firms, launched at the depths of the crash by many of the world's largest property investors, own something like three hundred thousand homes and counting. Some rental executives say single companies will be capable of managing pools that are multiples of that. With modern technology and a ruthless efficiency rarely displayed by the mom-and-pop types who long dominated the rental-home business, these companies have built a highly profitable industry so hungry for houses that the hunt has expanded from foreclosure auctions onto the open market. In many cases the big rental operations aren't waiting for houses to hit the market. They're building new ones in cities all over the South and in the West expressly to rent.

Their typical tenant is my age, earning about what I earn. From there we diverge. The rental-home companies' customers almost always have children, which makes apartments and urban settings less appealing. They prefer good suburban school districts at just about any cost. They're also usually too mired in debt to muster a down payment, too insecure in their employment to commit to a thirty-year mortgage. Sometimes both. And so they rent what a decade earlier they would have bought.

We're just the leading edge of postcrash America. There are tens of millions of millennials coming of age behind us buried in even more student debt, knowing full well that home prices can fall, and, thus far at least, not generally wedded to the notion of ownership. The rental companies' executives, as well as their investors, are giddy with the idea of high-earning, cash-poor, sharing-economy-steeped millennials making babies and alighting to the suburbs in search of nice schools and granite countertops.

Many of these young adults will appreciate that they can live in a well-maintained, family-sized suburban home and send their children to good public schools without committing to decades of mortgage payments, tying up their savings in down payments, or risking entrapment in another market collapse. By renting, though, they forsake the method through which most Americans build wealth.

Last decade's housing crisis threatens a more lasting and far-reaching impact on American society than other historic market meltdowns because the previous crashes have generally been in the stock market and share prices mostly affect the rich. The behavior of voters and consumers might be swayed by the direction of stock prices, but most people don't own much in the way of equities. When the masses suffer following a stock market crash, it's usually because of the knock-on effects of recession, such as job loss or lessened access to credit, not because their tech stocks lost 40 percent. The housing crash, on the other hand, delivered a direct hit to the middle class, widening the wealth gap in America.

Home-price appreciation has historically been how Americans achieve financial prosperity. A recent study of consumer survey data from the University of Michigan going back to the late 1940s found that rising home values fueled the surge in middle-class wealth after World War II. Unlike stocks and bonds, ownership of which is concentrated at the top, houses are widely held. Roughly half of housing wealth is owned by America's middle class, according to the researchers at Germany's University of Bonn who wrote the paper.

The other thing about stock busts is that unless you happen to be a hedge fund or some other big asset manager that's borrowed money to buy securities, shares fall only to zero. Houses, because they're such heavily leveraged purchases, can put buyers so far into the red when they lose value that it can take far more cash to extricate themselves from the debt than was needed to buy their houses in the first place. That's what happened to me when I plunged as deep as $70,000 in the hole on a house for which I had put up only a few thousand dollars of the $137,500 purchase price.

By early 2017, my situation began to brighten. I had been renting the house at a loss to help cover expenses while waiting for the market to rebound. Every so often I'd scan local listings and sales data to see how far I had to climb. Performing this routine one day that February, I saw a rental ad for a nearly identical house down the street listed for much less than what I was charging. My tenants saw the ad, too. They asked the company that managed both rentals if they could break their lease with me to move to the cheaper place.

To most landlords, this would have been a bad break. But in my upside-down situation, it was welcome news. Home prices in the subdivision had not fully recovered from the crash, but they had crept higher. Meanwhile, years of mortgage payments had worn down the balance of my debt. With my tenants on their way out, I had a chance to try to sell the house.

A real estate agent in Alabama with whom I had been consulting said that if I fixed the house up and put it on the market in spring, when buyers were out and the yard was in bloom, I might be able to get $115,000 for it. That was $22,500 less than I'd paid, but it would be enough to wipe out the mortgage debt and cover most of the sale expenses. At the end of March I took a week off work, packed a rental car with tools and a sleeping bag, and headed south.

# 2

## THE CONDO GAME

Alabama's beaches are among the most alluring in America. They are made of tiny bits of Appalachian quartz, glistening mountain dander that washed down to the Gulf of Mexico on glacial melt after the last Ice Age. The sand is sugar white and so fine that it squeaks underfoot. The shoreline's contour perpetually changes. The sand flows east from Mobile Bay toward Florida, conveyed by the current. In unspoiled places, the sand piles up around a gangly variety of live oak that spends its existence buried to the crown in hot sand, racing the accumulation toward the sun. The tops of sand live oak can create dunes taller than houses, and yet the trees never look like much more than a shrub from the ground level. Around them, sea oats sprout in a symbiotic relationship with a species of mouse endemic to Alabama's beaches. The effect can be Nebraska-by-the-Sea. The blue surf, gentle except during storms, is warm enough for swimming nearly year-round. Beyond the dunes, the coast is leafy with palms, longleaf pine, centuries-old live oak dripping with Spanish moss, and magnolias that squeeze out flowers as big and white as softballs.

Until fairly recently, most of Alabama's beaches were virgin. No one really had any use for them. They broil in the summer and they're crummy for farming. The city of Orange Beach, one of two municipalities on the Gulf between Mobile Bay and the Florida line, owes its name to a frostbit attempt long ago to grow citrus. The sandy vistas were uneasy to reach from all but a few regional cities. Foley, a Mayberry-type town to the north, was the end of the rail line. In the 1930s, the Army Corps of Engineers cut a ship lane along the coast as part of the Intracoastal Waterway, separating a spit of sand from Alabama's mainland.

For decades, locals scratched out a living fishing and running small motels and restaurants that catered to weekenders from Mobile and airmen on leave from the navy base across the state line in Pensacola. It wasn't until the notion of investment properties took root, in the early 1980s, that there was much in the way of development. Even then it came slowly, in speculative fits and bursts over the next two decades. By 2003, though, when I arrived and the national housing market was roaring into overdrive, developers were really making up for lost time.

Everything south of the Intracoastal Waterway was branded Pleasure Island. The low-paying and seasonal tourism jobs went mostly to high school students, people bused in from poorer neighborhoods across the bay in Mobile, and eastern European exchange students who arrived for their summer abroad shocked to find themselves in a summerlong indentured servitude flipping burgers and taking tickets while sleeping—in shifts and on air mattresses—a dozen to a house miles from the beach. Locals of working age usually made money one way or another from real estate sales and development.

They were mortgage brokers, builders, title agents, lawyers, landscapers, property managers, and countertop installers. Even the farmers north of the beach were in on it. They grew acres of sod that was sliced, rolled up like big earthy pastries, and trucked off to building sites and golf courses. Condominium developers and a cadre of übersuccessful Realtors occupied the social apex. Chief among them was a man named Bob Shallow.

In less than an hour one morning in early 2003, Shallow sold all sixty-six units in a twenty-six-story condo tower that was planned for a surf-side plot in Gulf Shores, Orange Beach's neighbor to the west. The condos fetched between $350,000 and $440,000 apiece even though they existed only on paper and wouldn't be ready to occupy for at least another sixteen months. Shallow had arranged the whole thing, buying out the owners of the existing low-rise complex and then selling the Gulf-front property to developers who would build the tower. Shallow's feat of salesmanship was mentioned in a Sunday real estate column of the *Mobile Register,* the newspaper I had moved south to join. It merited three sentences sandwiched between blurbs about a suburban shopping center changing hands and plans for a low-income housing project in Mobile, as if selling $28 million worth of nonexistent vacation properties in the time it takes to do a load of laundry was no big deal.

Slowed and slightly bowed by a bad back, Shallow wore a mustache and spoke at a sprint compared with the way most locals moseyed through sentences. He peppered his speech with light profanity and was startlingly blunt. "I like to cut to the chase, get to the point," he once told the *Register*'s real estate columnist. "I have no patience at all." He lived and worked with urgency. He liked reeling in big fish but loathed the quiet, waiting part of fishing. He was hooked on the feeling of accomplishment and said he felt physically ill when he went too many days without a sale. He swore that he could size up potential clients and know what they could afford within twenty or thirty seconds of meeting them. That usually meant skipping niceties and moving straight to the topic of money. Shallow seems unlikely to have ever blushed.

Like many other Realtors in town, Shallow advertised on billboards. But unlike those of his rivals, who posed in matching outfits amid sea oats or stood in the surf wearing suits, Shallow's signs featured just his contact information and knowing mug.

Most men in town drove big pickup trucks or sport utility vehicles. Though he might have actually needed a truck to tend to the bison and big-horned Ankole-Watusi cows he raised on a farm north of the beach. Shallow favored European luxury sedans. The dress code wasn't strict at Shallow's office. He cared more about how the employee parking lot looked, eyeing it to make sure the agents who worked for him were driving the right cars. Once, while addressing a gathering of Realtors from around the county, he said that the priority for any sales agent who wanted to amount to much was to buy a brand-new BMW, in white. That would show clients and the competition alike that they were not messing around.

You wouldn't find Shallow in city hall giving presentations to the planning commission, pleading with the city council to rezone property, or sucking up to the mayor. He left that to the developers and stayed in the background, working his golden Rolodex to find takers for all the condos that were being proposed. He was often seen in public. Some days all you had to do was look up.

For years he and his wife, Susan, who handles the books at his office, had a side gig in hot-air balloons. They had taken up the hobby after an enthralling family ride over Asheville, North Carolina, and spent many weekends traveling around the country to compete in balloon races. Bob was the top racer in Alabama and one of the highest ranked in the Southeast. A weekend's winnings might be $5,000. The paid expenses, roadblocks, and police escorts made him feel like a star. At home, the Shallows offered twice daily rides, an early morning flight and another in the evening. They'd wake at 3:30 A.M., check the weather, and, if conditions were right, call to wake their clients. They could take four in the basket at once. At $150 a head, it was a $600 payday before breakfast. They could nap a bit before the 5:00 P.M. ride.

When he became a RE/MAX agent, he had a balloon custom-made with the logo of the real estate brokerage so that on many mornings up in the sky just north of beach, there was Bob Shallow floating around in a faithful re-creation of one of the firm's advertisements. The Shallows also offered instruction to aspiring balloonists and had a hot-air balloon dealership. A natural salesman, Shallow was as good with balloons as he was with condos. He ranked among the world's busiest dealers ten years running.

Shallow had arrived in south Alabama at the dawn of the condo era, in 1981. He had been a dairy farmer in New Hampshire but was drawn to real estate at the beach. Hurricane Frederic had ripped through two years earlier, plowing away stick-built beach cabins and musty old motels. Industrious locals seized the opportunity afforded by stretches of newly empty beach—and insurance money—to build low-rise condominium buildings, which multiplied the amount of profit that could be made per waterfront lot compared with houses. "Every soybean farmer, anybody who could swing a hammer, could get a loan," Shallow told me. "Money, thanks to the savings and loans, was very easy to acquire and we had a liberal system with the good-old-boy stuff. So a lot of buildings went up. I mean a huge amount of buildings were built in 1980, 1981 and 1982."

Then the market crashed. The savings and loan associations that had fueled the boom with profligate lending imploded. Double-digit interest rates and proposals to eliminate the deductibility of mortgage interest on second homes kept demand for Alabama beach condos below the supply of new units. Shallow kept at it, though, hustling to sell houses and $95,000 condos on the beach. He bought a Coldwell Banker franchise and by 1984 he was selling more than a hundred houses a year. In 1985, he took out an ad in a regional real estate magazine describing himself as Baldwin County's number one agent, with $10 million in sales. The Baldwin County Association of Realtors called and scolded him. He could not run ads like that.

"Why not?" he asked.

The board didn't believe that he had sold so much and ordered him to appear at a hearing. "They had five of these grumpy little brokers from the Eastern Shore that I called the underachievers. All these fat little guys that sell four or five deals a year and manage ten agents and are broke all the time. You drive in and they've got these little twenty-year-old rusted-out cars and shit in the parking lot. I'm going, 'Oh, God.'"

The fat little guys on the board admonished Shallow for false advertising, and when they were done talking he pulled out sales records that he had brought with him and began tallying up his deals. He had sold 125 houses. The transactions amounted to nearly $12 million. The doubtful porkers were silenced.

In 1987, the market collapsed again. Prices plunged by as much as half along the beach, where properties had been bought as investments rather than primary residences. Foreclosures mounted, sending prices into a tailspin. Even prudent condo owners who had put 20 percent down were in a pickle. Units that had sold for $150,000 a year earlier appraised for half that. Someone who had paid 20 percent, or $30,000, up front might still have to come up with $45,000 just to get rid of their condo.

Mortgage companies listed in the local phone book were absent from the next year's edition. The more than 150 real estate companies shriveled to about 60. "Everybody was upside down. It was horrible," Shallow said. "The only way I survived was sucking up to all the bankers and selling foreclosures."

He took loan officers to lunch and cozied up to them in bars after work, hoping to win listings of repossessed properties. When Shallow learned that a mortgage insurer had foreclosed on fourteen units in an Orange Beach complex, he called a man in Tampa who worked for the insurance company and asked if he could list them. He was rebuffed. Instead of hanging up, Shallow mentioned that he had once lived in Tampa. That started a short conversation in which he learned that the insurance executive had plans to golf with two other men the next morning. Shallow wished him well, hung up, and dialed the airline.

He arrived at the golf course in Tampa early the next morning, palmed the clubhouse attendant a twenty and asked to be added to the next threesome. The mortgage insurance man and his buddies arrived at the clubhouse puffing cigars and joshing around. They obliged the attendant's request to add a fourth to their group. The round was half over before the mortgage insurance man with the repossessed condos figured out that Shallow was the Alabama real estate agent who had called the day before. He got a kick out of Shallow's chutzpah and invited him to lunch. Cocktails followed. Soon Shallow found himself in the insurance office signing listing agreements. Even better, Shallow had talked the guy into financing buyers.

Lenders were skittish after the crash, but Shallow felt he could find buyers if he could arrange loans for them. Cutting out banks also eliminated the risk that some persnickety appraiser might scuttle sales if he or she didn't think the condos were worth what buyers were willing to pay. Shallow put together other deals like that along the beach, unloading properties for builders who were stuck with unsold condos and desperate enough to dangle financing to buyers. He sold whole buildings' worth of condos and realized that a lot of money could be made in a crash. "Everybody else cries and gets out of the way," he said.

In 1991, Shallow paid another agent $10,000 for the file on a south Florida investment group that was moving up the Gulf Coast buying properties to serve as locations for its Surf Style beachwear shops. Shallow heard the rival agent was having a hard time with the Florida investors, so Shallow scribbled out a check and was handed a folder with their phone number. They proved to be lucrative clients willing to commit to deals in an instant. Right off the bat he arranged a $700,000 sale to them of some property at the Gulf Shores public beach. His commission was 10 percent, repaying his $10,000 gamble seven times over. When a commercial property across the street hit the market, Shallow called them and they agreed to pay the $1.8 million asking price on the spot. Shallow suggested they start with a lower offer, but the Florida men told him not to haggle. Nothing around had ever sold for so much.

In the mid-1990s, Shallow took over a local RE/MAX franchise. Condo prices had pushed comfortably into the six-figure range and builders had moved on from stucco-and-wood structures to concrete, which they poured into broad surfside towers. The prospect of vanishing tax breaks and high interest rates were faint memories. Borrowing costs had been lowered in response to the savings-and-loan crisis and the 1987 stock market crash.

Shallow was enlisted to sell condos in a huge high-rise resort that developers were planning out on the Fort Morgan peninsula, a finger of land that juts out thirty miles across the mouth of Mobile Bay. The Beach Club was the first development of its kind on Alabama's beaches, combining luxury condominiums, restaurants, and a spa.

Shallow sold ninety units the first week the condos were offered, some $14 million worth of real estate, with nothing but a brochure. Those sales gave lenders comfort, and ground was broken on the $200 million resort. A couple of years later, over toward the Florida line on Perdido Key, a developer named Larry Wireman proposed Caribe Resort. The four glassy condo towers would be even ritzier than the Beach Club. Shallow was tapped to sell Caribe as well.

The condos in the first Caribe tower were priced between $275,000 and

$450,000. A model unit was set up on the property to show off the granite countertops, custom cabinetry, stainless-steel appliances, and whirlpool tubs that would come in each condo. It also showcased a stunning setting where Perdido Bay drained into the Gulf of Mexico. Shallow had most of the condos sold before crews started sinking the tower's hundreds of huge concrete pilings into the bedrock beneath the property.

By 2002, Shallow was one of the top-selling RE/MAX agents in the world. He sold $126 million worth of real estate that year. The next year, he and the other agents in the three small RE/MAX offices he owned notched nearly half a billion in sales.

There are only about thirty-two miles of Gulf-front land between Mobile Bay and the Florida line, and much of it is taken up by the Bon Secour National Wildlife Refuge, state parks, and municipal beaches that are off-limits to construction. It was hard to fathom where Shallow and his crew were finding enough condominiums and houses to rack up nearly half a billion dollars of sales in a year. Certainly not with all the competition he seemed to have around town.

I grew up around the real estate business. My mother and both of her parents worked as agents when I was a child in Ohio. I fueled a baseball card habit with quarters they paid me to stuff mailers and lick envelopes. I did homework in the microfiche room at their office while whoever picked me up from school studied home listings and sales records. My earliest recollection of my mother cursing was when we would drive past a house with a FOR SALE BY OWNER sign in the yard and she would mutter, "Damn fsbo," over the lost opportunity for a listing. I was sometimes called on to keep a client's children occupied. That entailed outings such as a Cleveland Indians game, at which I attempted to explain what was happening on the field to a baffled Saudi boy about my age while my grandfather talked the boy's physician father through options in the suburbs.

Selling real estate was hard work for infrequent paydays. My mother would sometimes work with clients for months, dropping whatever she was doing to facilitate a showing or write up an offer, and wind up with nothing to show for the trouble. Panicked clients rang the phone at all hours. They were faced with some of the biggest decisions they would ever make, and it was not uncommon for them to lose their composure. One guy got so wound up that we had to change our home phone number. It could be months between paychecks. Selling a million dollars' worth of houses in a year was a big feat in the suburbs around Cleveland. Agents who achieved the milestone had special yard signs that touted their membership in the "Million Dollar Club" and got stars around their headshot in newspaper ads.

A standard 6 percent commission on the $28 million worth of nonexistent condos that Bob Shallow sold in less than an hour that January morning in 2003 is more than $1.6 million. Shallow was in a different Million Dollar Club from the one with which I was familiar.

Key to his success was the Dolphin Club, a coterie of wealthy real estate investors that he had cultivated. They were speculators for whom he bought and sold condo units—usually before they were even built—as if they were stocks or bonds. Under Shallow's tutelage, the Dolphin Club flipped condos like crazy. Shallow's eye-popping sales numbers weren't derived just from selling a lot of condos: he was selling many of the same condos over and over.

In order to get a construction loan, and sometimes even the cash to complete land acquisitions, developers needed to presell a certain number of the condos they planned to build. Doing so assures lenders that there is sufficient demand for the proposed building and that construction loans are likely to be repaid. Developers didn't need the full sales amount up front, but they required preconstruction buyers to sign purchase contracts and put up a 20 percent down payment. As with the Beach Club, all Shallow and his rivals needed to sell preconstruction condos was a nice, colorful brochure and an option on some property. Sometimes they didn't need even that. Prices were rising so fast at the Beach Club and Caribe as condos were flipped to waves of speculators that many buyers needed just a few numbers before they'd sign a purchase contract.

Within four years of the first Caribe preconstruction sales, prices doubled. Units that sold for $240,000 in the first tower were fetching nearly $550,000 by the time Shallow began selling them in the third building. One twenty-one-hundred-square-foot unit sold for $480,000. That was two buyers and four months after it was first sold by the developer for $295,000. Another unit at the resort shot to $735,000 from $399,000 in less than two years. It wasn't unusual for Caribe units to change hands four or five times as the towers were going up.

Prices followed a similar trajectory at the Beach Club. Two men from Traverse City, Michigan, closed on a fifteenth-floor condo there for $250,000. They signed it over the same day to a St. Louis couple for $282,400. Two deals later, the condo was sold again to a Georgia couple who paid $554,100.

When Shallow told his agents at a sales meeting that they were going to sell condos in the proposed Island Tower for around $420,000 apiece, they reacted as if he were joking. But when the time came to open the bidding in Island Tower, there were more than three offers for each of the sixty-six units. They sold so fast that the developer, the Surf Style group from south Florida, sent him back to buyers to tell them that the price would actually be $10,000 more per unit.

It wasn't long after Shallow sold the Island Tower condos that many of them were back on the market. A little over a year later, those units were selling for more than $700,000 apiece, even though the tower was still many months from completion. Word of the easy money spread and soon there were more people wanting to buy condos to flip than there were condos. Sales agents ached for condos to sell. One agent likened listing a Gulf-front unit to throwing meat into a pool of piranhas.

To feed the flippers, developers were frantically making way for new construction along the beach. Houses were being moved off the beach with regularity. Usually they were loaded onto trucks. Sometimes, when they were along canals or the back bays, they were plucked from their pilings by cranes, plopped onto barges, and floated away. One local lawyer had an entire condominium complex moved. His client, a local firm called Joe Raley Builders, had bought out everyone in the two-story complex and planned to build a luxury tower called Oceania.

The lawyer hired a company that specialized in moving industrial equipment and bought a lot across the beach road where he planned to stand the old structures on new pilings and renovate the units. The buildings weighed five hundred thousand pounds apiece. It was a days-long process to lower them gently from their pilings and onto a joystick-controlled bed with forty-eight wheels, which inched the structures across the street.

The old buildings were supported by concrete beams and had survived four hurricanes, but they were no match for rising real estate prices along the beach. They weren't ready for the landfill, but they were deemed unworthy of the Gulf-front property on which they sat. Surfside lots were bid up to as much as $40,000 per foot of shoreline. It took a lot of condos stacked on top of one another to cover land costs like that.

One group of developers had paid $20 million for a decades-old motel in Gulf Shores and were bashing away at it with wrecking balls to make way for an eighteen-story condo tower. The developers planned 251 residential units in the tower, a nod to the local telephone area code. They named the project Lighthouse Condominiums after the Lighthouse Motel, which dump trucks were lined up to haul away as soon as the crane operators finished walloping the old place to pieces.

Sales agents bragged that there were more than three buyers lined up for every one of the units, never mind that the property was just a heap of rubble. The Lighthouse developers announced plans to build another tower just like it a little ways down the beach. They paid $14.3 million for an old Holiday Inn and borrowed $55.5 million from a pair of banks to tear it down and build a condo tower called San Carlos. Like it's lookalike the Lighthouse, San Carlos was a hit, a nineteen-story bucket of chum for the flippers. Rick Phillips, one of the developers, told the *Register*'s real estate writer that he had a list of 650 people pining for the 142 units.

When Shallow wanted to get sales rolling on a proposed building, he would dial up members of the Dolphin Club. These were calculating investors who acted without the emotion typically involved in home purchases. "They make decisions based on an equation," Shallow said. "They don't care what the flooring is, they don't really care if there's an icemaker, they don't look at the plans. They're able to make a half-million-dollar deal on the phone in five minutes. All they need to know is price, square footage, and location within the building."

One of Shallow's flippers was a Pittsburgh steel executive. He had seen Shallow's name and telephone number posted at a construction site while he was vacationing in Gulf Shores. Before long, he and his wife had bought a lagoon-front condo that they kept as a retreat and were trading in unbuilt units along the beach. He said he trusted Shallow to bring them the right deals. "If he called me up and told me I need to do this, I'm in," he said.

The steel executive and a few friends with whom he invested had moved money out of the stock market after the dot.com bust and into real estate. They bought several condos and sold most of them before construction was complete. That was the ideal outcome, to flip the unit to someone else before it was finished so you wouldn't have to actually ever pay for it. "We don't want to own anything," he said. "We're happy with a positive return, to keep the money rolling forward."

Realtors boasted that the condo deals they peddled outperformed stocks even as shares were bouncing back from the tech bust. The S&P 500 index gained 29 percent in 2003. That was chump change compared with what could be made along the beach in much less time. Even the older condos that Shallow had worked months to sell a decade earlier for $95,000 were fetching nearly $400,000. Part of the appeal of these older units was the chance to be there when a developer with more ambitious plans for the property came along. That often entailed a big check and the rights to a condo in the new building. It was akin to getting in on a hot stock offering. "It's like when the NASDAQ was going crazy and you couldn't lose," the Pittsburgh businessman told me. In advertisements, one local firm urged those with "$100,000 or a million to invest" to consider Gulf-front real estate, "an investment you can touch and even live in—try that on Wall Street!"

In reality, it took much less than $1 million, or even $100,000, to get in on the action. For many, it cost nothing at all.

Though developers required 20 percent down payments to show lenders that there was ample demand for their buildings, they didn't actually need it in cash. A letter of credit from a bank sufficed. Lenders were eager to vouch for flippers' creditworthiness for a fee, usually around 1 percent of the IOU amount for each year that it stood valid. Good banking customers could get the fee waived altogether. They could obtain the rights to resell yet-to-be-built condominiums without a penny of their own at risk.

Say a preconstruction condo buyer had to pay the 1 percent annual fee, though. And say the buyer signed a contract to purchase a $500,000 condo in a preconstruction offering. A 20 percent down payment would be $100,000. So it would cost $1,000 to control the condo for a year. As hot as the market was, that was plenty of time to find another buyer. If someone agreed to pay $600,000 for the under-construction condo, the result would be a profit of $99,000, a heady return even after taxes and sales commissions were subtracted. Strings of preconstruction buyers would sometimes close their deals all at once, cash flowing like a waterfall from the end buyer who got the keys down to the original speculator who bought from the developer. Shallow would walk clients through an example in which $2,400 became $240,000.

Real estate is unique in that sense. Unless you're a Wall Street investment firm, you'd be laughed out if you walked into a bank and asked to borrow money to buy stocks or bonds. But because of government policies intended to spur homeownership among Americans and Wall Street's hunger for home loans that could be bundled into securities and sold to investors, banks happily facilitate speculative real estate bets.

The fountain of easy money alarmed some around town. Occasionally someone would invoke the empty buildings and bankruptcies during the savings-and-loan crisis. The condo game relied on there being someone—a retired chemical engineer from Louisiana, say, or a Birmingham banker—who wanted the keys to the condos once they were built and had the wherewithal to pay for them at their inflated postflip prices. Yet the instant riches to be made flipping condos were seductive. Everyone in town could do the math: the 6 percent sales commissions thrown off by the $497 million of sales from Shallow's office in 2003 amounted to roughly $30 million in pay for the agents involved. Shallow himself was responsible for nearly $100 million of sales that year, which would put his commission between $3 million and $6 million, depending on how often he worked for both the buyer and the seller in a deal. That was ballplayer money, not real estate agent money.

Developers could do even better. Larry Wireman, whose Caribe Resort on Perdido Pass had been such a hit, dreamed up something even more ambitious down the beach to the west. He proposed replacing a row of old beach houses with a pair of luxurious twenty-seven-story towers called Turquoise Place. The condos would start at an unheard-of $1.2 million. Before he could pump the preconstruction units into the frothy market, though, he had to convince enough Orange Beach City Council members—four, to be exact—to let him blow through the long-standing fourteen-story-building height limit. If he could, the financial rewards could be tremendous: tens of millions of dollars, maybe more.

# 3

## "THEY NEVER SING SONGS ABOUT A PILE OF RENT RECEIPTS"

Even with the benefit of hindsight, it's hard to say why I bought a house. It certainly wasn't just because I wanted to paint and plant a bunch of bushes.

I was twenty-five, with a fun job writing for the newspaper about the exploits of Bob Shallow and Larry Wireman, and I was newly married. Buying a house seemed like the logical next move, a rite of passage to full adulthood. It's more or less what our parents had done and theirs before that. I didn't buy a house explicitly to make money, as many did at the time. If anything, I was worried about home prices climbing beyond our reach. But that's really just another way of acting on a speculator's faith that prices were headed higher.

In hindsight, I had an alarmingly nonchalant approach to big decisions as well as a failure of imagination when it came to the potential downsides of buying a house. I blame the latter on my good fortune. By virtue of when, where, and to whom I was born, I'd never known bad times.

When I bought the house, rents were rising and borrowing costs were low. Owning also came with benefits, such as the ability to deduct mortgage interest and property taxes from our income taxes. We couldn't write off the rent of the ho-hum apartment we were leasing in a sun-baked complex behind the high school and a twenty-four-hour Walmart. The cost of maintaining a house and the possibility of repairs meant we'd have to watch our spending more closely, but it wouldn't be a strain. I had grown up working in my parents' hardware store. I knew a lot about home improvement and enjoyed it. Plus, the cottage was so small that there was only so much house to keep up. I had student debt, but it was manageable. There was no sense putting life on hold until after what projected as more than a decade of college loan payments. We were climbing the pay scales at work, adding to our cushion each year.

There wasn't really any reason to doubt that when the time came to buy a bigger house or move for new jobs, we would sell our little cottage near the beach. We'd probably even come away with a little cash to put toward our next home. That's what Americans had been doing for decades. Plus, swinging open the back door to let Pierre out into the yard sure beat saddling him up for a half-hearted walk around the apartment block first thing every morning.

Yet there was more that compelled me to buy a house: I was acculturated to do it.

Clifford Edward Clark, Jr., a college professor who in 1986 wrote a history of the American home, said he set out to understand why middle-class people like him spent so much time and energy remodeling their houses in small towns and suburbs. "Why were these homes, which seemed so similar, treasured as symbols of independence and personal identity?" he wrote in the *The American Family Home.*

Homeownership has been an American ambition from the onset. Alexis de Tocqueville, the Frenchman who traipsed through early America to describe the new democratic society for his European audience, cast the family home as the young nation's stabilizing force. Whereas Europeans of the time liked to escape their troubles at home by going out and stirring trouble, he wrote, the American withdrew from "the turmoil of public life into the bosom of his family." The family home seemed to instill in

Americans a love of order, which carried over into public life. Yet as much as Americans relished their homes, they had little trouble parting with them, Tocqueville noted. In French, he wrote something that translates roughly to, "An American will build a house in which to pass his old age and sell it before the roof is on."

By the time Tocqueville made that observation, in the 1830s, Americans had developed a rich tradition of real estate speculation. Benjamin Franklin, a successful property investor, took time in his autobiography to mention an encounter he once had with an old man around the time the founding father opened his print shop in Philadelphia. The city was already on the skids, the old man complained. Given the decay, he wouldn't even buy a house, let alone commercial property, as Ben Franklin had. He harped on Franklin for buying into a rising market that he was sure would crash. Franklin got the last laugh when the old man finally caved and bought property. "At last," Franklin snickered, "I had the pleasure of seeing him give five times as much for one as he might have bought it for when he first began his croaking."

Even in those early expansive days, real estate was no sure bet. Take Franklin's own father: when Josiah Franklin's heirs sold his four-unit Boston property in 1754, they received about 40 percent less than the patriarch paid for it in 1712.

Soon after Tocqueville's tour, housing in America was forever changed thanks to a Chicago lumberyard owner who developed what became known as the balloon-frame home, which standardized construction with two-by-four-inch wooden studs. Not having to rely on huge hand-hewn timbers dramatically reduced the cost and time needed to build houses.

In colonial America, the English love for the countryside prevailed over the Dutch preference for compact city living. As settlement barreled westward and transit systems allowed workers to live beyond a walk from work, more and more property became suitable for housing. Speculators built toll roads into the wilderness and trolley lines to the suburban communities that were springing up outside of cities. Tolls and fares were usually secondary to the profits transit tycoons could make speculating on land along their lines. Beside the obvious draw of escaping the squalid, crowded tenements and high costs of inner-city rents, Americans felt a sort of divine invitation to homeownership that, for most people, was achievable only if they really spread out.

Walt Whitman, the poet and essayist, captured the prevailing view on homeownership in an 1856 newspaper article about the downsides of living scrunched up in New York City. "A man is not a whole and complete man unless he owns a house and the ground it stands on," he wrote. "Men are created owners of the earth. Each was intended to possess his piece of it; and however the modifications of civilized life have covered this truth, or changed the present phase of it, it is still indicated by the universal instinctive desire for landed property, and by the fuller sense of independent manhood which comes from the possession of it."

(Perhaps buying my house had more to do with a deep-down urge to paint and plant bushes than I knew.)

There were people who disagreed with Whitman, naturally. The German philosopher Friedrich Engels, who helped Karl Marx frame communism, argued in the 1880s that to give factory workers their own houses was to effectively bind them to the land. The Industrial Revolution was supposed to have freed them from such bondage. How could laborers resist wage cuts at the factory if they had a house—let alone mortgage payments—to worry about? "The individual worker might be able to sell his house on occasion, but during a big strike or a general industrial crisis all the houses belonging to the affected workers would have to come onto the market for sale and would therefore find no purchasers or be sold off far below their cost price," Engels wrote. Early feminists didn't see the isolated domesticity of suburban housewives as a great step forward for women either.

These arguments were dismissed in the United States. Social control was sort of the point, after all. Pennsylvania Railroad executives preferred that employees owned their homes because then they couldn't really afford to strike. Willard Phillips, a nineteenth-century political economist, reasoned that homeownership gave individuals a stake in society. If the masses felt invested in the economy, he said, they'd be less likely to look upon it as "an inhabitant of a conquered territory looks upon a citadel of the conquerors.

"Give him hope, give him the chances of providing for his family, of laying up a store for his old age, of commanding some cheap comfort or luxury, upon which he sets his heart; and he will voluntarily and cheerfully submit to privations and hardships," Phillips said.

Privations be damned, homeownership became the norm as well as the prevailing manner in which Americans built wealth. Homeowners would be free from rent once they paid off their houses, which usually happened in a few years back then, not decades like today. As long as properties were kept in good repair, they would likely gain value. Whatever hurdles to homeownership hadn't been overcome by cheap land, transit, and balloon-frame construction, government policy began to address. Although it was a tax break not widely used for decades, Congress made mortgage interest deductible in 1913. Lending restrictions were loosened during World War I to juice home building.

"To possess one's own home is the hope and ambition of almost every individual in our country, whether he lives in a hotel, apartment, or tenement," President Herbert Hoover said in a 1931 address. "Those immortal ballads, Home, Sweet Home; My Old Kentucky Home; and The Little Gray Home in the West, were not written about tenements or apartments . . . they never sing songs about a pile of rent receipts."

By the 1940s, homeownership was basically a war cry. About a year into World War II, President Franklin D. Roosevelt sent a note to be read at a bankers' conference in Chicago on housing. "A nation of homeowners, of people who own a real share in their own land, is unconquerable," he wrote. The savings bank chiefs, whose specialty was home loans, resolved in turn to buy as many war bonds as they could afford.

When the war ended, soldiers returned home, started families, and the baby boom began. Homes were in short supply. Residential construction had collapsed during the Great Depression, when more than half of all mortgages defaulted. After Japan bombed Pearl Harbor, everyone was so busy with the war effort that there weren't many people available to build houses. Materials went to the war, too. Families doubled up in dwellings meant for one. Thousands of people lived in Quonset huts, a sort of prefabricated lean-to with an arched sheet of galvanized steel for a roof. Old trolley cars were sold as homes in Chicago. In North Dakota, people moved into grain bins. The war did, however, prepare some of the key builders who would address the paucity of housing.

Del Webb, whose eponymous subdivisions are still being built, cut his teeth—and began amassing his fortune—building Japanese internment camps during the war. He turned to residential construction around Phoenix when the fighting ended. Outside of New York City, a home builder named William Levitt used what he learned constructing barracks and war-worker housing and applied it to a swath of Long Island that he turned into a town. Levitt's crews were organized as though they were on an assembly line. They pieced together no-nonsense Cape Cods by the thousand in Levittown. "No man who owns his own house and lot can be a communist," Levitt once quipped. "He has too much to do."

Taxpayer-funded highways extended the range over which Americans could reside without exceeding the hour a day spent going to and from work that has shaped the boundaries of cities and civilizations for centuries and is named the Marchetti Constant, after the Italian physicist who popularized the idea. Broad swaths of cheap land were suddenly within commuting distance. Simple, inexpensive homes like those in Levittown swelled suburbs around the country.

The Federal Housing Administration, Veterans Administration, and Federal National Mortgage Association—an entity created in response to the Great Depression that is better known as Fannie Mae—greatly boosted the availability of credit by guaranteeing home loans against default. Most of them, anyway. Federal regulators drew lines around areas populated by minorities and refused to back home loans within the boundaries, a segregationist practice that came to be known as redlining and was eventually outlawed. Though sections of America were left out, the government guarantees gave lenders huge territories where they could write home loans with little risk. Down payment requirements plunged from what had historically been half or more of a home's appraised value. Interest rates declined. A decades-long boom in homeownership and home prices ensued.

By the time I was born, in 1980, to the proud new owners of a small postwar Cape Cod in a woodsy beach town in suburban Cleveland, nearly two-thirds of Americans were homeowners. They had taken on more than $1 trillion of mortgage debt to get there. But that was nothing compared with what was coming.

In 1978, a bond trader named Lewis Ranieri was assigned to the nascent mortgage desk at the venerable Wall Street investment firm Salomon Brothers. The housing market was never the same. Ranieri was one of the "fat guy" mortgage traders who engaged in the trading floor feeding frenzies with sacks of cheeseburgers and tubs of guacamole portrayed by Michael Lewis in his chucklesome Wall Street tell-all *Liar's Poker.* Ranieri, a loudmouthed Brooklynite who had worked his way up from the mailroom, helped investors around the world channel trillions of dollars into U.S. housing.

Historically, most mortgages were kept on the books of the savings banks that lent the money to the homeowner in the first place—think the Bailey Brothers' Building and Loan in *It's a Wonderful Life.* There wasn't much of a secondary market for mortgages. Individual home loans were unwieldy to trade, too small for big investors to justify the effort of vetting, and prone to being paid off early when homeowners died, moved, or refinanced. Ranieri and his colleagues at Salomon figured out how to pool similar mortgages in order to smooth the risks associated with each individual home loan and create a security substantial enough to entice big investors. Rather than expect each investor to pore over the individual mortgage documents, analyzing each property's characteristics and every borrower's finances, Salomon Brothers convinced credit-rating firms to vouch for the quality of the underlying loans just as they graded the creditworthiness of companies and cities that sold debt.

In 1979, Federal Reserve chairman Paul Volcker boosted interest rates in a move to rein in the era's runaway inflation. Short-term rates shot up. The savings banks that dominated home lending suddenly had to pay more to depositors than they were getting back from the interest paid on the thirty-year mortgages they'd made. The spigot of new home loans shut off. A lot of that $1 trillion worth of mortgage debt was suddenly for sale as savings and loan associations unloaded loans at fire-sale prices in order to stay afloat. Many were unable to manage and went out of business.

While most retreated from the mortgage market, Ranieri doubled down, hiring other institutions' laid-off traders and research analysts and buying all the mortgages he could find to bundle into bonds. In 1981, the federal government bailed out the savings and loan industry by allowing them to sell their mortgages at a loss, spread the loss out over many years for tax purposes, and steer the sale proceeds to higher-yielding investments such as construction loans or even another thrift's jettisoned mortgages. A trading frenzy erupted. Thrifts were often at the mercy of Salomon Brothers, though, which was more or less the only game in town. The firm printed money by shuttling piles of mortgages from one savings and loan to another. Ranieri had also loaded up on lobbyists in Washington, D.C., and eventually got rules changed to remove restrictions on selling mortgage-backed securities.

Mortgage-backed securities were a big hit with investors. There was little reason to be pessimistic about American home prices. They had been climbing for decades. And even if there was some economic shock that led to defaults, the debts were more or less guaranteed by the U.S. government, explicitly in the case of the Government National Mortgage Association (aka Ginnie Mae) and implicitly by Fannie Mae and the Federal Home Loan Mortgage Corporation (nicknamed Freddie Mac). With mortgages, the mantra on Wall Street went, it was a question not of *if* you'd get paid but of *when*.

At Ranieri's behest, Congress allowed big investors such as pension funds, insurance companies, and banks to start buying mortgages that failed to conform to the underwriting standards of the government-sponsored guarantors. Ranieri's grip on the mortgage-backed securities market eventually loosened as his competitors on Wall Street found ways into the lucrative and rapidly expanding trade.

The government, meanwhile, undertook initiatives to boost homeownership. The First-time Homebuyer Affordability Act of 1999 allowed funds to be withdrawn from retirement accounts, such as a 401(k), and put toward down payments. The next year, Congress passed a law that allowed low-income Americans to stockpile government rental assistance so that they could make down payments on houses. There was a rise in what's known as seller's assistance, in which the home price is inflated and the seller returns cash to the buyer as a gift for the purpose of being used as a down payment.

The administration of President Bill Clinton in 1994 convened the National Partners in Homeownership, which brought together bankers, builders, mortgage companies, real estate agents, and their regulators with orders to push homeownership to new highs. The group aimed to do this by "making homeownership more affordable, expanding creative financing, simplifying the home buying process, reducing transaction costs, changing conventional methods of design and building less expensive houses, among other means."

It worked. Within a few years, the homeownership rate topped the old high that was reached back in 1980. This feat was not without cost, though. Debt soared. Consumers became accustomed to spending more than they earned. The personal savings rate turned negative for the first time since the 1950s. The debt-to-income ratio per household shot to nearly 85 percent in 2000, up from about 64 percent in 1980.

For decades, most home buyers had been asked to put down around 20 percent of a home's value in order to get a mortgage. That number was shrinking. By 1999, more than half of mortgages had down payments of less than 10 percent. That had been the threshold for loans that Fannie and Freddie would buy on the secondary market. But the loan guarantors went lower with the market, accepting 5 percent down, then 3 percent, and finally, in many cases, zero.

The same low interest rates that were making home buying more attractive were also driving investors to seek out riskier investments to boost their returns. To meet the needs of aspiring homeowners and yield-starved investors alike, lenders lowered their standards. Mortgages to borrowers with iffy credit were known as Alt-A loans. Those extended to buyers with bad credit were called subprime. Speculators often took out regular old thirty-year mortgages, sometimes several of them at once, even if they intended to measure their ownership tenures in months.

In the past, lenders would likely be stuck holding their own dodgy home loans, worrying about whether the buyers would actually make the payments. The market for mortgage-backed securities enabled them to unload risky loans to the government-sponsored guarantors as well as eager buyers in the booming market for privately issued mortgage bonds that Ranieri and others on Wall Street had whipped up. Lenders were paid now to originate loans; collecting on them each month was someone else's problem.

In the new century, a lot of people who wouldn't have qualified for a mortgage before were now able to buy houses. For many Americans, it wasn't enough to own just one house. The emergence of millions of new house hunters nudged the homeownership rate past 69 percent, pushed up home prices, and made mortgage-backed securities even more attractive. That in turn increased the amount of money that investors made available to home buyers.

Rising home prices, falling interest rates, and the rich fees that could be earned making home loans and bundling them for investors created ripe conditions for homeowners to pull cash out of their homes by refinancing at higher values or taking on second mortgages. In 2000, $460 billion worth of refinance loans were written. In 2003, with interest rates lower by about a quarter, the volume of refinance loans rose sixfold, to a value of $2.8 trillion.

By 2004, nearly every corner of the country had flipped into a real estate tizzy. Builders held lotteries to winnow the buyers for tract homes that hadn't been built yet in the deserts outside Phoenix, Las Vegas, and Los Angeles. In south Alabama, people lined up outside the doors of real estate offices hoping to plunk down $10,000 deposits for nonexistent condominiums planned along a shipping channel.

Across the country, average home prices were up more than 50 percent from a decade earlier. In particularly fevered markets, such as those in the Sun Belt, prices had risen a lot more than that. People like me who were looking mainly for affordable shelter a reasonable distance from the office seemed to have a choice: buy or be left behind.

# 4

## SWIM WITH THE DOLPHINS

As lucrative as 2003 had been, 2004 was shaping up to be even better for real estate interests at Alabama's beaches. Developers' ambitions grew. Prices soared. So did the rooflines. The condo fever spread north to the Intracoastal Waterway, where some truly audacious developments were drawn up.

Developers from Atlanta, northern Alabama, and Destin, Florida, came together and borrowed more than $20 million to buy about a thousand acres of pine woods along the Intracoastal Waterway in Gulf Shores. They announced that they would build a town within a town called Bon Secour Village. It was hard to keep up with all the features and amenities the developers would rattle off whenever they talked about the project. There would be an amphitheater, a medical center, a marina, one hundred thousand square feet of office space in buildings that wouldn't look out of place in Paris or Porto, grids of neat houses that would evoke the elegant districts of New Orleans, a hotel and conference center, shops, and residential buildings sitting flush at the edge of a boat basin. A Redneck Venice for the Redneck Riviera. A local community college abutted the northern property line, so the developers decided they'd build student housing up that way. "We think of ourselves as town founders," one of them told me. "Now that may seem a little corny, but we do see ourselves not as developers but as facilitators."

There was originally going to be a golf course, but after the town founders got a look around and realized how many golf courses there were already in the existing town, they doubled down on the Venetian theme. They proposed a canal system and water taxi service. Aside from a few weedy drainage ditches that pointed toward the Intracoastal Waterway, there were no canals on the property, but no one questioned them.

The developers enlisted an *en vogue* architect who was known for his pastel master-planned communities on the Florida Panhandle, including Seaside, where Jim Carrey's *The Truman Show* had been filmed. The watercolor renderings depicted an old-world port city on the north side of the ship channel. As the developers envisioned it, Bon Secour Village would cost more than $500 million to build and take many years to complete. They started digging out a boat basin and plotted an auction for the first batch of residential property: a few blocks of narrow single-family lots and a building full of $500,000 condos.

Bon Secour Village was just west of the Alabama 59 bridge over the Intracoastal Waterway. Up until a few years earlier, it was the only way across the canal. But now, a few miles east in Orange Beach, there was a new, privately owned toll bridge to Pleasure Island.

The Foley Beach Express toll bridge had opened to fanfare a few years earlier and was hailed as a much-needed second route to and from the beach. It also opened swaths of out-of-the-way and empty land, mostly sod farms and swampy woods, to development. Unlike neighboring Gulf Shores, Orange Beach was walled off by water from the expanses of undeveloped and unincorporated land north of the canal. There were miles of undisturbed waterfront across the back bays that could be developed just like the marina-lined bayous and coves in Orange Beach. The toll bridge gave Orange Beach a link to the mainland, even if it cost a couple of bucks to cross.

In 1996, then governor Fob James signed a law making it easier for developers to build private toll roads in Alabama. Soon his sons and a family friend with a road-building business emerged with plans for a short span over the Intracoastal Waterway and a four-lane thoroughfare up to Foley. They had agreements in hand to acquire rights-of-way from rural landowners along the route. The prospect of an expressway going through their land prompted nineteen of twenty landowners along the route to donate roadway to the cause. The only landowner that had to charge the governor's sons for the right-of-way was a land trust that wasn't legally allowed to give away acreage. During the waning days of his administration, in early 1999, Governor James signed a road construction deal between the state and the city of Foley and released $7.5 million in federal highway funding. The tax dollars extended the expressway north past all the congestion and traffic lights in Foley, which made the toll to cross his sons' bridge more palatable to drivers.

Tim James, the bridge project's leading brother, was worried about finding the $36 million it cost to build the bridge and start the expressway. The investment bankers they hired at Dillon, Read & Co. made a list of twenty-three potential financial backers. One after another, the investors passed on the Foley Beach Express. The recent track record for toll road investments had been poor. The bankers couldn't get anyone to look at the Orange Beach bridge.

It seemed like a risky deal given that drivers could use the expressway for free and then skirt the toll by driving three miles east along the waterway to the free-to-cross state-owned bridge. James wasn't worried about that, but he did lament not snapping up more property along the route while it was still cheap. By June 2000, when local dignitaries and the state highway director gathered to cut a ribbon and open the toll bridge, developers were already platting subdivisions for the old turf farms and land prices were soaring.

In 2004, Tim James approached city officials about helping to refinance the bridge debt. He and his partners offered to annex into Orange Beach their bridge and their land at the bridge's northern landing and to pay the city a royalty for every car that crossed the span for thirty years.

They really wanted a deal. So they added an option for taxpayers to buy the bridge after three decades or to just keep collecting royalties for another thirty years. After ten years, the city's cut per car would be thirty cents. During the first decade, the amount paid per car depended on annual traffic totals. The more cars, the higher the city's royalty rate.

Orange Beach would get twenty-one cents for each of the 2.1 million cars that crossed the bridge in 2003, or more than $440,000. But that payout would boom if the bridge builders' projection of 10 percent annual traffic growth came to pass. If 4 million cars crossed the bridge, the city would receive forty-six cents a pass.

The bridge builders wanted $12 million in return, payable in equal installments over ten years. A $1.2 million annual pledge from Orange Beach, with its excellent credit, would enable Tim James and his partners to refinance the $36 million they'd borrowed to build the bridge at about half the interest rate they were paying. Orange Beach was flush from all the building permits and sewer connection fees that developers were paying, but the city of fewer than five thousand full-time residents didn't have that kind of cash. The city council would have to borrow millions of dollars to hold up its end of the bargain.

Mayor Steve Russo, who ran a marina supply shop and filling station when he wasn't at city hall, favored the deal. He was sold on the bridge owners' spreadsheets. They showed the city making its money back during the deal's first decade. "None of it is supposed," he said.

Some of the city council members were apprehensive. Jerry Davidson, chronically sunburned from the sailboat excursions he guided in his day job, said he thought the traffic projections were solid. Yet he was wary of setting precedent. If the city cut a deal to help the bridge investors, other businesses were sure to come asking for their own financial aid.

It was also a puzzling position for the city, borrowing money just to turn around and lend it to someone else. Davidson came around, though. He broke a 3–3 tie in favor of a bridge deal. Six decades of toll royalties was a worthwhile investment, he decided. Plus, a toehold north of the Intracoastal Waterway would help Orange Beach in another deal.

The city itself was among the speculators that snapped up land along the expressway before the bridge was built. In 1999, Orange Beach paid $5 million for 144 acres at the bridge's northern landing, planting a flag and pushing the municipal border onto unclaimed waterfront.

The plans for Orange Beach RiverWalk were unveiled on a Monday night in March at city hall. Joe Raley Builders, the local construction firm, had agreed to buy the city's property and build an $85 million mixed-use development. There would be a marina, restaurants, nightclubs, about four football fields' worth of retail space, theaters, a hotel, a water park, and a go-kart facility. The main attraction would be a Gulf World Marine Park. It would have shark tanks, seals, and a swim-with-the-dolphins attraction ringed by grandstand seating and condominiums. Scott Raley, president of the family firm, wouldn't disclose the retail tenants but said he had a deal in hand with an art gallery and two small museums attached to on-theme restaurants. One would be dedicated to golf and the other to automobiles.

Rather than filling the wetlands, Raley proposed boardwalks through mushy parts of the property. He'd leave the trees and marsh and post bird sanctuary signs. There'd be a facility affiliated with the marine park to provide care for marine mammals wounded in the wild, the grazing manatees, whose odds of being minced by boat propellers were rising with each new marina that was built along the waterway.

Most of the condo buyers in coastal Alabama were retiring baby boomers. It was difficult to picture the sorts of buyers that RiverWalk's developers had in mind. The condos were a closet or two over seven hundred square feet, cost $250,000 a pop, and looked out onto a big pool where dolphins would be coaxed to jump through hoops before bleachers full of vacationers. The man-child that Tom Hanks plays in *Big* came to mind.

The RiverWalk plans were the only blueprints Orange Beach building officials ever saw with sea lion pens. City hall signed off. It was an election year and city leaders were eager to show some return on their $5 million investment in the property. RiverWalk also promised to boost Orange Beach's bridge investment by drawing beachgoers past the toll booths.

There were rival Florida Panhandle resorts to consider as well. Panama City Beach, 115 miles to the east, had a Gulf World Marine Park. With a marine park of its own, no prospective vacationer would cross Orange Beach from their list for a lack of dolphins to swim beside or a tank full of stingrays to poke. The council unanimously approved the plans. The developers promised RiverWalk would open for the summer of 2006.

Across the bridge from RiverWalk was a big wooded tract that had been bought by a mall builder from Birmingham named Alex Baker. He had the financial backing of American International Group, the insurance conglomerate known as AIG, and came forth with his own ambitious plans. In May, the mall builder teased AIG Baker's plans for a big mixed-use development called the Wharf. He gave an interview to the newspaper. There'd be a movie theater. Condo towers. More than seven hundred thousand square feet of retail space. An open-air concert venue. Three miles of boardwalk, and—God save the manatees—a marina with more than two hundred boat slips.

A few months later, Baker, a beefy man in shorts with big visions, came before the Orange Beach City Council. He wanted to build what they'd read about in the newspaper. He just needed help.

Baker wanted Orange Beach to rebate half of the sales and lodging taxes generated by the Wharf for as long as it took for him to recoup $25 million. That was basically what he'd spend building the boardwalk, installing sewers, and paving the 220-acre property.

He could just give all that to the city as part of the deal: $25 million worth of sewers, streets, and boardwalk. He'd still build the Wharf if the council demurred. But not to the full glory that he envisioned and had described in the Sunday edition.

"We would not do the amphitheater, we would not do the boardwalk, we would not do the public-access boating," Baker told a crowded city council meeting.

The council didn't need much convincing. The pine trees and wetlands on the property weren't producing sales or lodging taxes. There was nothing to lose in agreeing to give up half of whatever was made there. Half of something was more than all of nothing, one councilman argued. Tim James and the other toll bridge owners had given the city spreadsheets showing that if the Wharf was built as Baker intended, the additional traffic would add $25 million to $37 million of toll revenue to the city coffers. "If I may be presumptive," Baker said, turning to the standing room crowd, "I see this becoming the downtown of Orange Beach."

The way lofty development plans were stacking up along the canal, the waterway's banks seemed destined for a downtown skyline.

Tim James sought permission to build four residential towers on a slice of property at the northern landing of his toll bridge.

A founder of the Checkers fast-food chain had 285 acres along a bend in the canal and proposed a development called Waterdance with about a dozen residential buildings houseing more than three thousand condos.

Former Krispy Kreme Doughnuts chief executive Mac McAleer was flush with millions after selling shares of the doughnut company he had taken public. He bought a parcel beneath the bridge in Gulf Shores, dug a boat basin, and had condo plans drawn up.

A group from Florida paid $9 million for two dozen acres nearby and said they envisioned several high-rise residential structures.

# 5

## THE BEACH PAC

The prospect of all this construction had dollar signs rolling in the eyes of a lot of locals. Yet many others were appalled by all the ostentatious towers and sprawling tourist traps on the drawing board. The development promised to dramatically alter the area's character and do irreversible harm to the coastal environment. Alabama's beaches would not just look a lot different, be devoid of wildlife and more crowded with people, the price of living along them was rising as well.

Condominiums that hardly anyone in town could have afforded a few years earlier were being stacked to the clouds. Out-of-towners had shown up to build a faux French Quarter in the woods along the barge channel and were asking big-city prices for tiny lots within walking distances of huge swaths of vacant land. It didn't make any sense. An old man from Mobile paid nearly a million dollars for a shape-shifting, twelve-and-a-half-acre splotch of sand at the mouth of Perdido Pass and wanted to build thirty or so tiled roofed McMansions on it with docks instead of driveways.

Even the public beach in Gulf Shores, the center of gravity along Alabama's coast, was poised for a dramatic makeover. Bob Shallow's investor group from south Florida had bought out, to the tune of $20 million, a cluster of small businesses at the public beach in Gulf Shores. They planned residential towers and sidewalk cafés in place of an old motel, a costume jewelry shop, a daiquiri bar, and a dive that was popular with bikers. No one was going to miss the cruddy motel or a couple of places best known for fistfights, but it was a dizzying leap from that to glassy towers and cappuccinos.

This gold rush had grave ecological consequences, a reality not lost on the sensitive and science-minded segment of the population. Wetlands, the coast's kidneys, were filled in to support foundations. Orange Beach's sewer system was overwhelmed and overflowed during busy summer weekends. Sewerage installed by a lightly regulated private company in subdivisions beyond city limits routinely failed and fouled nearby creeks and bays. In one large and out-of-the-way subdivision upstream from Orange Beach, downpours resulted in sewage spraying from manhole covers in geysers of shower water and toilet flushings. Residents had to pick toilet paper out of their shrubs after heavy rains.

The dunes that fortified the shoreline were bulldozed, dooming taxpayers to the never-ending expense of what the civil engineers called "beach renourishment." The practice involved prospecting for ocean-bottom deposits of white quartz and pumping it ashore into plump, albeit unanchored, mounds at a cost of tens of millions of dollars every few years. The human-occupied stretches of Alabama's beaches had no room for the gnarly oaks that had evolved to serve as the shoreline's pilings. The civil engineers and public works directors always budgeted for mass plantings of sea oats to help hold the man-made berms in place, but without the nearly extinct Alabama beach mice around to nibble seeds and spread the oats in their scat, the plants usually didn't propagate fast enough to have much function beyond serving as a backdrop for family vacation photos.

The Alabama beach mouse and its rarer cousin, the Perdido Key beach mouse, became lightning rods. Environmentalists and locals in favor of limiting development sued the federal government to force a reconsideration of the endangered species' habitat and range, which if expanded would limit development. A new phase at the Beach Club on the Fort Morgan peninsula became entrapped and construction was delayed for years. In Orange Beach, a persistent rumor was that a particularly bold developer unwilling to risk losing property rights on account of a mouse became quite the cat lover, adopting several from the county animal shelter, and encouraged those in his employ to do the same—and then to let them loose in the dunes. The tale seemed true given the number of feral cats that roamed the western tip of Perdido Key, near Caribe, and the disheartening number of beach mice that U.S. Fish & Wildlife Service biologists could turn up. Biologists and environmental advocates argued that the beach mouse was a bellwether. Their extinction signaled the ecosystem's collapse. The argument for extermination put forth by developers and the lion's share of locals was this: It's a mouse.

Sea turtles wired to lay eggs on the very beaches from which they had hatched arrived at their natal grounds after decades at sea to find trampled vistas upon which there was too much human activity and the sand too compacted for them to nest. Many turtles faced with this dilemma aborted their eggs in the surf and turned away. The odds were against those eggs that were laid. Sea turtles hatch at night and scramble toward light the moment they burp from their sandy birth pits. For millennia, light had shown the way toward the sea, where the moon and stars reflected. Over more and more of Alabama's beaches, the brightest light beaconed hatchlings to pool decks and parking lots. Disoriented hatchlings would desiccate, be mauled by cats, or get run over by cars. Biologists and volunteers walked the beach looking for nests. They put stethoscopes to the sand, listening for activity. Once they heard the faint scratching that indicated birth was near, they sat up in shifts to turn around any turtles that raced off in the wrong direction.

During certain times of year, resort managers made groundskeepers start work early enough before vacationers awoke to have time to collect the songbirds that thudded into the towers en route to or from the Yucatán. Broken scarlet tanagers, painted buntings, a rainbow of warblers and rose-breasted grosbeak dotted the landscaping around the high-rises that had been erected in their migration path.

None of this is to argue that Gulf Shores and Orange Beach were on the cusp of losing their quaintness. They were far down the road to barrenness. When I arrived in April 2003, I was floored by the sudden skyline that emerged as I crossed the Intracoastal Waterway. A few weeks earlier, I had flown into Mobile to interview for a reporting job at south Alabama's daily newspaper. The *Register*'s managing editor, Dewey English, had responded to one of the dozens of letters I'd sent to newspapers around the country seeking work after I graduated from college. He left a message on my parents' answering machine in an intriguing drawl. He said the paper was looking for someone to write about Alabama's beaches.

I didn't even know Alabama had beaches. Nor did I have any specific reason for seeking employment on the Gulf Coast. I was up for adventure and eager to forge a writing career no matter where it took me. When Dewey English called, my job prospects were as bleak as the Cleveland winter I was shivering through. A paltry paper in nearby Lorain, Ohio, that made reporters share computers wouldn't budge on the $20,000 salary. I could sign on as a grunt with a Great Lakes barge crew and find out if my seasickness was curable. Or I could keep unloading trucks and waiting on customers at my parents' suburban hardware store, which had been my after-school occupation since I was thirteen or so.

The beaches were too far from the Mobile newsroom to visit when I came to town for my interview. But the weather was balmy by March, the *Register* was flush, had a writerly reputation, and from the moment I met him, I was dying to work for Dewey English. I accepted the posting sight unseen.

It took two days of driving in my shiny new Nissan Sentra, stuffed with books and clothes, to get from the shore of Lake Erie to the Gulf Coast. It was a straight shot south through Columbus, Cincinnati, Louisville, Nashville, Birmingham, and finally Montgomery. Two hours later I crossed into Baldwin County, where Alabama's beaches are located, and exited the interstate at a place called Perdido. There were no smartphones to guide me, no satellite maps to offer a look around. My road atlas wasn't detailed enough to be much use navigating from here.

Perdido, which means "lost" in Spanish, seemed like a put-on. The only thing to break the pitch black was a dingy Chevron station. I went inside and bought a county map.

Back in the car, I unfolded the map over the steering wheel and flicked on the dome light. There wasn't much on it: a small crosshatch every so often along the main north–south highway, Alabama 59, and shallow grids of streets along Mobile Bay to the west and the Gulf of Mexico to the south. There were a few patches of pale green to signify wildlife preserves and parks. But big sections of it were empty, just plain white. I'd never seen a road map with so little on it.

It turned out I had found the wrong Perdido. Perdido Bay, Perdido Pass, and Perdido Key, on the Gulf near the Florida border, were where I wanted to be. I was in plain old Perdido, a speck amid pine forest and pitcher plant bogs roughly ninety minutes north.

There wasn't much on the way to the beach. Stretches were astonishingly dark. Occasionally I could glimpse some ramshackle homestead set off the road flickering through neat rows of skinny pine trees. Signs of life emerged in Foley. A Winn-Dixie. A massive all-hours Walmart. An outlet mall. Farther south in Gulf Shores, the runway of a little airstrip was illuminated near a miniature golf course and a multistory go-kart track. At the top of the bridge over the canal, a wall of residential buildings came into view along the water's edge.

I drove until the highway ended at the Gulf Shores public beach. It was spring break and I met a rambunctious scene. My Nissan felt petite among pickup trucks mounted on oversize wheels. Huge rebel flags flapped behind some of them. Young women dressed for swimming were packed into the truck beds. Their bikinis bore the colors and logos of the Confederacy, Corona, and college football teams. The guys all had the same haircut, bangs combed flat down their foreheads a finger's width above their eyebrows. Hondas outfitted with spoilers and neon undercarriages rattled with bass. They circled the beach parking lot, peacocking.

I flipped through a free apartment finder guide outside a grocery store and was surprised not to find anything in the towers along the beach listed for rent. Most of the buildings had a proletariat apartment block look to them. I was curious who lived in them. Maybe no one. It wasn't that late, yet there weren't a lot of lights on inside the towers. It seemed too far to commute to Mobile for work each day, and at a glance it was hard to fathom how anyone might earn enough around town to afford oceanfront residences, even if they were just honeycombs in unsightly edifices. It seemed like the kind of place where everyone who isn't on vacation is employed catering to those who are.

More than any other grandiose development plans, it was Larry Wireman's proposal to swap a row of old beach houses with a pair of opulent skyscrapers that tore apart locals. Wireman was a midwestern businessman who had seeded his Alabama real estate pursuits with money he made working on the Trans-Alaska Pipeline. He started with a cluster of beach houses on Perdido Key and then moved to towers with Caribe. Wireman was flush with the resort's success and kept the condo game going with even higher stakes at Turquoise Place. Like Caribe, Turquoise Place would be painted white, wrapped in blue glass, and stand in sharp contrast to the other buildings along the beach, which tended toward boxy and beige. No expense would be spared in what he promised would be the finest pair of buildings on the southeastern seaboard.

Pledges of quality didn't stop Turquoise Place from becoming the breaking point for those uneasy with the jump from an out-of-the-way fishing village, where the dominant profession was charter captain, to a speculator-centric resort with some of the biggest buildings in the Southeast. This faction was troubled by all the deals that city officials were cutting with developers and put off by the magnitude of the construction boom. The thought of the traffic was enough to make some old-timers tremble. People who lived nearby calculated the hours that their homes would sit in the towers' shadows.

Yet for many residents, livelihoods were at stake, not to mention the town's tax base. There was perpetual concern about keeping up with the Florida Panhandle resorts with which Alabama's beaches competed for vacationers and second-home buyers. The pro-growth group accused the not-in-my-backyard crowd of being self-centered, of not wanting to share paradise.

In order to build twenty-seven-story stacks of residences on land zoned for single-family homes, Wireman needed the Orange Beach City Council to assign the property special zoning that would allow him to ignore a lot of rules, like the fourteen-story building height cap.

There was a lot to consider for the elected officials who had to decide on Turquoise Place. On one hand, there would be sewer connection fees paid to the city for each of the hundreds of units, municipal sales taxes levied on the building materials, as well as property and lodging taxes to be collected once the condos were built. Plus, the towers were objectively more stylish than the other buildings on the beach. Yet rezoning the property would set a precedent. It would be difficult to turn down other nonconforming towers.

The matter was the subject of several weeks of heated public debate until Wireman put forth an offer that city officials couldn't refuse. He would deed to the city a strip of Gulf-front property to serve as public beach access and also build a park on six acres across the highway. The property sat on a slender slip of water called Cotton Bayou, and he agreed to install a fishing pier and build a small firehouse up by the road. Most important, Wireman would resolve a thorny legal matter that had been hanging over city hall for years.

An extended family from a timber town ninety minutes to the north had been feuding with Orange Beach officials, whom they accused of plotting to drive down the value of their property by rebuffing its rezoning requests. The family alleged in a suit filed in Mobile's federal court that the mayor and others at city hall wanted to restrict what could be built on the property to keep the price low so that the city could buy the land itself and build a convention center on it. The family sued the city, seeking $40 million in damages. Wireman agreed to buy the land from them for $40 million, contingent upon his getting permission to build Turquoise Place. If that happened, the lawsuit would be moot and abandoned.

The city council voted 4–2 in favor of Turquoise Place. The resentment between the "for" and "against" factions grew in May when Wireman came back to the city council hoping to add two more towers to Turquoise Place and to build three stories higher. This time he had the neighbors on his side. Once the first two towers were approved, the owners of several beach houses to the west dropped the fight and decided to sell to Wireman. They pleaded with the city council and residents who had sided with them earlier against Wireman not to doom them to live in the shadows, to let them take the money—upward of $5 million apiece—and leave. City council members were sympathetic to the sellers' pleas and enticed by Wireman's offer of another twenty acres for the park across the street on Cotton Bayou. With the neighbors on board and the city council in hand, Wireman had one remaining obstacle to a four-tower Turquoise Place.

His old buddy Bob Shallow had bought the parcel right next to Turquoise Place and told Wireman that he would build an intentionally ramshackle burger joint and beach bar unless his asking price for the property was met. Shallow and Wireman had fallen out after making a fortune together at Caribe. Shallow went so far as to hire an architect to draw plans for a two-story haunt called Bob's Cabana and deliver the designs to city hall for review. The plans called for a big neon sign out in front that would flicker as if it were on the fritz, crackling like a bug zapper. Shallow admitted that it was "just to fuck with Larry." Yet the sincerity with which he pursued Bob's Cabana, going so far as to sit through a planning commission review of the designs, made it unclear how far he was willing to take the ruse. Rather than learn, Wireman gave Shallow keys to two condominiums at Caribe and some cash in exchange for the lot.

The angst among residents boiled up over the summer with the approach of the municipal elections in August. An enterprising man named Dean Young turned the rancor into a cottage industry.

Young was a conservative political operator who had moved to town and launched a political action committee called the Beach PAC. He was a Mississippi native who had made a name for himself as an angry and oft quoted attendee of antigay rallies in the 1990s. His notoriety grew when he helped vault a county judge in rural Alabama named Roy Moore to national fame as "the Ten Commandments Judge."

Young had created an organization called the Christian Family Association PAC and launched a website selling Ten Commandments memorabilia to raise money for Moore's defense in a widely publicized legal battle the judge was fighting with the American Civil Liberties Union. The ACLU objected to Moore leading jurors in pretrial prayers as well as to a homemade Ten Commandments plaque that he had hung in his north Alabama courtroom. A higher court ordered Moore to stop the prayers and remove the plaque. Rather than bow, Moore campaigned to become Alabama's chief justice.

Moore won the state's highest judicial position with Young playing a prominent role in the campaign. The two fell out when Young grew frustrated with how long it was taking Moore to make good on a campaign promise to put a Ten Commandments monument in the Alabama Judicial Building in Montgomery. Moore eventually installed a two-and-a-half-ton granite Ten Commandments monument in the lobby of the state's high court and had a velvet rope run around it so that no one could miss it. It looked like a big gravestone. A passerby might assume that some old titan of jurisprudence lay in state below. It was too late for Dean Young, though. He was already gone, bound for the beach.

In early 2004, Young filed paperwork with state election regulators to launch the Beach PAC. One of the forms he submitted had a space in which filers were asked to describe the political action committee's purpose. "To promote good government," he wrote in pinched print.

With the market as hot as it was, anyone could sell condos or houses near the beach. The key was winning approval to build enough of them to become filthy rich even after accounting for the exploding costs of property. All it would take to shut off the money party was for four out of six members of the city council to have unfavorable views toward the tract-by-tract rezoning of the city. Keeping friends on the council was crucial to developers, real estate agents, lenders, and everyone else with a stake in the game.

Young raised more than $100,000 from local real estate hotshots. Bob Shallow and one of his Florida investors, Shaul Zislin, gave to the Beach PAC. So did Larry Wireman. Daniel Sizemore, the founder and chief executive of Vision Bank, which lent to developers as well as flippers, was a donor. So were executives with Brett/Robinson, a firm that had been walling off Alabama's beaches with buff-colored condo towers since the late 1970s.

The Beach PAC paid nearly all of the money it raised to a political consulting business that Young owned. Some cash was paid to his teenage sons. Young promoted a slate of pro-development candidates led by incumbent mayor Steve Russo and waged a nasty campaign against their opponents.

A councilman named Brett Holk, who worked as an electrician and voted against most of the big developments, challenged Russo for the mayor's job. Holk was an earnest man with a knack for profound statements and mispronunciation. He was a man of the people and nearly as much a fish out of water on the council as I was in south Alabama.

We met when I introduced myself after the first council meeting I attended in my new job as a reporter for the *Register.* For the occasion I had bought a gray suit at the mall and was wearing it with a tie from TJ Maxx. He asked me why I was dressed like a lawyer. I told him I was the new reporter from the paper. He asked where I was from.

"Cleveland."

Holk cocked his head back to get a good look at me through the glasses at the end of his nose and asked, "Cleveland, Mississippi, or Cleveland, Tennessee?"

Holk himself, like many of the grown men on Pleasure Island, preferred to wear shorts to public functions. Even if he wasn't dressed for it, he took his duties deadly seriously. He carried his notes and meeting materials under his arm in a bundle and flipped through them as the council moved through their agendas of Safe Boating Week proclamations, liquor license renewals, budget requests from the recreation center, and nine-figure real estate development plans. Like the other council members, he was paid $10,000 a year for his trouble.

The group that got behind Holk was, like him, generally against high-rises and mega-developments. His supporters created an organization called Concerned Citizens of Orange Beach Inc. to raise money and get out the vote. They were badly outgunned by the Beach PAC, though. The Concerned Citizens were mostly retirees and raised money hosting bake sales and barbecues. They handed out photocopied leaflets outlining the positions of the candidates they supported to people who turned out for the free hot dogs.

Holk kicked off his candidacy with a fish fry at a small park in a neighborhood of old cottages. He greeted attendees and shook their hands. The closest he came to a speech was to announce to the mostly geriatric crowd that the fried mullet was ready to eat. With the developers' dollars, Young made chum of the Concerned Citizens.

Right away Young sicced the secretary of state on his opponents, insisting upon an investigation into the Concerned Citizen's cookouts. He claimed they were illegal fund-raising activities.

Young also drew up inflammatory ads for print, local television, and radio. One mailer sent to everyone in town teased Holk for once voting against spending that included mosquito spraying. The cards in everyone's mailboxes had a drawing of a giant mosquito wearing a Holk campaign button and attempting to suck the blood from a figure cowering under a bedsheet. Young wouldn't say whether he or one of his children had drawn the picture, but he was quite proud of it. Another mailer featured photos of union pickets and told residents they could expect similar scenes in Orange Beach if they elected to the city council a retired mill executive who had been a union official early in his career. There was phone polling in which the callers purported to be conducting anonymous surveys. Residents learned the polls were not anonymous when they received follow-up calls from pro-development candidates trying to convince them to change their minds.

Young was relentless and made a lot of people uneasy. He wore his hair buzzed and moved in a clenched march. Whether he was popping into a store at the outlet mall to pick out a new pair of shorts or heading into a planning commission meeting, he looked as if he were late for an appointment to punch someone in the face. When Holk ran a full-page ad in the *Register* criticizing developers' sponsorship of Russo, Young was incensed. He called me and fumed. The Beach PAC was not any developers' doing, he insisted. It was all his idea.

No one could really explain Young's arrival or his intense interest in the municipal election. One after another, the candidates whom Young supported with his campaign denied knowing much about him. Some even said, with little credibility, that they had no idea who he was. Yet they all expressed gratitude that they were not on his bad side and reported his advertising as in-kind contributions on their campaign finance disclosure forms. Larry Wireman had funneled tens of thousands of dollars to the Beach PAC through his girlfriend, and I asked him one night after a council meeting how he had settled on Young to support his allies in city hall. “I think Dean kind of picked us,” the developer said.

Russo was obviously pleased to have Young’s support. His campaign received cash from other real estate investors and he used some of that to hire his own political consultant, a man who normally worked statewide races. The mayor took every chance to chide Holk for his propensity to vote no. “This is a guy who voted ‘no’ to adjourning a meeting one night because he’s so used to having his name called and just voting ‘no,’” Russo said.

The mayor promised that if reelected, he’d keep squeezing parkland and cash from the developers, reduce taxes, and build another bridge so that Orange Beach could expand across the back bays.

Russo won reelection, outspending Holk two to one in what was by far the most expensive election in the city’s short history. The two mayoral candidates’ combined spending worked out to more than $30 for each of the 2,326 ballots that were cast. That was a lot for a $25,000-a-year job. But it was a high-yielding investment for real estate interests. The council positions were again split in a way that made the mayor’s vote crucial for developers to win zoning votes.

# 6

## TROUBLE ON MONKEY ISLAND

On September 2, 2004, a tropical wave off Cape Verde turned into a tropical depression. The storm strengthened as it moved west, and a few days later it was Hurricane Ivan. The storm bowled past Cuba, up through the Yucatán Channel, and into the Gulf of Mexico as a Category 5. It weakened a bit as it spun toward the coast, though meteorologists warned that Ivan was nonetheless of uncommon strength and likely to cause catastrophic damage. It was headed straight toward Alabama's beaches.

Alabama's governor, Bob Riley, ordered everyone living within about thirty miles of the coast to evacuate. My girlfriend, and future wife, had moved south earlier that year following her own college graduation. We packed up her car and she drove north to stay with friends. Being the newspaper's beach reporter meant that I was staying. I drove toward the shore against a stream of evacuating vacationers in sport utility vehicles with cooler chests and boogie boards banded to their rear bumpers.

Snarls of traffic spilled out of the gas stations. People were nailing plywood over windows and pushing carts piled with water jugs out of grocery stores. In the parking lot of the Alabama Gulf Coast Zoo, a sweaty man rolled a cage holding a slumped baboon into an Atlas Van Lines tractor trailer.

The nonprofit zoo had put out bulletins on local television stations the night before pleading for help evacuating its animals. The zoo was on a low-lying swamp-adjacent tract about a mile off the beach. The man carting the drugged ape was a trucker who lived over the state line in Pensacola. When he heard the call for help on the evening news, he enlisted his daughter, her husband, and a neighbor and drove his rig over from Florida first thing.

In the zoo's kitchen, keepers were injecting grapes with sedatives. The spiked fruit was going to be fed to the smaller monkeys to knock them out for the trip. For safety reasons, the keepers kept their destination a secret. The small zoo had just 268 inhabitants, yet moving even a modest menagerie turned out to be a huge challenge. Darting the larger primates, like Umba, the twelve-year-old baboon who was zonked out in the moving truck, was one of the initial steps.

It was important to take the primates first, and to do so stealthily, the zoo's director, Patti Hall, explained. Hall, a smoky-voiced redhead who was never seen in public without her zookeeper's vest, was narrating for a small film crew that was documenting the evacuation.

Everything had to seem stasis around the aviary. The birds went last. They are the natural world's emergency broadcasters. Once the birds got a sense that something was amiss, it would be impossible to get them to shut up.

"If they hear the birds screaming, then the monkeys will know something's up," Hall said.

That's why the keepers were doping grapes and moving furtively with the dart gun. Messing with an excited monkey was a good way to get bit. The last thing the keepers needed as they raced against Ivan was trouble on monkey island.

Once the primates, bears, a pair of Siberian tigers, two African lionesses, and a couple of cougars had been sedated and carted off, the keepers went for the birds. Sure enough, they burst into cacophony. The old pet parrots and parakeets cawed and howled. A few squawked "hello" over and over. From inside the dark moving truck, one kept shrieking, “Hey, darling!”

The keepers left behind boa constrictors, pythons, and other reptiles in their bunker-like building. The alligators stayed as well. They were native and would have to fend for themselves in the storm.

Hurricane Ivan made landfall overnight. I spent the night at the county emergency management bunker, which was packed with uneasy elected officials, fire chiefs, sheriff’s deputies, utilities executives, and public works directors. National Guard members paced about, waiting for the storm to pass so that they could take up posts at the beach. The bunker was squat and storm-proof, set in a clearing twenty-five miles north of the beach. A pair of giant antennae were braced by huge cables that criss-crossed high above.

The center of the bunker housed a control room, which was walled with computer monitors and weather maps. The innermost space was ringed by long rooms filled with bunk beds. Reporters on assignment were given an outer lobby in which to wait out the storm. It happened that my patch of floor placed my head right next to a snoring cameraman’s fragrant wet feet, so I spent most of the night just outside the bunker entrance, listening to the hurricane’s low roar and watching power transformers explode in the distance.

In the morning, the sky was blindingly clear. The air was cooler than it had been and drier. The storm had sucked up all the undesirable traits of late Alabama summer and carried them off. But it left behind astonishing wreckage. The air smelled powerfully of fresh-milled pine on account of all the trees that had been snapped by the wind. Broken power lines hung like tinsel. Unfamiliar insects that seemed to have blown in from the tropics fluttered around. The closer to the beach, the worse it got.

About a mile north of its actual terminus, there was a new filthy beach of bamboo that had been carried up from the Caribbean, decking lumber and garage contents, like gas cans and beach chairs. There were an unusual number of lightbulbs lying around unbroken, set gently atop the rest of the debris by the receding storm surge. Toward the beach waves crested in the roadway and a police officer puttered around on a Jet Ski.

Flounder dried on sidewalks. Over at the zoo, eels and sea bass were found stuck in tree branches. A few of the zoo's alligators, including one alarmingly large specimen, were unaccounted for.

Along the beach, stretches of highway were shattered like ice and covered with head-high sand drifts. Stick-built houses and small condo buildings had been reduced to heaps. Waves had blown through souvenir shops, and there were foam coolers and neon water noodles all over town. At first glance, a lot of the waterfront condo buildings didn't look too bad.

Two colleagues and I finagled our way down to the beach and were trying to call the newsroom back in Mobile to tell them what we found. The storm had downed overhead phone lines and toppled cell towers. A satellite phone the paper equipped us with was the only way to reach the photographers who awaited our instructions and our colleagues who sat in the *Register*'s generator-powered headquarters, ready to take dictation for the next day's paper. We walked toward the surf in Orange Beach, hoping that the finicky satellite phone would make a connection over the unobstructed ocean sky. We were huddled around the phone for a few seconds before I looked down the beach.

The Gulf had risen up and peeled away ocean-facing walls in buildings all along the beach. They looked like life-size dollhouses. Tile floors draped over the edge of upper floors as if they were rugs. What hadn't been ripped away remained eerily intact. A bed was still made in one room. In another we could see the condiments in a refrigerator door that swung ajar. Cupboards that had been cracked in half exposed glasses still neatly stacked. So much sand had been scoured away by the surge that in-ground pools lay atop the beach, cracked like eggshells five and ten feet tall. Smoke detectors and battery-powered alarm clocks chirped. There were boats on the roads and cars in the water.

The Bon Secour National Wildlife Refuge, some seven thousand pristine and wild acres out on the Fort Morgan peninsula, was trashed. There were drifts of storm debris the length of football fields left at the ocean's point of retreat. Chunks of houses and their contents had been blown out across the lagoon. The wreckage would have to be removed gingerly, so as not to further disturb the preserve's fragile habitats. It would take U.S. Fish & Wildlife Service workers months. The tops of huge dunes had been sheared off by the surge along the beach, exposing the defoliated and twisted middle sections of the anchoring oaks.

One big Mediterranean-style mansion vanished in Orange Beach. Some of its distinct and hefty roof tiles turned up about a half mile away in the state park. Other than that, the best anyone could figure was that it had all been sucked into the ocean. No one died along Alabama's beaches during Hurricane Ivan, but several people did just over the state line in Florida.

A week after the storm, I bumped along the busted-up beach highway in a military transport with Gulf Shores residents. The city was chauffeuring them to the beach so that they could see their homes, or at least what was left of them. It was a fitting ride.

The beach highway looked like a war zone. Search teams were still walking dogs through wrecked homes, spray-painting symbols on the doors once they were cleared. There were a lot of dangers yet. The zoo's alligators were still on the lam, venomous snakes were turning up in strange places, and power lines were submerged. Bulldozers buzzed about with loads of beach sand. A huge operation was launched to collect the sugar-white quartz from roads and private property and put it back on the beach. The sand was the big tourist draw, the place's claim to fame. It was worth a fortune. The bulldozers scooped it up and pushed it into big piles, where it was sifted for impurities and carted back toward the surf. The breeze stung.

As we rumbled past an intact house, a man sitting across from me pumped his arms and howled, "We have a home!" On the next block, a couple found their home ruined. The roadside wall was missing. We could see right into their bedroom. Their possessions looked as if they had been tossed around in a giant washing machine.

Dozens of houses were destroyed and more than a hundred multi-family buildings suffered significant, typically irreparable, damage. There were a lot of older people who wouldn't bother rebuilding. They'd take the insurance money and sell out to developers. There was nothing sentimental about a bunch of snapped pilings and rotting carpet.

I found a young couple that I knew digging their barbecue grill out of a four-foot drift. The duplex they rented across the street from the beach was already slated to be demolished to make way for a tower. Now they were going to have to find a new place a lot sooner than they had anticipated. They gathered salvageable possessions—a plastic laundry basket, fishing poles, toiletries—and used dresser drawers as makeshift moving boxes. The steps up to their half of the duplex had been swept away, so they shinnied around some missing planks in their deck and cut through their neighbors' place to climb down the only set of intact stairs on the property. The inside of their home stank from two weeks shut in the sun without air-conditioning. No one dared open the fridge. There was a dull thud outside. We looked across the street and a man was shoving rolls of waterlogged carpet out the window of a bright green beach house.

Over in Orange Beach, an old man named Cecil Young, whom I knew from city council meetings, gripped some hand tools and walked up into his house. It had been ripped from its pilings and deposited in his neighbors' front yard. It might have drifted farther, but a palm tree had wedged into a doorway and stopped it. Inside he inspected his books, which were sopping wet but still on their shelves.

Pretty much everything inside was trashed. The kitchen sink was about the only thing worth salvaging. He set down his tools on the cockeyed countertop, selected the basin wrench, and bent under it to loosen the sink.

Bob and Susan Shallow rode out the storm in their penthouse atop a new tower on Perdido Key called Legacy Key. The real estate agent's million-dollar boat was in tatters below in Old River, not far from where authorities were fishing bodies out of the water on the Florida side of the state line. The Shallows were well provisioned and out of harm's way perched on the fourteenth floor, though.

There were a few reasons they stayed while everyone else fled. For one, the balloonist in Bob wanted to see the violent sky. Plus, it was good marketing for the type of concrete condo towers he sold. Sheltering in place during a direct hit from a Category 3 as though it were just another rainy day was a good endorsement of the latest construction methods. He had a firsthand account of the storm for news reporters and could plug himself as well as Alabama's new breed of residential towers in the process. But the biggest reason he stayed was that he knew what was coming. Once the floodwaters receded there'd be another deluge, this one of deal-seeking disaster capitalists. Staying at the beach during the storm put Shallow on the right side of the National Guard barricades so that he could jump on redevelopment opportunities before all the blow-ins arrived and drove up the prices.

From his balcony, Shallow could see a swath of devastation across the street on the Gulf. A small condominium complex called Sandy Cove was an unsalvageable mess, ripped open along its surf-facing side. Contents of upper units barfed out onto the beach. Alarms were still chirping in the rubble when Shallow's phone rang.

It was the president of the Sandy Cove owners' association. The owners decided to sell after getting a look at their heap of second homes. They wanted $10 million.

"It's worth more than that," Shallow said.

They wanted to sell quickly and move on, he said. Ten million got the deal done.

"Great," Shallow said. "I'll buy it."

Shallow had $1 million in earnest money wired over and called Shaul Zislin, the beachwear merchant and property investor.

"You want half of it?" he asked.

Zislin did. Next, Shallow called a man in Mobile whom he knew to be in the market for Gulf-front land to build a condo tower.

"Hey," Shallow said, "I just bought this land at Sandy Cove, I'll sell it to you for fourteen and a half million."

The man in Mobile said he'd take it. Shallow never even had to buy the property himself. He simply sold it for $14.5 million and then passed on the $10 million he had agreed to pay to the owners of the caved-in condos. The difference, $4.5 million, was his. He took a $500,000 fee for putting the deal together and sent Zislin a check for $2 million. When Zislin received the check, he called Shallow.

"What the hell is this two million for?" he asked.

"Sandy Cove," Shallow said.

"You blew it?" Zislin asked.

"No, I didn't blow it."

He said he'd already sold it. The $2 million was Zislin's half of the profit for agreeing to be fifty-fifty partners with him, Shallow said.

Shallow had been waiting for an opportunity like this since the savings and loan bust, when office buildings, condominiums, airplanes, and even Rolex watches were dumped by desperate sellers. Unlike then, he now had the means to take advantage of this market dislocation and the opportunities it presented, chiefly a lot of Johnny-come-latelies with cheap and nearly unlimited credit who were itching to get in on the condo game.

# 7

## "LIKE WORKING AT WENDY'S"

Condo flipping went full throttle after the storm. Shallow was selling units at Island Tower for the sixth time and the building wasn't close to being finished. They fetched $875,000, more than twice the price paid the year before when the first round of buyers gobbled up the proposed condos in less than an hour. Anyone who'd scoffed at the star sales agent's audacity was now agog.

People were ditching their service jobs in droves and studying for real estate licenses. The average price of a preconstruction condo unit rose to about $500,000. Realtors bragged about having lists of hundreds of eager buyers for any waterfront unit that came available. It took just a day for Tim James to collect deposits on the five-hundred–plus condos he wanted to build at the foot of his toll bridge. Encouraged, he bought an option on a cement plant near the bridge's southern landing and sought permission to stack more than nine hundred condominiums on the dusty property.

On the day that AIG Baker offered preconstruction contracts on the Wharf's first condos, buyers clutching $10,000 checks for the deposits lined up out the door of a local real estate firm that had been tapped to handle sales. "It was like working at Wendy's," said one of the sales agents on duty that day. "They were just coming in."

The 190 condos in the planned mall's canal-facing Levin's Bend building were gone in moments. About thirteen hundred people signed waiting lists should any more condos become available or if anyone who'd gotten a condo ahead of them dropped out. Those who didn't want to risk being left out could shop on the aftermarket. By the end of the day, people who had been first in line with their deposit checks had already listed their future condos for sale. Some were asking $100,000 over what they had agreed to pay that morning.

The group developing RiverWalk across the waterway from the Wharf doubled the number of condos included in its plans. A local real estate agency called Joan T. Realty ran late-night television commercials touting the riches to be made flipping condos as well as houses near the beach.

The Orange Beach election didn't much alter the dynamics of the city council, but it did allow Russo to restock the planning commission, which vetted building plans before they went on to the city council. Russo appointed a young woman who had married into a prominent local fishing family and was an aspiring real estate agent, a churchy man who ran a small home-building business, and Dean Young, the fierce campaigner who plowed real estate money into the mayor's reelection bid.

Russo said he realized that the appointment would raise hackles among his detractors, but he said he wasn't really doing Young any favors. Planning commissioner was an unpaid position and came with a healthy dose of wrath from other residents. "I'm not giving him anything," the mayor said. "A headache, maybe."

Young didn't mind. "You do things like that because you want to help the city," he told me. "Orange Beach is getting ready to rebuild, so I think it's important that it's rebuilt in the correct manner."

Rick Phillips and his partners who were building the Lighthouse and San Carlos towers in Gulf Shores moved into Orange Beach with ambitious plans. Years earlier, they had bought a restaurant near Perdido Pass. Now that Ivan had wrecked the eatery and several old houses nearby, they saw an opportunity to redevelop the stunning oceanfront property with a residential tower. The city owned a few parcels along the seawall and was known to be on the hunt for a few million dollars.

Orange Beach officials had agreed to pay more than $4 million for the small island at the mouth of the pass to keep the old man who owned it from building a bunch of houses on it. The federal government was interested in preserving the island as a heron rookery and pledged $1 million toward its conservation. The city had to come up with millions more to repay the bank loan it had taken out to cover the rest.

Phillips offered to buy the city's parcels along the pass for $3.5 million. That left only one holdout, who was refusing to sell to the developers. Money wasn't the issue for the unwilling seller. He believed that his deceased wife's spirit inhabited the place, and therefore he would not allow it to be demolished. When the developer explained the situation at city hall, one municipal employee wondered aloud, "Was the spirit attached to the property or just to the house?"

The widower was asked. Sure enough, the ghost was bound to the house, not the sand beneath it. Phillips arranged for the haunted house to be moved to another lot and bought the property.

Phillips and his partners, a man with a construction company and another who had made a fortune on Terminix franchises, also locked down twelve acres near the center of Orange Beach.

It was the storm-blasted stretch where my colleagues and I got our satellite phone working for our first dispatch after Hurricane Ivan and where President George W. Bush was later photographed surveying damage with local leaders. Phillips and his partners wanted to scrap all the damaged buildings and build two thirty-six-story buildings, which they called Mandalay Beach. They would have five hundred condo units between them and top Larry's Wireman's peak at Turquoise Place by about 5 feet. They offered to turn a 325-foot-wide strip of their property into a public beach and hand it over to taxpayers in exchange for lenient zoning.

One of the developers told the planning commission that at $100,000 per waterfront foot—a price they had helped set with their own purchases—

they were essentially giving taxpayers a $32.5 million gift. The offering was the latest of $100 million in public gifts pledged by developers needing to skirt city zoning rules. The planning commission was unanimous in waving the plans through.

Shallow sold his Orange Beach and Gulf Shores RE/MAX franchises that summer to two younger agents he had been grooming and decamped for a small office in Orange Beach to focus on arranging development deals. "Controlling inventory," as he put it. Though he was no longer in charge of seventy-some sales agents, his days were no less hectic. He received around two hundred phone calls a day and employed two administrative assistants to take most of them. A pair of licensed agents, including his daughter, worked at his side. They referred many of the inbound calls to Shallow's former employees.

Even turning business away he tallied $172 million of sales himself, good for third best among RE/MAX agents worldwide. Shallow had brokered about three hundred deals to achieve that volume and was working hard to line up more. At one point he had seven condominium projects underway and three more on the drawing board.

The agents he left behind managed well without him. On average they earned $440,000 that year. Shallow was particularly proud of his protégés who had earned their own seven-figure paydays. "Thirteen of them made over a million," Shallow said, beaming. "Thirteen of them!"

Among the superlative performers were a father-daughter duo who sold $65 million worth of property. He worked clients on the golf course and she built a website and juggled phones at home with a baby. An agent who racked up $63 million in sales gathered his team every morning for breakfast at 7:00 A.M. "Five years ago I was working for fifty thousand a year," he said. "Last year I made two million." Three others of Shallow's former employees each exceeded $45 million in sales.

Even Shallow's mistakes were minting money. He sold Zislin's Florida group a piece of property on the north shore of Perdido Key for $3.5 million, but when they came to town to see it, they went looking along the beach in Gulf Shores. That's where they thought they had bought.

They called Shallow and told him they couldn't find their parcel. He told them that it was over in Orange Beach, near the Florida line. They drove over to it and called him back. They didn't want that property.

"No problem," Shallow said. "I can sell it for five million."

That afternoon he did just that. The Florida investors made more than a million dollars for their trouble and Shallow produced another six-figure commission for himself.

# 8

## FLIPPED

It was the latter part of 2005 when I became part of the story that I was covering for the newspaper.

The wreckage from Ivan was still being cleaned up when Hurricane Katrina struck. The monster storm made landfall in Louisiana that August and wiped entire towns off the map there and in Mississippi. Alabama, especially east of Mobile Bay, was mostly spared.

Vulnerable structures had already been knocked down or sucked into the sea by Hurricane Ivan the year before. Hurricane Katrina buried the beach highway in sand again and brought more debris, like the real estate yard sign from Mississippi that I found washed up on an Alabama beach. But debris cleanup workers and the dredging crews who had been pumping millions of dollars' worth of white quartz ashore to rebuild eroded stretches were still in town. They were simply enlisted to stay longer.

I waited for the storm to pass at my apartment, watching from the balcony as the wind peeled the vinyl siding from an identical building across the parking lot. My college sweetheart and I had married a few weeks earlier and we returned from our honeymoon just in time for the hurricane. She had been hired to teach kindergarten at the beach, and in the interest of establishing our careers we had decided to stay in Alabama longer than we had originally anticipated. We were tired of our humdrum apartment, though.

We lived in a ring of broiling asphalt, paper-thin walls separating us from an ever-changing cast of neighbors. It was a drag having to hop in a car to go anywhere except the YMCA, a Walmart Supercenter, and a treeless tangle of look-alike houses. I would jog with the dog in the adjacent subdivision and get turned around no matter how many times we ran the route. The houses were ornamented with an unusually large amount of college football paraphernalia. I came to believe all the LSU and Auburn insignia had as much to do with making the houses recognizable from one another as it did touting rooting interests. We were ready for better living and probably a little eager to reward ourselves for getting through college and landing the jobs for which we had studied. There wasn't much we could afford, though.

One night I went to a party that the Bon Secour Village developers held to launch sales of their town within a town. They had rented a big wedding tent and set it up in the parking lot of a furniture store in Orange Beach. A checkered dance floor had been laid down over the asphalt, a band was hired, and a bar was stocked. One of the developers took the mic and teared up as he offered a rendition of his "town founder" spiel. Sales agents were positioned like cocktail waitresses. On their menu: a few dozen condos that averaged $560,000 and narrow home lots that cost $450,000.

The watercolor renderings looked nice, like something from New Orleans or the old downtown neighborhoods in Mobile, but besides the fact that they didn't exist yet, Bon Secour Village was so far out of my price range that I had a hard time imagining something nice would ever would be within reach.

Anything near the beach was out of the question. So, too, I was finding, was any new construction within ten or twenty miles of the shoreline. I couldn't afford those cookie-cutter tract houses where I jogged with Pierre. I wasn't sure who could. My wife and I had seemed to have some of the more desirable and decent-paying jobs in town.

Affordability was a big problem, and not just for us. Businesses at the beach were already having to import people to fill service jobs. Resorts and retailers bused in workers from sixty miles away. Restaurants, hotels, and amusement parks relied on students from Bulgaria and Russia to get through the busy summer season. Now the next rungs on the pay scale, where a lot of civil servants and public employees stood, were having trouble finding places to live.

When a lawyer for Tim James made his case to council members in Orange Beach for the condo towers at the toll bridge's northern landing, he said rezoning the property would add inventory to the lower end of the market. "It will facilitate affordable condominiums for John Q. Public," said the lawyer, Greg Leatherbury. After the property was rezoned for the towers, James presold all 507 units for between $400,000 and $500,000. Whoever John Q. Public was, he didn't work for the police department, the fire department, the elementary school, or, for that matter, the newspaper.

City leaders were receiving a lot of complaints from business owners about the lack of affordable housing. It was alarming to city officials that emergency responders such as police officers and paramedics were having to live miles away from the city, where they might be needed at a moment's notice should a fire break out in one of the skyscrapers or a swimming vacationer was sucked out to sea.

Working for Orange Beach was like working for a hot tech company. Early employees who had gotten in and bought homes before the boom were way in the money. But city hall was having trouble replacing them because the cost of housing had soared well beyond the means of most municipal hires, particularly those just starting their careers.

Jeff Moon, a jovial man who ran Orange Beach day to day as its city administrator, told me about a municipal employee who had bought a small home two years earlier in an old section of town called Bear Point. The house was about twelve hundred square feet, perhaps forty years old. She had paid $74,000 for it and was now selling it for $249,000. She had made way more money owning the old house for two years than she had working for the city. At $249,000, that was about as cheap as anyone could expect to find a house in Orange Beach. Yet it was beyond the reach of most working people in Orange Beach, where the median income was about $47,000.

"I talked to a real estate agent today who closed on two lots in Bear Point with a forty-year-old trailer on them," Moon said. "A hundred and ninety-nine thousand dollars!"

Instead of spooking me out of the market, this sort of information nudged me toward buying while I still could. My wife and I began our house hunt in earnest soon after Hurricane Katrina.

Unsure what we could afford, we took our pay stubs, my student loan repayment books, and account statements to the local Regions Bank branch. We waited in the lobby for the mortgage banker, and when he was free he examined our paperwork, asked us to fill out some forms, and gave us a list of additional documentation he would need before he could tell us what the bank would be willing to lend us to buy a home.

My wife got a letter from the school board attesting to her employment. I fetched one from my bosses on newspaper letterhead. A few days later, the mortgage banker got back to us with a number. It was the amount we were preapproved to borrow. I don't remember exactly what the number was, but it was less than $200,000. Certainly nowhere near the $350,000 that was being offered as affordable by subdivision developers in Orange Beach.

There weren't a ton of options in our price range. There were double-wide trailers and a lot of chintzy apartments being sold off as condominiums. We were trying to move out of one of those nondescript complexes, not buy into one. Houses in the sticks usually came with so much land that they got pricey. I wanted a yard but wasn't looking to buy a tractor. Houses in the old central part of Foley were the sort of fixer-uppers that could turn into money pits. Many homes we looked at were deeply flawed. I couldn't imagine how I'd ever remove the mildew or pests from some. One had little half-sized windows like a jail. An old cottage seemed suitable until it came time to discuss the rotten pilings upon which it sat. We arrived for a few showings only to learn that the houses had already been sold. Katrina had stirred up a lot of demand from people who lost homes in Louisiana and Mississippi, especially families who were rushing to set down new roots in time for their children to start the school year.

Our real estate agent took us to a neighborhood called Audubon Place. It seemed nice when we pulled in. People were outside in their yards, walking dogs and retrieving the mail from the front where the letter boxes were clustered. Children drew on the sidewalk with chalk. A pack of kids circled the neighborhood on bikes.

Audubon Place was not yet ten years old. That all the houses had already been built and occupied seemed like a plus. There weren't any crews nailing frames together in staccato claps, portable toilets at the curb, or red, muddy tire tracks all over the streets as there were in the subdivisions that were still being built.

Audubon Place was manicured without being sterile. Some of the landscaping was downright lush. Bottlebrush and oleander stood the height of two men near the front of the subdivision. The periphery of the neighborhood was set aside as common space. It served as a vegetated buffer as well as a flood-control basin. Giant longleaf pine trees that looked straight out of Dr. Seuss swayed in the sky above the houses. Most newer neighborhoods around town were treeless, built over farmland, or clear-cut by developers who didn't want to work around obstacles. There were only a few different models of houses in Audubon Place, but at least they were different colors. Many subdivisions were made of identical brick houses.

The neighborhood sat just west of Alabama 59 off a country road that made the border between Gulf Shores and Foley and led to Bon Secour, where the shrimping fleet harbored. A big home builder from Mobile had parceled out the 109 lots and started popping up houses in 1996. There were a few two-story houses in the oval, but most were single level. They were built on slabs, wrapped in vinyl siding, and significantly cheaper than anything builders were offering in newer subdivisions. As such, the houses in Audubon Place were a hot commodity and selling at a rapid clip when we arrived.

The back windows of the houses in the middle of the oval looked into the windows of the houses behind them. We ruled those out. Along the outer circle, there were a couple of choices. The pitched roof of a two-story house we went through rendered the second floor a lot less useful than the square footage and the price would suggest. We really liked the next one we toured.

It was near the entrance of the subdivision. Instead of someone else's windows, the view over the back fence was of a line of trees. Beyond them was an older house on a farm-sized plot. It wasn't a working farm, but a few horses were kept there and could be heard faintly whinnying. Even if houses were built over there, we'd still have the fifteen-foot drainage buffer and most of the trees. A huge hedge along the driveway basically hid the house next door, offering a modicum of privacy in a neighborhood where the houses were just a few passes of a lawn mower apart.

It was also the least expensive of the houses for sale in Audubon because the garage took up space that was used as a third bedroom in other models. The living space was only about a thousand square feet, but we barely had furniture for a second bedroom. A third would have been wasted space.

The house appeared hardly lived in. The carpet was fresh. The walls were painted with the sort of chalky white favored by builders operating on skimpy budgets. The ceiling fans and faucets were an assortment of the cheapest and most basic models available at Home Depot. There were a lot of inexpensive things, including new paint and nicer lighting, that we could do to improve the house and make it our own.

The yard was uninspired and the lawn a bit weedy, but it had promise. The hand-built shed in the backyard needed a coat of paint, but it would free up space in the garage so that we could keep one of our cars out of the sun. Two massive longleaf pine trees with thick, crackly bark were excellent landscape features to work with. Growing up at the hardware store in Ohio gave me a good sense of what it would cost to spruce up the place, and I was eager to undertake what would be a largely aesthetic renovation.

The real estate agent guiding our house hunt was a charming older woman. She told us we'd probably have to make an offer quickly before anyone else did. The house was owned by a couple from north Alabama. We were told they used the place sparingly during fishing trips. Hence the small boat in the garage and the sparse furnishings. A few men's shirts hung from cheap metal hangers in the walk-in closet off the master bathroom. There was nothing but cans of diet soda in the fridge, and the tiny television in the corner looked to be about as old as me. They were asking

$145,000. On the way out, I noticed that one of the scrawny azaleas in the front bed was plastic. Someone had shoved it into the ground in lieu of filling in the empty place in the row of ornamentals with an actual bush. We went home to sleep on it.

What our real estate agent had not told us—and what I learned only much later—was that the sellers had bought and sold two other houses in the neighborhood. They had already made more than $50,000 on a couple of quick flips when we came along.

Deed filings in the county courthouse showed that they had bought a house down the street in March for $118,000 and sold it in July for $154,000. In August they paid $125,000 for another and sold it in September for $145,000. They bought the one I was mentally remodeling in July. They paid $120,000, putting $12,000 down and borrowing the rest from a California lender called Countrywide Financial, which had recently eclipsed Wells Fargo to become the largest mortgage underwriter in the country.

According to county records, the north Alabama couple were the house's third owner since June. A local man acquired it in 2002 after it was repossessed by a lender. He paid the bank $61,500 and agreed to cover the previous year's unpaid tax bill. Three years later, in June 2005, he sold it to a Gulf Shores man, who sold it to the couple from north Alabama a few weeks later. I showed up in October, took a look around, and offered $137,500.

Our agent had sent another agent in her stead to meet us with offer documents to sign. Someone else from her office called us to say the sellers had accepted, so long as we paid the closing costs. We called our agent to ask about that and she discouraged us from countering. It was too hot of a market to quibble over the closing costs, which amounted to a few thousand dollars, she said. We struck a deal on a Saturday morning and delivered a $1,000 check to our agent's office to serve as earnest money.

On Monday morning, I went to the Regions branch and spent a couple of hours with the mortgage banker as he prepared the financing documents. Because we were first-time buyers and since the house was in a zone covered by a Department of Agriculture program aimed at spurring homeownership in rural areas, we qualified for financing that required no down payment. There were two loans, a first mortgage for $110,000 and a second, essentially a maxed-out line of credit, in the amount of $27,500. We used what we had saved for a down payment to cover the closing costs. Including those, we effectively paid a little over $140,000 with something like 2 percent or 3 percent down. We had some cash left over to rent a moving truck, buy a new couch to replace the one Pierre had chewed up as a puppy, and get started making the home our own. The monthly payment, even with taxes and expensive hurricane insurance added, wasn't much more than our rent.

It was a week before Thanksgiving. Our apartment lease would be up at the end of the month. On my way to the closing, I stopped at an Ace Hardware and filled my car with paint, drop cloths, and a ladder. Once we signed the papers at a title company office in Gulf Shores, I drove back to the house, changed the locks, and began painting.

I knew the housing market was heated. And not just in south Alabama. After Shallow told me about his Dolphin Club, in the summer of 2004, I filed a lengthy story to my editors that described the speculative mania and laid out the mechanics of the condo flipping that was transforming Alabama's beaches. We headlined the story "The Condo Game," a nod to *The Money Game,* George Jerome Waldo Goodman's masterful market explainer from 1968. My editors put the story above the fold on the front page of the July 4 edition so that it would be stacked in hotel lobbies, on grocery store racks, and in street corner newspaper boxes when the beach would be most crowded.

The amount of money speculators were making with so little of their own cash at risk shocked a lot of people and caught the attention of economists at the Federal Deposit Insurance Corporation, who cited it in a report they published at the end of the year on consumer behavior and the housing market.

The agency created by Congress amid the Great Depression to maintain stability and public confidence in the financial system and known as the FDIC deemed the housing market to be "most impressive." The U.S. homeownership rate had reached new heights, north of 69 percent.

Existing homes were changing hands at the highest rate ever, and prices had risen in every corner of the country that spring. New houses were being built at the fastest pace in a quarter century. Roughly one out of every eight new jobs being created in the United States was in construction. Mortgage debt piled up.

Besides taking out loans for all those new houses, homeowners were borrowing hundreds of billions of dollars against the gains in value of properties they already owned. The volume of these loans, called home-equity lines of credit, or HELOCs, was growing by about a third each year. Homeowners were blowing into the sails of the broader economy by spending their home equity on cars, college tuition, vacations, and at the mall.

The FDIC's regional economists reported all sorts of superlative and puzzling situations. In New England, home prices were climbing more than 10 percent a year. The number of homes in Orange County, California, that were being flipped within six months of purchase, was soaring. Speculators from the mainland were overheating the market in Hawaii. In San Antonio, foreclosures were at record highs, yet so, too, were building permits. High home prices in Baltimore inspired homeowners to flood the market with a 20 percent year-over-year increase in listings, which didn't seem to have any deleterious effect on prices, as would be expected by a surge in supply. Houses around Annapolis had become so expensive that teachers, police officers, and other civil servants who worked in Maryland's capital were having to move so far away to afford houses that they were driving an hour to work each morning. In doing so, they were bucking thousands of years of habit by spending twice as much time commuting as the hour-a-day average that has dictated human range since ancient times.

The FDIC economists pointed to changes in mortgage underwriting. Interest-only mortgages and piggyback loans, which reduce the amount needed for a down payment, were allowing house hunters to buy more than they would otherwise be able to afford. Low credit scores and histories of defaults didn't seem to disqualify borrowers as they once had. Home buyers were securing "no down payment" mortgages even though they had defaulted on home loans a year earlier. In Alabama and parts of

Florida, the economists noted, people were getting their hands on yet-to-be-built luxury condos with little to no money down and trading them like securities.

Home prices had been rising faster than wages for five years running, and some economists started throwing the B word around. Bubble. If the typical worker couldn't afford the typical house, something had to give.

The FDIC said starter homes were worth watching closely. If interest rates rose, a lot of new homeowners who'd signed adjustable-rate mortgages might find themselves unable to make monthly payments. Rising home prices were also a risk to buyers at the margin because of the accompanying increases in property taxes. Yet low interest rates and lenient lenders made owning a home more attractive—sometimes even cheaper—than renting in many markets. The national vacancy rate for rental properties exceeded 10 percent for the first time on record. Empty apartments were especially numerous in the Midwest and the South.

A friend noticed the report's citation of my article and sent it to me. I read it and understood every word of it. Nonetheless, a few months later I was vacating an apartment in the South and signing papers to buy a starter home in a scorching market with almost no money down. I thought what we were doing was outside the game that flippers were playing. We weren't buying a house to sell, we were buying one in which to live. Besides, what was the worst that could happen with a house that was already near the bottom of the market?

# 9

## WANNA BUY A BRIDGE?

Bob Shallow wound up selling $173.3 million worth of real estate in 2005, earning him the top spot among the world's one hundred thousand–plus RE/MAX agents. He beat out agents from more expensive and much larger markets in south Florida and Northern California and was crowned the global brokerage's sales king at its annual convention in Las Vegas.

Television shows and financial magazines called. Another high-powered RE/MAX broker asked Shallow to come out to California to speak to his staff. He offered to send a private jet to fetch Shallow and to pay him $20,000 for his time. Shallow turned it down. He was making more than $20,000 a day in Alabama, where he preferred to spend his spare time tending to his cattle. "Selling real estate is not rocket science," he told the *Register* for a story about his feat. "You have to show up. And you gotta work."

Selling real estate in coastal Alabama was indeed requiring a lot more work than it had a few months earlier, when buyers were lined up outside of agents' offices waving checks. By the end of 2005, more than twenty-six hundred condos had piled up on the market. Many of those listed for sale were in buildings that were scheduled to be completed in the new year.

Wishful flippers were on the hook to actually pay for them unless they could find a buyer.

The hurricanes had begun to take a toll. Thirteen of them had struck the United States between the summer of 2004 and late 2005. Katrina, which filled New Orleans like a tub, petrified would-be buyers. Property insurers were sapped. Premiums soared, forcing some who owned homes along the water to sell and move inland.

The owners in a pair of nine-story buildings in Orange Beach opened their wind insurance renewal letters and were aghast to find their buildings' premium jump from $40,000 to $1.1 million. Each owner in the complex would have to come up with an extra $15,000 a year to cover the increase. That was a problem for retirees who had bought condos years earlier and lived in them on fixed budgets. Meanwhile, property taxes were soaring to catch up with sale prices. Every time a developer like Larry Wireman or Rick Phillips paid a new record price for land, the tax value of all the other property around it rose as well. The sharp rise in prices was really good only for sellers. For everyone else it just made owning more expensive. For some, the higher costs could be covered only by selling, which added more listings to the backlog.

Word spread that buyers were starting to wriggle out of their commitments to buy condos at the Wharf, the AIG-backed mega-development on the Intracoastal Waterway. For a while, sales agents backfilled the building with people who'd put their names on the waiting list. Rick Phillips and his partners were having a far more difficult time trying to sell the five hundred condos they wanted to build at Mandalay Beach than they had at the Lighthouse or San Carlos, which sold out immediately.

Developers, real estate agents, and city officials seemed unfazed by the cracks starting to show in the market. It was just a correction, a shaking out of the undercapitalized speculators that would reset prices to more sustainable levels, they said. Lots along West Beach in Gulf Shores that were fifty feet wide and had been selling for $1.3 million were now fetching $1 million. The 30 percent drop was steep, sure, but someone was still willing to pay a million dollars for fifty feet of sand and a huge insurance bill. The widely held expectation was that as Ivan and Katrina receded further from the public's conscious, insurers would return and bring the price of coverage back down, which would lift the market. Developers didn't slow down.

Though it was happening directly across the Intracoastal Waterway, the flight of condo buyers from the Wharf did not seem to register with the developers of Orange Beach RiverWalk. As they started knocking down the pine trees and building the dolphin-show grandstands, their ambitions grew. They hired a photogenic young woman from one of the local TV stations, where she reported feel-good community stories for the morning news. They made her RiverWalk's spokeswoman. She gave regular public briefings about the status of the ever-expanding development.

The convention center would be bigger. A massive water park had been added. The precise designs weren't ready to reveal, she said, but the developers had engaged water park designers who'd worked on Blizzard Beach and Typhoon Lagoon. There'd be a coral reef for snorkeling. A wave pool. Huge waterslides. Flamingos. Aquarium-themed restaurants. The best part, she said, would be a lazy river in which visitors could splay out onto inner tubes and float leisurely around the property on a rivulet of chlorinated water. There would be a transparent acrylic tunnel that would take the floaters through a shark tank. The development's price tag had risen beyond $300 million, up from just $85 million a couple of years earlier. It all called for a new name. RiverWalk was rechristened Bama Bayou.

Audacious development proposals arrived one after another like waves. On Perdido Key, a flurry of proposals for thirty-story-plus condo towers threatened to turn the spit of sand into a Manhattan-style canyon. A big Chicago developer paid the family of a Mobile lawyer nearly $19 million for about 150 acres out on the Fort Morgan peninsula that included the site of a nineteenth-century settlement called Pilot Town. It was named for the navigators who lived there, memorized the contours of Mobile Bay, and were hired to guide ships up from the ocean to the Port of Mobile in the days before proper ship channels were dredged. Now the Chicago firm wanted to dredge up some 55 acres of Mobile Bay for a big marina, mound sand to make a 38-acre beach, and erect condominiums. The Fish & Wildlife Service had tried to buy the ecologically sensitive and historic property a few years earlier from the lawyer's family, but the government's $2 million offer was rebuffed. The family had paid $620,000 for the land in 1998, outbidding a group of local preservationists in an auction, and had a much greater return in mind.

Nearby on Bon Secour Bay, the developer of the Beach Club, the resort that started the high-rise boom, pitched another set of towers. The property was well north of the beach, up toward where I lived, but units would be priced as though they were at surf's edge, between $459,000 and $1 million. On another stretch of bay-front woods, a doctor from Tuscaloosa sought permission to build a thirty-story tower with four hundred condos and a yacht club.

An oddball with apparently deep pockets wanted to tear up a privately owned tract of coastal forest on the Fort Morgan peninsula to build a high-rise surrounded on all sides by the Bon Secour National Wildlife Refuge. He wanted to name his towering hotel the Sanctuary. Officials up to the federal level shot down the plans and were unmoved by the developer's offer to build a $1 million boardwalk leading from his hotel down to Alabama's last remaining virgin beaches. Nor did his offer to spend $200,000 on a welcome center for the wildlife refuge change their minds. The point of a wildlife refuge seemed lost on the guy. "I'm offering to do something really nice here and all I'm getting is a hard time," he complained after a public hearing that didn't go his way.

All the developers and real estate investors flying into town on private jets strained the small airport in Gulf Shores, and the city embarked on a $38 million expansion. In Orange Beach, so many of the old marinas along the bay fronts were slated to be turned into private dock space for condo owners that municipal officials paid $7.6 million for an old storm-battered marina in a bid to save the charter fishing fleet. For-hire fishing boats had always been one of Orange Beach's biggest businesses and remained one of its top tourist draws. Yet the salty old fishing captains were faring no better in the real estate boom than the endangered Alabama beach mouse. The beach mouse's oaty dunes were sprouting condominium towers. Now the same thing was happening to anglers for hire.

Tim James had taken deposits on the 507 condos he planned to build near his toll bridge, but he began to harbor doubts about the project as well as the other residential complex that he had planned for a cement plant across the canal. Schoolteachers were flipping condominiums that should have been well out of their price range. Something was amiss in the market. James pulled the plug on both residential projects and even sold his toll bridge.

Macquarie Group, an investment firm often described as the Goldman Sachs of Australia, paid James and his partners about $150 million. The Alabama men cleared more than $70 million before taxes. That was nearly twice what they had borrowed a few years earlier to build the bridge. The investment bank's plan was to bundle the Foley Beach Express toll bridge with three other Alabama toll roads and the operator of the Detroit–Windsor Tunnel, line up long-term debt financing, and flip the package to other investors. When Tim James hunted for money to build the bridge, he had struggled because of the poor record toll bridge investors had compiled. By the time Macquarie was shopping the bridge around, the bad road deals were far enough in the rearview mirror that they had apparently been forgotten on Wall Street.

Investors' interest in toll roads has risen up in fevers on and off since the country's early days. In 1792, there was a speculative frenzy over a stone carriage path between Philadelphia and Lancaster, Pennsylvania. Shares of the road were a huge hit when they were offered to the public, like a hot tech-stock offering today. In a letter to a friend, a Pennsylvania court official described a chaotic debut for the toll road's shares. His employees, "having been infected with the Turnpike Rage," skipped work and went to the stock offering. "My office was deserted the whole day," he said. At the sale there were way more orders than there were shares. A riot ensued.

Turnpikes proliferated since states didn't have much in the way of resources to build public roads. But because they were so often built ahead of settlement and tolls were easily skirted, turnpikes rarely paid dividends.

In the middle aughts, turnpike fever raged anew. Big investors including pension funds, college endowments, and supremely wealthy families had poured money into private funds that invested in infrastructure. Such funds aimed for steady but unspectacular returns associated with necessities such as sewage, electricity, and gas pipelines.

Macquarie lined up nearly $500 million in debt that investors could use to buy its bundle of toll roads. The investment bank paid a firm called Syncora to insure the bonds against default. To make its case that tolls from the Foley Beach Express, three shortcuts in upstate Alabama, and a tunnel connecting Detroit to Canada would cover the payments on a half billion dollars of debt, Macquarie turned to an Australian traffic consultant called Maunsell.

The Australian consultant produced a report that estimated traffic on the five roads would nearly double by 2015 and that revenue would almost triple in that time if the tolls were increased.

Much of the added traffic was expected to come from the bridge in Orange Beach as cars shuttled between Bama Bayou and the Wharf. The Australian firm's projections added millions of cars to even the rosiest of estimates Tim James had used a few years earlier to convince city officials to invest. Maunsell and Macquarie told the bonds' insurer and the big investors who were considering buying the roads that they could expect more than fifteen million cars to cross the bridge by 2020. That would be an unfathomable leap in traffic, of course. A simple comparison to publicly available traffic figures for San Francisco's Golden Gate Bridge, which about forty million cars cross a year, proved the projection ludicrous. There weren't yet three million cars using the Orange Beach bridge and already the island's few thoroughfares were gridlocked on summer weekends. Anyone who looked at a map of the watery place would see that there was not enough land, let alone roads, to quintuple traffic. Apparently no one did.

By October, Macquarie had sold the toll roads to an infrastructure fund manager called Alinda Capital Partners. Alinda embraced the Australians' suggestion to raise the tolls as well as their optimistic traffic forecast. The firm relayed the projections to bond investors, who bought roughly $500 million of debt, the repayment of which depended on the predictions coming true.

# 10

## "THERE'S A MILLION DOLLARS TO BE MADE HERE"

One morning during the summer of 2005, a builder named Jim Brown walked into Steve Russo's store in Orange Beach, as he often did, to fetch breakfast.

The mayor was waiting for him at the deli counter, clutching a land-auction brochure. It advertised two adjoined lots along Wolf Bay, a resplendent body of water plied by dolphins and osprey. The mayor had already spoken to the auctioneer. The property could probably be bought for $900,000 or so.

"Somebody hasn't done their homework," Brown said. He thought the property was worth twice that. "There's a million dollars to be made here."

The mayor waved Brown back to his office and shut the door. Out of earshot of others at the store, the mayor asked Brown if he would buy it with him.

Squat, fair-haired, and perpetually ruddied by the Alabama sun, Brown had built a small empire as a contractor and real estate investor in Orange Beach. He owned an apartment complex and offices. He had built a subdivision, a high-end recreational-vehicle park, beach houses big enough to sleep entire church groups, a shopping center, and a bank.

By the time he was fifty, the high school dropout was worth more than $30 million. He owned a jet, which he kept in Dothan, 180 miles northeast of Orange Beach, and hired a pilot whenever he wanted to go somewhere. He had a house in Cabo San Lucas and several properties in central Florida.

Much of Brown's business crossed the mayor's desk. The Wolf Bay lots in the brochure were an easy way to earn a few hundred thousand dollars while pleasing the mayor, he thought. Though the lots weren't quite as mispriced as Brown first thought, he was able to buy them for $1.2 million. That was still low enough for the two of them to make hundreds of thousands of dollars' profit flipping the property.

Brown had known Russo since the early eighties. They'd see each other around, usually at Russo's store, where Brown bought gasoline and sandwiches. Not long after Russo became mayor, he asked Brown to build a mother-in-law suite and a swimming pool at his house. Brown did the work but never sent a bill. When the mayor asked what he owed, Brown told him to consider it a campaign contribution. The mayor followed up with requests for a concrete driveway, a screened porch, a tiled patio, a fence, a backup generator, roof repair, yard sprinklers, ceiling fans, sod.

The unpaid odd jobs at the mayor's house were a small price to pay to protect his livelihood in Orange Beach, Brown reasoned. There were millions of dollars to be made all over town buying property and then convincing the city council to rezone it for greater density or bigger buildings.

Russo knew this. His support was critical to such schemes. He was the swing vote on the council, with a mandate from voters to keep the money party rocking. Yet he wasn't getting any of it. He was like the bouncer sitting outside the bash, deciding who got in but never able to enjoy the revelry himself. Every time he cast a tie-breaking vote a developer's way, the developer made millions. Russo got $25,000 a year, long hours, and a lot of grief. Brown's price was going up.

One day when they met at the store, the mayor rose from his desk, walked in front of it, and stood over the much shorter builder. He looked down at Brown. "You need to find something to make some money," he said.

Brown obliged. He was preparing to deliver his biggest ask yet to city hall and couldn't risk running afoul of the mayor. He and a business partner named Ken Wall wanted to build a $300 million oceanfront resort called the Water Club. Doing so involved a complicated series of land swaps. Houses had to be moved down the beach. The divided city council would have to acquiesce to several requests. Tens of millions of dollars were at stake.

Brown had a more pedestrian deal over in Gulf Shores. He could cut the mayor in on that to stay in his good graces. Brown and another man had bought an option to buy an old beach house, which they planned to knock down and replace with a newer, much larger house to sell. Brown had the profits pegged at six figures. That seemed plenty to retain the mayor's tie-breaking vote.

Brown had to get his existing partner out of the way. He told him that he had received a nice offer for their option to buy the house. It would net each of them a $45,000 gain. Brown suggested they take the quick haul and not mess with construction, which couldn't begin until after the last of the summer reservations had been satisfied. There really was no offer. Brown cut his partner a check for $45,000 and told the mayor that he'd found a way to make some money.

Larry Sutley, a country lawyer who had drawn up Orange Beach's incorporation papers in 1984 and served as city attorney, caught wind of the beach house and wanted in. Brown didn't care for Sutley, and it would mean splitting the profits three ways instead of two. But he figured at least the lawyer, unlike the mayor, could cover his share of expenses and help with the paperwork. Brown was paying the mayor's share and had been stuck with all the work.

To cloak their participation in the speculative endeavor, the city attorney assigned each of the men a one-third interest in a company called American Hot LLC. It was a legal entity he had created on behalf of two city employees who never followed through with plans to bottle a hot sauce recipe.

Brown went to Vision Bank and opened an account in the name of American Hot and borrowed $1.6 million. That would cover the cost of the existing beach house, demolition, and construction of an eight-bedroom, eight-bathroom replacement. As soon as the vacationers were out of the old house, Brown would tear it down and begin building the new one.

Meanwhile, they had a political matter with which to contend. Jerry Davidson, the sailboat-captain councilman, had once been Russo's ally but lately was relishing his role as high-rise opponent. His concerns about strained roads and sewerage were widely shared and he was a threat to the mayor's reelection. Brown heard Davidson might stand down and move out of town. Particularly if he could find someone to buy his house in Orange Beach and help him buy a bay-front place beyond the city limit.

Davidson had voted against Brown's interests, and the builder was as eager as the mayor to see the councilman gone. Brown bought the house Davidson liked across the bay for $355,000 and told Davidson he'd pay $755,000 for his house in Orange Beach, which was about $200,000 or so more than it was likely to fetch on the open market. The arrangement was conditioned on Davidson not running for mayor.

The day after the deadline to qualify as a candidate in the city election, Davidson got the keys to his new house and $400,000 in cash from the house swap. In one of his last acts on the city council, Davidson blew Brown a legislative kiss, switching his vote to "yes" on a marina Brown was building.

The mayor paid his thanks with lucrative storm-debris cleanup contracts after Hurricane Ivan. Brown was paid $170,000 for one job even though city employees did the work. The mayor assured Brown that the payment was no mistake, but he made clear that he expected Brown to share.

One morning when Brown stopped by the store for breakfast, the mayor was waiting for him at the deli counter. Russo was headed to a BMW dealership in Mobile to trade up for that year's 530i. He needed $10,000. Brown pulled a checkbook from his pocket.

A few hours later, Russo strode into the BMW dealership with $10,000 in cash, bundled neatly in five stacks. When he paid, the mayor slid a $100 bill from one of the bundles and folded it into his pocket. Then he handed the rest, a stack that was $100 short of triggering an IRS notice, over to the salesman.

It wasn't long after that scene at the BMW dealership that FBI agents showed up at Brown's office in Orange Beach. Brown wasn't there and was summoned. On his way to meet the investigators, the builder got on the phone with Russo. The mayor asked Brown to stop by his store before he met the agents. Russo was waiting outside when Brown pulled in. The two of them were walking around back of the store when the mayor turned to Brown and asked if he was wearing a wire.

"No," Brown cried. He thrust his arms into the air, inviting inspection.

Russo spun away and stormed off into a wooded area behind the store. He was panicked. The FBI knew about the $10,000 check. Agents had dropped by the store earlier to question him.

Though they were being investigated by the FBI, Russo and Brown proceeded with their plans to flip the lots on Wolf Bay. Brown couldn't afford to lie low. He and Wall had something like $15 million tied up in the Water Club. Even a delay could be devastating. If their options to buy the property expired before the plans won approval, they'd be financially ruined. If they pulled it off, the wealthy men would be even richer. They estimated that their profits on the Water Club could be $64 million.

Brown and Wall sometimes worked with a pair of investors from Louisiana, for whom they would scout land deals and manage construction in exchange for a cut of the profits when whatever they built was sold.

The Louisiana men had a tract in Orange Beach where they wanted to build a bunch of houses. They had mentioned that if the right property became available, they would be interested in expanding the subdivision to Wolf Bay to the north. The lots that the mayor wanted to buy with Brown were perfect. Brown sent Wall to pitch them.

They agreed to pay $1.6 million, totally unaware that they were being pinched for $400,000 so that their Alabama business partners could bribe the mayor.

In January 2006, a federal indictment against the mayor was unsealed. State prosecutors leveled their own charges against Russo, as well as against Sutley, Brown, and a crusty old former councilman named Joe McCarron. Prosecutors alleged that he traded votes in exchange for business at his insurance agency before he was voted off the council in the 2004 election.

Sheriff's deputies rounded up the men on the morning the charges were made public and booked them at the county jail in Bay Minette.

They each had a mug shot made against a glossy block wall and then were allowed to post bond and leave.

The mayor faced a litany of charges. There were accusations that he hid and illegally spent some $33,000 of campaign contributions on suits, computer gear, and trips to the casino boats in Biloxi, Mississippi. He was accused of spending taxpayer money on limos and other personal expenses during a trip to New York City to butter up credit-rating firms before a municipal bond offering. The most serious counts were allegations of bribery related to the BMW, the beach house, and Brown. The feds didn't even know about the Wolf Bay land flip yet. Wall wasn't charged until March.

When Russo was arrested, he was in a second-floor condo in one of Wireman's Caribe towers. The mayor had sold his house and moved into Wireman's luxury tower. Russo would live there while Brown finished building him a bigger house on land bought with his Wolf Bay flip profits.

It was a bad look for Russo to be living at Caribe, even if he was paying market-rate rent, as he swore he had been. Russo had been beating back accusations that he was in Wireman's pocket ever since it came out that he had been using the developer's condominium in downtown New Orleans for weekend getaways. Jerry Davidson let that one loose at a crowded and testy public hearing about a big condo plan. Davidson was no longer on the council, or even a resident of Orange Beach, yet was still perfectly capable of being a pain in Russo's ass. The mayor eventually admitted to crashing at Wireman's New Orleans pad a few times but insisted that the hospitality had not influenced his support for Wireman's giant Turquoise Place condo towers.

Russo was using Wireman's New Orleans place more than he let on, though. The mayor was there enough that the cable bill was in his name. Worse yet, prosecutors accused the mayor of paying for the television service at Wireman's apartment from a stash of pilfered campaign contributions.

Wireman was named in the indictments. FBI agents questioned him twice. The U.S. attorney in Mobile asked a federal judge to order the IRS to turn over years of his tax returns, along with those of Brown and Sutley. In court papers that were kept under seal, Wireman was listed as a defendant along with Russo. When agents arrived at Caribe to apprehend the mayor, Wireman figured he was going to be arrested as well. There had been a report on the local TV news to that effect the night before. The guard down at the resort's gate called up to tell him the feds had arrived. He emptied his pockets and went outside to where the agents had gathered around the tower where Russo was living.

Wireman recognized one of the agents from his questionings.

"You looking for me?" the developer asked.

"Why would we be looking for you?" the agent said. "We're here for the mayor. He's up there. If you don't want your door broken down, you'll let us in."

Davidson, though his exit from Orange Beach became central to the federal bribery case, was not charged and became a cooperating witness for prosecutors.

Two weeks after the arrests, the Orange Beach City Council convened a special meeting. It opened with a prayer and the Pledge of Allegiance. Russo remained standing and read from a typed two-page statement.

"I ask everyone, both in Orange Beach and south Alabama, to resist the urge to jump to conclusions," the mayor said. "If you merely read the paper and watch the news, it is easy to conclude that I am guilty and should hurry on off to jail."

Unbeknownst to the mayor, he would be whisked off to jail again. Within the hour.

Investigators had happened upon some weed stashed inside a vase when they combed the mayor's Caribe condo after his first arrest. Sheriff's deputies had been dispatched to haul him in again, this time on misdemeanor drug charges.

When the deputies arrived, the mayor was in a closed session with the city council to discuss the corruption charges against him and the city attorney. News cameras were waiting behind city hall when deputies escorted him out to a patrol car, tipped off by someone on the side of the law. The marijuana citation paled in comparison with the seriousness of the felony corruption charges, but the embarrassment hit a tipping point with city employees and residents. Russo resigned a couple of days later and then drove to Mobile in his new BMW to plead not guilty to the federal charges.

The trial lasted two weeks in late August. Brown pleaded guilty beforehand and became the government's star witness.

His testimony spanned three days, during which he told all about how he had cowed to the mayor and tried to enrich him in hopes of currying favor at city hall. "I was afraid for my livelihood," Brown kept saying. He explained how Russo had helped him with matters related to the Water Club, how he had moved Davidson out of town and the mayor had rewarded him with lucrative storm cleanup contracts for relocating his biggest obstacle to reelection.

The builder recited the jobs that his crews did gratis at Russo's old house and how he'd cleared land, had an architect draw up plans based on a magazine photo the mayor had given him, and was getting ready to start building Russo a Mediterranean abode when he was arrested. He acknowledged that he, Sutley, and Russo had made matters worse for themselves trying to move money around after the indictments came down.

Brown said his net worth had plunged to about $12 million from the more than $30 million the year before. An expensive option ran out on a valuable tract on the Fort Morgan peninsula and he had sold some other property for less than he had expected. There had been all sorts of expensive complications at the beach house in Gulf Shores.

The cost of materials and labor skyrocketed after Ivan. Workers were in such demand that they could command twice what they earned six months earlier. Prices for plywood, drywall, and wiring were way up. The house was already over budget when Hurricane Katrina blew out windows, soaked the inside, and knocked some of the footers askew. Near the finish line, inspectors from Gulf Shores decided that the house was eighteen inches too tall, so Brown lifted off the metal roof and refastened it a foot and a half lower at a cost of more than $40,000. Days later, the city guys returned and said they'd made a mistake. There was no need to lower the house eighteen inches after all.

It came out that Russo had done more for Brown than throw debris work and rezoning votes his way. Brown told about the time that he, Vision Bank CEO Daniel Sizemore, and a man from a local mortgage company paid $1.6 million for a lot on the beach before they realized that the property didn't go all the way to the ocean and that their view was about to be blocked by another building going up between them and the surf. The developer of the view-obstructing tower offered to buy the land from Brown and his partners for what they had paid.

Brown and the lending chiefs weren't content with that, though. They wanted to profit. Brown called the mayor and explained their predicament. Russo told him that he'd talk to the other side. The offer was raised. Before long, Brown and his buddies were divvying up a $600,000 profit. Brown subtracted $25,000 from each partner's portion and set it aside for the mayor. He told his partners that the deduction was a management fee. The mortgage company executive asked Brown what exactly there was to manage. All that there was at the property were remnants of a house that had been destroyed by Hurricane Ivan.

"Just don't ask," Brown said.

Brown was a prodigious dealmaker. Prosecutors and defense attorneys alike had a hard time untangling his web. Brown had his name on so many limited liability companies and owned so many properties around town at one time or another that even he couldn't keep track. The lawyers spent hours asking him about legal entities and partnerships even if they didn't appear to have anything to do with the case at hand.

"What about Southern Strategy Investments LLC?" one of the lawyers asked.

"He's not a part of that," Brown said.

"And who are your partners there?"

"I honestly don't remember right now if I have any partners in Southern Strategy."

"What about Canal Lands?"

"Canal Lands—"

And on it went. Wall's lawyer must've asked about every LLC he could find with Brown's name on it. He was trying to establish for the jury that Brown worked a lot of deals that had nothing to do with his client, that just because Brown was up to something crooked didn't mean Ken Wall was involved.

"What about Confederate Money LLC?" Wall's lawyer asked.

"Confederate Money is a hotel in Gulf Shores," Brown said.

"That's the name of it? That's not the name of the hotel, is it?"

"No, sir," Brown said. "I think it's La Quinta."

The defense attorneys wore seersucker suits in contrast with the government lawyers' dark wool. One of them toted around a thick de Kooning biography and read from it during breaks. Their strategy was mainly to paint Brown as a serial liar who would tell prosecutors whatever they wanted to hear in order to save his own neck. Russo never took the stand in his own defense.

After six hours of deliberation, the jury returned guilty verdicts against Russo, Sutley, and Wall. The lanky mayor stood slump shouldered in his billowy suit. His mother wailed behind him. Outside, the mayor's brothers led the family through a cluster of television cameras and reporters with microphones like lead blockers at the goal line. The gaggle re-formed and pursued the mayor's family down the street toward their car.

When I called Russo the next morning, he was calm and reflective. "It's just hard to absorb, honestly," he said. "I'm glad my kids weren't old enough to be there."

After the verdict, he and his family made the hour-long drive back to the beach in silence. He thought the government's case was bullshit, but he couldn't compete with its unlimited prosecutorial resources. Most of his assets had been frozen. The trial had drained him, and he now had to come up with funds for his appeal and to provide for his children while he was locked up. He was unapologetic about trying to get a piece of the action, though.

"I didn't do anything that a lot of other people haven't done as far as buying property and selling property," he said.

That was probably true, but it suggested that much more of the local real estate market was rigged, underpinned by blind greed and deceit. Even after everything he'd been through, the former mayor didn't acknowledge that he, the rule maker, was different from the common speculator playing the game.

The Water Club's fate was sealed in December 2006 when the city council voted down the rezoning request from Brown and Wall. The denial had nothing to do with the developers' indictment and pending imprisonment. It failed on a technicality. City law required that rezoning applicants own the subject property, or at least have it under contract to buy. Brown and Wall's options on some of the land had lapsed. The Water Club was dead.

Prosecutors had drummed up a letter-writing campaign in Orange Beach urging maximum sentences for the former city officials. "Can you imagine if every public official in the country did what this defendant did?" Assistant U.S. Attorney Steven Butler told the judge at the February sentencing. "Our republic would go the way of the Roman Empire."

Friends and relatives of the defendants as well as some prominent citizens wrote letters of their own requesting leniency. Tim James, the toll bridge developer whom Russo and Sutley had helped make a millionaire many times over, came to the sentencing and spoke on their behalf. "Orange Beach is a small town and you hear all the secrets," James said. "I've never heard anybody say Steve Russo or Larry Sutley are on the take. . . . There's never been one iota of them doing anything but benefiting the public—as a developer it's been expensive, but it was always for the public."

Judge Kristi DuBose told Russo and Sutley that she had read the letters written in their support. By the sentences she handed down, it didn't appear she was much swayed: she gave Russo ten years and Sutley twenty-seven months. "The conduct for which you've been convicted may not define you. But nevertheless it has been sufficiently proven," she said. "It is part of your history. It is now part of who you are."

Wall wound up getting a year and a day. Even after he'd testified against the others and helped investigators in another matter upstate, Brown still had to serve a year in prison. The ill-gotten gains, including the Gulf Shores beach house and accounts at Vision Bank, were forfeited to the government.

This was all incredible fodder for a newspaper reporter, and I was glad that my wife and I had decided to stick around.

At home, I installed French doors that swung open to a backyard where we planted azaleas, Arbor Day cedar saplings from the Boy Scouts, and a

New Zealand tea tree that flared up in fiery-pink flowers. We mounded soil into a garden bed and raised bell peppers, cucumbers, and arugula. By the side windows, we planted fast-growing and poison-leafed oleander for privacy and shade. I dressed up the front yard with big ferns and lined the flower bed with river rocks. We ripped out the drab linoleum and laid ceramic tile in the bathrooms and kitchen. I made a big mess using the wet saw in the garage, so even it got a paint job. We traded the chintzy faucets and ceiling fans for sturdier, stylish models.

Though the cottage was shaping up nicely, the marriage was another story. After two years, in the summer of 2007, my college sweetheart and I split up and agreed to sell the house as part of our divorce. Unfortunately, the market had unraveled before our marriage.

# PART II

# II

## INTERESTONLY™

Home prices peaked nationally in the summer of 2006. It hadn't been a year yet since my wife and I had bought our house. We were blissfully unaware of how mistimed our purchase had been. In fact, I still felt we had made a sound, conservative purchase given the frothy market. I knew what we earned—together more than twice the area's median household income of about $45,000—and what we could afford. I was familiar with the wages paid by the municipal governments, which were among the largest employers around. Whatever riches the real estate folks were raking in, my wife and I were typical of the area's salaried workers. Yet somehow few of the roofs that were mushrooming around us were priced anywhere near the $137,500 that we could afford.

At about $250,000 each, the small brick houses of a subdivision being built off the next county road over were among the cheapest around. Yet the houses cost $100,000 more than those on my street. I felt it unlikely we'd ever have much competition in our price range, especially given how land and labor costs had risen following Hurricane Katrina.

Though my county map showed swaths of empty space that implied no scarcity of developable land, lot prices surged to more than $75,000 apiece. The average house price in the county hit $250,000. And that was over a mostly rural area that was larger than Rhode Island. Down by the booming beach, where I lived, home prices were well above the county average. Lots alone could cost $225,000 even if they were well inland. Just about any house listed under $150,000 sold within days of hitting the market as Katrina refugees resettled.

It was a different story on the waterfront. Mansions on Ono Island, a gated community off Perdido Key, were priced 25 percent less than a year earlier and still wouldn't sell. Secluded beachfront lots on the Fort Morgan peninsula fetched half what they had in 2005. More than thirty-three hundred condos were listed for sale in July 2006, compared with fewer than one hundred the summer before.

Real estate agents blamed the condo glut on stubborn speculators who were clinging to the idea that someone would buy them out at last year's highs. Condos would still sell. It was just that the seller might have to shave $100,000 or so off the asking price. That was problematic if it was less than they had agreed to pay and they didn't happen to have a spare $100,000 to fork over to whomever they had agreed to buy the condo from.

Given the stories circulating about $30,000-a-year clerical workers on the hook for condos that cost several hundred thousand dollars, it seemed likely that many preconstruction buyers might not be able to afford to walk away without a fight. All eyes were on the Lighthouse, which had been completed in June.

Three years earlier, when dump trucks were still carting away the remnants of the demolished Lighthouse Motel, it took just a day for the developers to find buyers for all 251 of their proposed condo units. The big question now was whether buyers would hand over hundreds of thousands of dollars for keys to the finished condominiums. Prices had surged during the three years it took to build the two-tone tower. The first wave of buyers agreed to pay between $215,000 and $485,000. But many of the residences had been flipped in the ensuing years. Subsequent buyers had agreed to pay more than $700,000 in some cases. Then prices fell. Condos that had changed hands for $650,000 before Hurricane Katrina were turning up on the market for less than $500,000. Either way out—selling for a loss or walking away from the 20 percent deposit—could cost six figures.

By July, about fifty Lighthouse units had closed and one of the developers, Rick Phillips, told the *Register* that he hadn't heard from anyone who wanted to back out. "We've had a couple of buyers say they would not like to close," he said, "but they plan to close unless they find a buyer."

The Lighthouse was the first of a few towers where developers would summon buyers to the closing table in 2006. Larry Wireman's latest Caribe tower was nearly ready. So was a sleek crescent down Perdido Key called Bella Luna, where Shallow had handled sales. Others nearly ready for move-in included Crystal Tower in Gulf Shores, a twenty-story tower abutting Gulf State Park called the Colonnades, and San Carlos, a 142-unit building that had the same paint job, swimming-pool-blue windows, and developers as the Lighthouse.

That August, the S&P CoreLogic Case-Shiller U.S. National Home Price Index declined for the first time in a decade. On a conference call with Wall Street stock analysts, Angelo Mozilo, a hard charger who had built Countrywide Financial into the largest mortgage lender in the United States, struck a rare note of caution. "How low are they going to go?" he said. "It's hard to tell. But the trend is down."

The year before, in 2005, Countrywide had lent almost a half trillion dollars to home buyers, including the couple from north Alabama who flipped my house to me. That was up from about $67 billion of home loans that the California company originated five years earlier, in 2000. Mozilo pledged to tap the breaks in 2006, but some investors were still worried.

Countrywide had promoted a type of loan, known as option ARMs, that offered low teaser rates and multiple payment options each month, including one that wasn't even enough to cover the accruing interest. Choosing that option meant adding to the loan balance instead of reducing it with a payment. Countrywide had trademarked the term InterestOnly for a variety of loan that forestalled principal payments for several months.

Loans like these were popular with people who didn't plan on hanging on to the house or condo they'd just bought. InterestOnly loans allowed flippers to pay peanuts to hold properties for a short period of time. Ideally, home prices rose fast enough that they could sell higher before the teaser terms expired. That's how it worked out for the folks who sold their house to me. I took them out of their InterestOnly Countrywide loan a couple of months before they would have had to start making bigger monthly payments, according to the terms of the document on file with the county.

What if these borrowers weren't able to sell or refinance before the introductory terms expired? What if someone like me never came along wanting to make a home out of their flip house? Would those borrowers be able to handle higher payments once interest rates reset or principal was added? Mozilo didn't know. "I'm not sure exactly what will happen then," he told the analysts.

For the most part, the Lighthouse buyers honored their commitments and signed closing papers over the course of the summer. In October, Rick Phillips summoned the buyers of his look-alike tower, San Carlos, to do the same. By the end of 2006, twenty San Carlos buyers had closed their deals. A dozen put up a fight.

Some wanted out because they said that Phillips hadn't delivered the high-end condos they'd bargained for when they agreed to pay as much as a million dollars. A trio of surgeons from Mobile said that they had discovered all sorts of problems with the unit they had put a deposit on. A toilet didn't flush. Doorknobs and a bathroom mirror were missing. A drippy fire sprinkler had made a moldy mess. One of the patio doors wouldn't open.

The surgeons' lawyer argued that the work was done hastily to beat a deadline in the purchase contracts that gave buyers an out if the building wasn't finished by a certain date. He insisted that the surgeons' lawsuit had nothing to do with weak resale prices or any failed effort to flip. "These people are big-time investors, they have money and they're not afraid to close," the lawyer told me. "They're worried about if the developer pulls out and they're caught holding the bag on a pig in a poke."

Another batch of aggrieved buyers sued explicitly because they had been unable to flip their units. They were real estate agents, formerly employed by the brokerage that Phillips owned, and they were fighting to keep their old boss from collecting on the letters of credit they had put forth as down payments. The sales agents said they signed up for San Carlos preconstruction units so that their old boss could show his lenders there was enough demand to begin construction. They had no intention of actually moving into the building.

As their closing dates approached, the agents slashed their asking prices. One said he had agreed to pay Phillips $723,000 for a three-bedroom unit but after he found no takers cut his asking price to $670,000. That would amount to an ugly loss, but it would be better than forfeiting a six-figure down payment. "We were trying to lose $50,000, $60,000, instead of $150,000, $160,000," the agent said.

It would be a major problem for Phillips and his partners if the condos started selling for less than what other buyers had agreed to pay for the same units. If three-bedroom units sold for $670,000, that pretty much set the bar for the collateral value of the similarly sized condos in the building. Lenders would be unlikely to finance someone who had agreed to pay the developers $723,000.

The agents said their boss made them pull their discounted units from the market so as not to derail sales to buyers who actually wanted keys to their condos. The agents felt that absolved them from having to go through with their purchases. Phillips disagreed and went after their deposits.

In addition to being a developer and a real estate broker, Phillips served as a director at Vision Bank. To beat back the San Carlos lawsuits and pursue the balking buyers' deposits, Phillips turned to a fellow bank board member. Julian Brackin, whom everyone called Buddy, was a local lawyer feared around town as Gulf Shores' unforgiving municipal judge. Brackin denied the agents' claims and successfully pushed the San Carlos disputes into arbitration proceedings outside of open court. Even if

Phillips was winning in court, the reception from buyers for the finished product at San Carlos was not a good sign for other towers topping out along the beach.

It was clear the air was whooshing out of the condo bubble, but I still hadn't made the connection between surgeons trying to wriggle out of a regrettable investment over some mildew and my own fortunes.

# 12

## OVER THE HEDGE

A timeline of the housing crisis prepared by the Federal Reserve Bank of St. Louis points to February 27, 2007, as an early sign of the brewing calamity when Freddie Mac announced that it would no longer buy the riskiest types of subprime mortgages.

For me, the first hint of trouble was the smell of hot garbage wafting over the hedge. It was coming from the house next door. The young couple who owned it were gone. They paid $153,000 for their house around the same time we'd bought ours, setting a new high-water mark in Audubon Place. Now it was as if they had vanished. There was no note, no FOR SALE sign. They hadn't even bothered to take out the trash. Inside, a half-eaten pizza festered on a countertop.

At first the stinking house next door was mostly an annoyance. I cut the lawn with a few extra passes of the mower and had a sweaty tangle every now and then with the big hedge to keep it from overtaking my driveway. By summer, as I was preparing to list my house for sale, the empty house next door became disquieting. It was dawning on me that its abandonment wasn't isolated but rather something of a trend. That it wasn't just overzealous speculators on the beach who were being clobbered.

On Wall Street, the housing market had shifted from a source of jubilation to one of serious concern. With home prices falling, people who had counted on refinancing out of interest-only or pay-option loans before their monthly payments shot up found themselves stuck. They couldn't borrow enough to clear the existing debt. Many were unable or unwilling to make much higher mortgage payments. Countrywide, New Century Financial, and other lenders that had fueled the housing boom with suspect loans were buckling under mounting losses.

In June 2007, a dozen anxious creditors gathered at a Park Avenue office tower to meet with executives from Bear Stearns, the venerable Wall Street investment bank. The creditors were worried about the faltering performance of two of Bear's hedge funds, which had bet more than $20 billion on mortgages granted to home buyers with poor credit.

Bear had launched one of the hedge funds in 2003 to invest primarily in collateralized debt obligations, or CDOs, which pooled large numbers of individual mortgages into single securities. They were mind-bogglingly complex, but the bottom line was simple: If borrowers paid their bills, investors made money. By August 2006, the fund had earned a 36 percent cumulative return as home prices soared, so Bear launched another fund that layered on even more borrowed money in hopes of boosting returns. The more leveraged fund managed less than $700 million in investors' cash, yet it had about $15 billion in assets when the housing market spiraled lower in the spring of 2007.

The same leverage that juiced returns also amplified losses. When the funds' assets dropped below their collateral value, the banks that had lent the funds billions to buy CDOs called the debts due. Selling assets to repay the banks meant dumping these complex mortgage-backed securities into the market and pushing prices even lower.

Representatives from the troubled funds' lenders were given an eleven-page handout when they arrived for the meeting with Bear Stearns executives. The handout detailed the funds' troubles and listed the margin calls it faced from lenders. Bear wasn't going to bail out the funds. Instead, the investment bank asked creditors to impose a sixty-day moratorium on margin calls while the situation was straightened out. Attendees were stunned. They wanted their money back before there wasn't any left. A risk management executive from JPMorgan Chase & Co. raised his hand. "With all due respect," he told the men from Bear, "I think you're underestimating the severity of the situation."

A few days later, Bear had a change of heart and said it would bail out the older of its ailing funds with a $3.2 billion loan to stop the bleeding. The newer, riskier fund was too far gone. By the end of July, it had lost all value. The less leveraged fund fell further, with assets worth pennies on the dollar. Both declared bankruptcy. The funds' collapse jolted Wall Street.

Given the high grades that credit-rating firms had given them, CDOs were supposed to be as safe for investors as U.S. Treasurys. They were not. CDOs were opaque and relatively illiquid. That hadn't really mattered while home prices were surging and their continued rise was taken as an article of faith.

During the first half of the decade, there had been such strong demand for CDOs from investors around the world that lenders began to cut corners in order to produce enough loans to pack the securities. Sometimes lenders didn't verify borrowers' income. Appraisals were fudged and values inflated. Mortgage underwriters didn't care much about the consequences because they were able to unload the risk to Wall Street operations that were pooling the home loans and selling slices of the mortgage bundles to investors.

On the same day that Vision Bank lent my now missing neighbors $137,700 to buy their house, the local lender turned around and sold the mortgage to ABN AMRO Mortgage Group, a Dutch-owned concern that originated, serviced, and bundled into securities hundreds of billions of dollars' worth of U.S. mortgages. Vision was off the hook for the loan before it opened for business the next day. The local bank had earned transaction fees and could give a hoot whether the loan was repaid.

Investment firms, AIG chief among them, also sold credit default swaps, which were essentially insurance against losses in CDOs. There were also synthetic CDOs used to bet on the performance of actual CDOs. As a result, a single ill-advised mortgage might play a role in the performance of dozens of securities. The trillions of dollars invested in securities backed by subprime mortgages represented a bet on U.S. housing that was considerably higher than the value of the actual property involved. Timothy Geithner, the soon-to-be Treasury Department secretary who was head of the Federal Reserve Bank of New York when the real estate market collapsed, once likened dissecting a CDO to untangling "cooked spaghetti."

Consider CMLTI 2006-NC2, a mortgage-backed security created by Citigroup in June 2006. Citi asked to buy about a billion dollars' worth of loans from New Century Financial, a high-flying home lender headquartered in Irvine, California. New Century delivered to Citi an assortment of about forty-five hundred mortgages to fulfill the bank's order. There were loans to house flippers on Oahu, home buyers in Boston, some funded refinancings in Des Moines, Iowa, and interest-only mortgages made around Miami. There were concentrations of loans in California, Florida, and Arizona, but really they were from all over. Cleveland, Tennessee; Cleveland, Mississippi; and Cleveland, Ohio, were all represented. So were Arkansas and Alaska. A few of the mortgages were originated where I lived in south Alabama.

Someone in Foley with a pretty poor Fair Isaac Corp. credit score of 654 borrowed $209,000 to buy a house for $220,000. New Century accepted the borrower's word as to income and agreed to an adjustable-rate mortgage with a balloon payment after two years. Another person, who was slightly more creditworthy with a FICO score of 681, took $50,000 cash out of an Orange Beach home using a second mortgage.

Citi employees set aside $4.3 million worth of loans to borrowers who reported no income and no assets. About a dozen of those "NINA" loans were removed from the pool as unacceptable. The rest were bundled into the bond, which was then carved into smaller batches of loans according to their perceived risk. Fannie Mae took the safest chunk. Buyers of other slices included the People's Republic of China, Kentucky Retirement Systems, bond funds managed by Fidelity and State Street, Banca Commerciale Italiana, France's Société Générale, a multibillion-dollar British investment fund, a big German savings bank, a hospital in coastal Mississippi, Seattle's Washington Mutual, an arm of JPMorgan Chase & Co., and several hedge funds.

The riskiest slices were bought mostly by CDOs, including one called

Kleros Real Estate CDO III, a billion-dollar security that Switzerland's UBS Group created by wadding together bits of various mortgage-backed securities and then dicing them anew. A few synthetic CDOs—with names such as Auriga and Glacier Funding V—held credit default swaps, or insurance against losses, on segments of Citi's CMLTI 2006-NC2.

Not even Lewis Ranieri, who had pioneered mortgage-backed bonds in the 1980s at Salomon Brothers, was sure he understood CDOs. There wasn't much information about what collateral they held. Plus, CDOs often invested in other CDOs, which made things muddier. There wasn't really any way to tell who was holding the riskiest slices of the securities, which were the first to lose value when home prices fell. "I don't know how to understand the ripple effects through the system today," Ranieri said at a real estate seminar in early 2007.

As the abandoned pool in the backyard next door filled with roof shingles and palm fronds, I put our house on the market. To cover sales commissions and other expenses, we'd have to sell it for more than we'd paid. That seemed unlikely to happen given that home prices were amid a tumble unmatched in modern times. Even if someone came around who liked the azaleas we'd planted or the new tile floors so much that they were willing to pay the price that we needed to clear the mortgage debt and transaction fees, they probably wouldn't be able to get a loan to do it.

The real estate agent who had sold us the house didn't think it was worth the trouble to try to sell it. I didn't have a choice. No matter how bleak the prospects, I had to at least list the place and try to sell it to comply with my divorce agreement.

I turned to Pam Anderson, a coworker's wife, who had just become a real estate agent and was eager for a listing. On November 19, 2007, the house was listed for $149,000 with the understanding that we'd accept much less. If I had to, I could drain my retirement account at work to make up the difference between what we owed and what the house fetched.

In anticipation of the first open house, I scrubbed inside and out, planted fresh flowers, and dabbed a bit of paint by the front door. My real estate agent mother taught me that trick. House hunters would be struck by the scent of newness upon arrival. My mom had lots of open house horror stories, like the roommate who didn't get the message and was lounging in his underwear smoking a joint when she arrived. Another time she showed up to host an open house for some family friends and found them in a heated argument. The wife was furious with her husband for leaving water drops in one of the huge house's many sinks. I gave my kitchen sink one last wipe just in case. I didn't want any drops derailing a deal.

Pam pounded arrows into the subdivision's entrance to point the way and tied balloons to the yard sign. She baked cookies and wrote her mother's name in a guest book so that it would not be empty for the first arrival. I wished her luck and made myself scarce. It rained that day and Pam sat alone for hours in the impeccable house, listening to the drizzle. Her foray into real estate was as ill timed as mine. Not even the cookies got a nibble.

After a few fruitless months trying to sell my house, she pulled up her sign and moved on. I stuck a FOR SALE BY OWNER sign in its place, hoping, along with ever more Americans in similar predicaments, for a quick rebound.

# 13

## "WE'VE HAD QUITE A FEW PEOPLE WALK AWAY"

I wasn't the only one having a hard time selling a house. A few weeks before I put mine on the market, the American Hot beach house, the eight-bedroom box that had helped sink the mayor of Orange Beach, was auctioned off.

The fifty-three-hundred-square-foot house had been sitting on the market for nearly a year. It was listed for $2.9 million by a local firm pursuant to an agreement between its owners—Steve Russo, Larry Sutley, and the builder, Jim Brown—their lenders, and federal prosecutors. With no real interest from buyers, the U.S. Marshals Service scheduled an auction.

The house was painted fog green and stood on a surfside lot about five miles west of the center of town. Improbably, the massive house was on stilts. Each of the three floors featured living areas outfitted with wet bars. There was an elevator and a swimming pool out on an elevated deck. Each room had a balcony on the back looking out to the Gulf. It looked more like a small condominium building than a house. It slept twenty.

About fifty people packed into the second-story great room for the auction. The house that Brown built to bribe the mayor had yet to be lived in but was in rough shape nonetheless. Trim pieces were missing. There were empty spaces where kitchen appliances should've been, and the windows were without screens. The pool was empty save for a puddle of rotten rainwater. The top two floors smelled strongly of backed-up sewage.

Local real estate brokers had submitted offers beforehand and $950,000 had been the highest. A twangy auctioneer from Georgia addressed the gathered bidders from the kitchen's granite countertop and started the bidding there, at $950,000.

"One million!" someone in the crowd shouted.

"One million fifty thousand!"

"One million one!"

The price moved up like that, $50,000 at a time, until bidding sputtered at $1.5 million. Another man from the auction company whispered with the marshals off to the side. They broke their huddle and the auction company man told the crowd they'd accept bids in $10,000 increments.

A man up front bid $1.51 million, and then across the room someone blurted, "One point five and a quarter." That wasn't a $10,000 increment, but it didn't matter because it didn't last. When the price hit $1.54 million, there was another pause.

"I'm going to look everyone in the eye," the auctioneer said. He bent forward and scanned the room slowly, like a rooster. Everyone stiffened. "Who wants to bid one million five fifty?" His eyes met shaking heads.

Someone broke the silence with a bid. After a few minutes of back-and-forth and goading from the auctioneer, a couple from Columbia, Missouri, won the American Hot house with a bid of $1.65 million.

A man from Vision Bank stood in the corner of the kitchen, looking beside himself. Jim Brown, via American Hot, the company that the city attorney used to conceal the mayor's involvement in the house, had borrowed more than $2 million from Vision. The bank would be receiving the bulk of the $1.65 million auction price but would still have to absorb a six-figure loss. Those were piling up at Vision, which had been bought seven months earlier by a bank holding company from Ohio called Park National.

Park National had paid about $170 million for Vision in March in an effort to jump-start growth to its bottom line. Executives wanted to be lending money in places that people were moving to, not places from which people were moving, like the Ohio and Kentucky towns where Park operated. Investment bankers brought Vision to their attention, and an acquisition was announced in September 2006, right before home prices began to deteriorate around the country.

Park hadn't owned a bank farther from its central Ohio base than the Cincinnati suburbs. Now it had fifteen branches in coastal Alabama and the Florida Panhandle as well as more than half a billion dollars of iffy loans tied to real estate along the Gulf, like the American Hot beach house. Park had caught the proverbial falling knife. By the end of 2007, about 10 percent of Vision's $639 million in loans were nonperforming. Daniel Sizemore, the CEO who had started and steered Vision, resigned from Park National and quit its board about fourteen months after the merger.

Other big players from out of town were getting clobbered as well. Condo buyers were balking at the Wharf, the entertainment district that insurance giant AIG was developing on the Intracoastal Waterway with a Birmingham mall builder. The Wharf's first condo tower, Levin's Bend, had sold out in a flash a couple of years earlier when buyers lined up out the door of the real estate office to put down deposits. Now buyers were heading to court to get those deposits back. By the time contractors put the finishing touches on Levin's Bend in the summer of 2007, buyers of about 20 percent of the building's 190 units were suing to get out of purchase contracts.

They argued that they were entitled to walk away with their deposits because construction had taken longer than promised. The developers countered with "act of God" provisions in the sales contracts that pushed out deadlines in the event of disasters such as Hurricane Katrina. Buddy Brackin, the baleful municipal judge and bank director who was battling remorseful buyers on behalf of other developers, took the buyers' side at the Wharf. He argued that his clients weren't getting what they bargained for from AIG Baker.

Though condos at the Wharf were cheaper than those on the beach, the 20 percent deposits were still a lot more than most people could afford to lose. Among those who'd taken their fight to court was a Louisiana couple that wanted to avoid forking over the $90,000 deposit on the thirteen-hundred-square-foot unit for which they'd agreed to pay $450,000. Some litigants had put deposits on more than one Wharf condominium. It was early on, but after a few weeks of attempted closings, two buyers had chosen court for every one that took keys. More than $20 million in sales were at risk, and the number was growing.

"I'm sure there are folks that never thought they'd close on a condo," AIG Baker's regional boss told me. "They just wanted to flip, and then we got into this soft market."

At the end of September, Colonial Properties, a Birmingham real estate investment trust that was building an open-air shopping mall with the help of Gulf Shores taxpayers, took a $35 million loss on two residential projects in Orange Beach.

The publicly traded firm had partnered with two thirty-something brothers from Orange Beach to build a 350-unit residential project next to the Wharf's amphitheater and across the street from the city's notorious sewer plant. Cypress Village was to be built over a decade on eighty-four acres. Town houses were offered from $425,000 and home sites for $200,000.

The arrangement called for Colonial to buy the property and fund construction while the brothers did the building and selling. It was not unlike the arrangement Jim Brown and Ken Wall had with their Louisiana investors. Colonial Properties spent millions paving roads, installing utilities, and mounding dirt so that building foundations were situated on firm ground above flood lines. The first eighty town houses were built and painted tastefully in mossy greens and earthy yellows. They were meticulously landscaped with Aztec grass and dwarf oleander. A stand of cypress was planted at the entrance. It looked great. But it stank thanks to the sewage treatment plant across the street.

Three miles down the road, across from the former mayor's store, the brothers and Colonial were also building Grander, a thirty-unit residential marina project with the same palette as Cypress Village. The four-story condos each had its own elevator and were arranged in pairs on a slope down toward Terry Cove, where there were covered boat slips.

Colonial's corporate filings showed a $75.5 million investment in Cypress Village and $20.4 million in Grander. Nearly $100 million was at risk. Less than half of the $730,000 Grander condos were sold. It was even uglier at Cypress Village. The developers hadn't been able to close a single deal for any of the 80 town houses they built. They managed to sell just 5 of the 188 single-family lots they'd staked out.

"We've had quite a few people walk away from their deposits," a Colonial executive told analysts on a call to discuss the company's third-quarter earnings. The firm had written off any chance of recouping $35 million that it had sunk into the Orange Beach projects. "What we have invested down there is greater than what we think we can sell the properties for," he said.

I could relate.

# 14

## SYSTEM ERROR

When John Thain arrived at Merrill Lynch at the end of 2007 to take over as the wealth management firm's CEO, he had a reputation as Wall Street's Mr. Fix-It. Merrill had lured him away from the New York Stock Exchange, where he was also CEO. Thain replaced Stan O'Neal, whose five-year tenure atop Merrill ended that autumn when the firm recorded an $8.4 billion loss.

The loss was staggering, one of the largest ever on Wall Street. It amounted to something like an eighth of the firm's total value. Two weeks earlier, Merrill had warned investors to expect a $5 billion loss. But its mortgage-related securities soured with shocking speed. Moody's Investors Service and Standard & Poor's had cut their ratings of the mortgage-backed securities underlying CDOs as defaults mounted. For years, CDOs had been some of the most in-demand assets on Wall Street. Now they were hot potatoes that no one wanted to be holding.

Problems in the billion-dollar CDO called CMLTI 2006-NC2 were typical. The borrower in Foley with bad credit who in 2006 took out a $209,000 loan with a two-year teaser rate managed to pay off the mortgage before the payments ballooned. That wasn't ideal for investors hoping for payments over years, but it was a lot better than what happened to many of the other loans with which the Foley refi had been bundled in Citi's doomed creation.

The CMLTI 2006-NC2 borrower who pocketed $50,000 by putting a second mortgage on an Orange Beach home in 2006 stopped making payments the next summer. That resulted in a $51,895.26 loss for CMLTI 2006-NC2, or at least for whatever slice of the mortgage bond it was that held the unpaid cash-out loan. Any CDOs that owned that slice would also take a hit. So, too, would other CDOs and synthetic CDOs that owned or tracked the performance of slices of the CDOs that were exposed to the tranches of bonds that held the bad loan in Orange Beach. And so on.

In the first half of 2007, home loans were blowing up within mortgage-backed bonds and ricocheting through the financial system in unpredictable ways. Thanks to CMLTI 2006-NC2, a $312,000 loan to someone in Cathedral City, California, who hadn't been required to prove income and possessed a credit score that should have made it hard to sign up for a cell phone plan became a problem for investors around the world. That loan in Cathedral City and the smaller loss in Orange Beach were just two of more than one thousand defaults suffered by CMLTI 2006-NC2. That security was just one of the more than $500 billion worth of CDOs created in 2006.

CDOs were already difficult to value and to sell. They weren't like stocks, which have so many buyers and sellers and change hands in such volume that there are constantly trades from which to derive a market value. CDOs weren't listed in the price tables in the back of the morning paper. They didn't zip by along the bottom of the television screen. Someone with a mortgage-backed bond or a derivative had to survey dealers of such securities to formulate present value. It was an educated guess at best as to what a lot of the securities were worth. By late 2007, it didn't really matter.

Defaults laid waste to the underlying bonds and forced the credit ratings firms that had originally judged the securities as safe as Treasurys to downgrade them. Investors dumped the securities. Hardly anyone was buying. Prices plunged for even those slices of mortgage bonds and CDOs that had been rated as the least likely to lose value and been scarfed up by Fannie Mae and other government-backed mortgage guarantors.

John Thain studied electrical engineering at MIT and had a Harvard University M.B.A. He ran Goldman Sachs's mortgage bond trading desk in the late 1980s and ascended to the legendary firm's presidency. He left that lofty perch to lead the stock exchange as it went digital and global. At Merrill, his priorities were to raise capital to fill the hole blown in its balance sheet by bad mortgage bets and to figure out how to extricate the firm from the mess. There were more than $50 billion of mortgage-related securities on Merrill's books. The entirety of its positions were long, or investments made in expectation that home prices would continue to rise and that borrowers would keep paying their mortgages. Five years earlier, Merrill hadn't owned any of these securities.

"Why is it okay to own $50 billion of these assets?" Thain asked Merrill's board of directors soon after he started. Because they were graded AAA by the credit-rating firms, same as U.S. government debt, he was told.

Thain dug deeper and examined the computer model that analysts used to predict how mortgage-related securities would perform under various economic conditions. Among the variables that the financial analysts could toggle was the rate of home-price appreciation. There was a box where various rates of growth could be typed in, but the computer program wouldn't accept a negative number. Whoever had built a model used to value trillions of dollars of mortgage-related securities hadn't considered a scenario in which American home prices declined.

By early 2008, a full-blown crisis was unfolding in New York City. Big banks rang in the new year with tens of billions of dollars in mortgage-related losses. Bank of America thought it was buying at the bottom when it paid $4 billion for Countrywide. A year earlier, the wobbling mortgage lender's market value was six times that much. Countrywide's loans kept blowing up, though, and Bank of America's purchase became regrettable no matter the price.

Bear Stearns, near bankruptcy, fell into the arms of JPMorgan Chase in March. Five months later, the U.S. Treasury Department took over Fannie Mae and Freddie Mac and the more than $5 trillion in mortgages they held or had guaranteed. The mortgage giants had eased their standards during the housing boom, trying to stave off Wall Street rivals who were gaining market share by bundling mortgage bonds without Fannie's or Freddie's stamp of approval. Investors, including central banks around the world, were at enormous risk if either Fannie or Freddie failed. The implicit government guarantee they offered to buyers of mortgage bonds now needed to be explicit.

Lehman Brothers Holdings, the country's oldest investment bank, with roots as a cotton brokerage in antebellum Alabama, filed for bankruptcy protection a week later. Washington Mutual, with $307 billion in assets, became the biggest bank failure in U.S. history. It was seized by the federal government, which sold what was left of the country's largest savings and loan to JPMorgan Chase for $1.9 billion.

Charlotte's Wachovia had been on an acquisition bender, wolfing down smaller lenders with an eye to becoming a national financial services firm. It choked on its $26 billion takeover of a California lender called Golden West Financial. A septuagenarian husband and wife named Herb and Marion Sandler had built Golden West into the country's second-biggest savings and loan by peddling the same types of choose-your-own-payment loans that Countrywide cranked out. Golden West's shares were trading near an all-time high when Wachovia came knocking in 2006. The loans began defaulting in early 2008. In April, Wachovia disclosed a $350 million loss mostly related to the option ARMs it acquired when it bought Golden West. Between the big quarterly loss and the Washington Mutual failure, depositors were unnerved and withdrew $15 billion from Wachovia. The bank's creditors tightened their reins and charged it more to borrow. In July, Wachovia reported a $9 billion quarterly loss. Wells Fargo agreed to buy the reeling lender in October.

There was turmoil in Europe, too. Banks had to be bailed out in the United Kingdom, Belgium, and Germany. They failed in Iceland, Denmark, and Spain.

The U.S. government bailed out AIG, which had sold about $79 billion of protection against losses from mortgage-related securities without putting nearly enough cash aside to cover the obligations, not to mention the insurance giant's suspect dalliances with real estate development, as at the Wharf in Orange Beach.

Citi, which in early 2007 bought the Dutch mortgage giant that owned the loan on the abandoned house next door to me, had a $43 billion hoard of CDOs and wound up with its own monumental losses. It had to be bailed out by the government in November.

Thain couldn't untwist Merrill from its house trap fast enough and had to sell the firm to Bank of America. Thain took a lot of heat when it came out that upon arriving to try to save the firm, he had outfitted his new office with a $68,000 credenza and a $35,000 antique commode. He was out within weeks of Bank of America's takeover.

Congress and the administration of President George W. Bush reached agreement on a $700 billion banking rescue package that autumn. The Troubled Asset Relief Program, or TARP, enabled the Treasury Department to buy distressed assets from financial institutions that were choking on toxic mortgage-related securities. The aim was to keep banks solvent and able to lend to businesses and consumers. If banks stopped extending credit, the whole economy would seize up.

The biggest infusions went to Wall Street institutions: $90 billion between Bank of America and Citigroup; $25 billion apiece to JPMorgan Chase and Wells Fargo; $10 billion each for Goldman Sachs and Morgan Stanley. Overall, more than nine hundred financial institutions received government assistance. Regions Financial, the Birmingham, Alabama, bank that lent me the money to buy my house, took a $3.5 billion bailout in November. Ohio's Park National received $100 million in December to help it withstand the tens of millions of dollars in losses on Vision's bad loans at the beach.

The Federal Reserve cut interest rates to try to slow the bleeding, but it was no use. Mortgage rates remained stubbornly high given the risks of lending into a declining market. Foreclosures swelled as droves of underwater homeowners walked away.

# 15

## "THE WHOLE CAPER WAS OVER"

On Alabama's beaches, the condo game screeched to a halt. More buyers bailed and prices plunged. Subdivision developers disappeared and cranes idled at surfside towers. Jobs vanished. It was a bonanza for bankruptcy lawyers.

Rick Phillips, the condo developer who was having trouble convincing buyers to finalize sales in his San Carlos tower, went bust in April. He filed for Chapter 7 bankruptcy protection with debts of more than $124 million, against assets—ranging from condominiums and life insurance policies to the miniblinds and lamps at his primary residence—that added up to a little over $8 million. The debts were claimed by a roster of rattled lenders with whom he'd mortgaged condominiums and other properties. He owed more than $1 million each to Washington Mutual, Wachovia, and Lehman Brothers and $550,000 to Countrywide. He owed $4 million to Vision Bank, where he had been a member of the board of directors' audit committee. The IRS sought $885,000. Phillips owed Compass Bank more than $9 million, Colonial Bank in excess of $22 million, Bank Trust $14 million, and my lender, Regions, about $17 million. The larger debts were related to his plans to build the massive Mandalay Beach project in Orange Beach and a tower on Perdido Pass, where he bought land from the city and removed a haunted house.

Mandalay Beach also generated significant obligations to individual investors. Phillips and his partners owed millions to a local developer who had helped them assemble sixteen acres of beach for Mandalay after Hurricane Ivan and was now owed $7 million for his services. Jim Mattei, a Mobile native who made a fortune founding the Checkers fast-food chain, had foreclosed on a big chunk of the surfside property at the start of the year.

During the frenzied land grab after Hurricane Ivan, Phillips and his partners needed $35 million to complete their Mandalay land purchase. They turned to Mattei, a friend of some of them. They showed Mattei their plans for Mandalay Beach and told him the project would net more than $100 million in profits. The drive-through tycoon agreed to lend them $35 million if they paid him a $10 million fee in addition to interest.

When the loan came due during the summer of 2006, they owed Mattei more than $29 million, a debt that was accruing interest at a rate of about $9,600 a day. In the foreclosure sale, Mattei put in the high bid, about $15 million, and subtracted that from the developers' debt, which was still about $15 million and growing.

A North Carolina development firm told Orange Beach officials the year before that it would be taking on the troubled project, but city hall hadn't heard a peep since. Banks and their appraisers started calling to ask the building department what they could do with the portions of the property against which they had lent. City hall had been banking on a luxury tower, conference center, and municipal beach. It was unclear what would happen now. As it sat, the oceanfront property was littered with dead palms and debris from storm-damaged buildings. The unsightly scene stretched for about twelve hundred feet along the beach highway at the terminus of Orange Beach's sole north–south artery and was cordoned with a ragged combination of fluorescent plastic fencing, chain link, and remnants of decorative walls.

Behind the scenes, the situation was as messy as the property. Multiple lenders had foreclosed on pieces of the financing. One conference call that city employees joined had nearly thirty different bankers and lawyers on the line. At some point, the project's name was changed to Mandolay Beach. However it was spelled, city leaders were willing to give the lenders time to try to revive the development. "We'll take anything with a pulse right now," the mayor said.

Heavily indebted developers were folding up and down the beach and beyond. Bon Secour Village, the town within a town drawn up for the woods along the Intracoastal Waterway, went belly-up. During the summer of 2007, the developers enlisted the former mayor of Gulf Shores to lobby the new mayor and council for help jump-starting the old-world waterfront they envisioned. They needed something in the neighborhood of $30 million, maybe $40 million.

The former mayor, a grumpy old bull who ran a real estate firm and liked to wear softball shorts, cited his administration's aid to Colonial Properties, the real estate investment trust that brought a shopping mall and Publix to town. The Bon Secour Village developers had in mind something similar to the city's arrangement with Colonial: they'd sell bonds to pay for roads, sewers, and riprap along the canal, and Gulf Shores would rebate to them tens of millions of dollars of sales and property taxes generated at Bon Secour Village. The developers would use the rebated taxes to repay bondholders. The council agreed to entertain a more detailed proposal, but it never came.

The Bon Secour Village developers—or town founders, as they preferred—stopped paying their largest lender around then. Wachovia sued them in December 2007 in Mobile's federal court, claiming to be owed $21.2 million, plus interest that was accruing at a clip of about $4,000 a day.

Until then, the developers had projected an image of health. Though Bon Secour Village was little more than the start of a boat basin and a colonnaded sales office that looked like an unfinished bank branch, the developers had paid $15,000 for the lead sponsorship of the National Shrimp Festival that was held every fall down at the public beach. The first house built in Bon Secour Village got a spread in *Coastal Living* magazine. Once the fanfare and awe ebbed, though, the thirty-five-hundred-square-foot Acadian-style spec house started to look less like the first house built in Bon Secour Village and more like the only house.

An entity owned by three of Bon Secour Village's five developers spent $1.9 million building the lonely manse. It was made to fit into one of the decadent streets in New Orleans's French Quarter, yet it sat in the woods between a sparsely traveled county road and a barge channel. It was the sole structure in sight, unless you counted a portable toilet that workers had left behind down the street. A launch party the developers hosted at the Birmingham Museum of Art, as well as the one in the furniture store parking lot in Orange Beach, had been well attended but apparently hadn't done much for sales.

Privately, the Bon Secour Village partnership was splintering. The men who built the spec house ran afoul of one of the other developers, a Birmingham man who raced cars. He had separately sold them a stake in a Florida resort deal for $1 million. The arrangement was for them to pay it off in monthly installments of $10,000. After they missed a payment in the summer of 2007, the race car driver fired off an email threatening to sue if they didn't square up pronto. The payments constituted the bulk of his income, he said. He needed to be at the front of their line of creditors.

"We are not choosing to not pay you," one replied. They couldn't pay anyone. They were scrounging for investors and had a lead on someone who might infuse their flimsy real estate empire with some cash. "I have a friend from college," he typed.

The spec home trio filed for bankruptcy protection in April 2008. One of them, from Florida, reported more than $120 million of debt. The other two, from upstate Alabama, claimed liabilities in excess of $160 million. A bunch of the debt was tied to Bon Secour Village. That was the largest of the many deals and limited liability companies in which they had become entangled. In addition to aspiring town founders, they were prolific condo traders.

They were holding dozens of units in Alabama and Florida when prices dropped. Introductory terms on loans lapsed before they could sell, and they were spread too thin to keep up with the higher payments with rental income alone. One of their companies, which filed separately for bankruptcy protection, controlled more than thirty condominiums as well as a house on a private island in Miami. They had used that entity to buy more than fifty condominiums—and sell thirty-five—in Alabama alone.

Blowing up a condo empire that large was not a neighborly thing to do. The bankrupt brothers had stopped paying owners' association dues and shared expenses, which meant other owners had to pick up their part of the tab to keep the hallway lights on and insure the buildings. *Condo Owner,* a glossy magazine dedicated to the local vacation property business, hosted an event for subscribers to learn from an expert lawyer about how to best collect dues from the lenders who were repossessing condos along the beach.

"I've had more bankruptcy notices come across my desk in the last month than I had in the twelve years before," the lawyer began. Going after the Bon Secour Village guys, omnipresent as they were, consumed a good deal of his time.

The race car driver and an Atlanta developer that served as Bon Secour Village's public face tried to hold the project together. They hosted investors from New York and flew out west to woo potential partners, to no effect.

Down at the beach, Larry Wireman was having trouble at Turquoise Place.

A neighboring hotel and the estate of a couple who once owned the land where Wireman planned his third and fourth towers came forward with old deed restrictions that limited building height on the property.

Lawyers for the estate and the hotel, which had an interest in preserving its sunset view, said they'd tear up the decades-old deed restrictions if Wireman paid them $22 million. He refused. They countered with $10 million. Wireman opted to fight them in court. He was successful, but he had to wait until his opponents had exhausted their appeals.

By January 2008, when he was cleared to break ground by the state's highest court, Wireman had just days to decide whether to go forward with buying the land for his second pair of towers. He had agreed to pay several neighbors about $50 million altogether for their old beach houses. The way things were going with the first two towers made it worth reconsidering his plans for four.

The first Turquoise Place tower was opening that summer. It was a splendor, wrapped in blue-green glass and balconies, some of which were bigger than my entire house. Each was tiled with porcelain and had a hot tub, gas grill, and bar sink. That was just the balcony. Inside, the condos introduced a new level of luxury to Alabama's beaches. The bathrooms had boxy little toilets designed by Philippe Starck with vanities and faucets to match. There were teak-trimmed Jacuzzi tubs, some of which filled from spouts in the ceiling. There were squiggly blown-glass chandeliers in the Dale Chihuly vein. The fourth floor had a meandering lazy river, and the gym took up three thousand square feet. A few units came with separate, smaller units for nannies or in-laws. There was an indoor pool equipped with underwater speakers. For a while, at least, residents would have to use the indoor pool or swim in the Gulf of Mexico. The outdoor pool wouldn't be ready for a bit.

Orange Beach building inspectors didn't want to risk construction debris falling thirty stories onto sunbathers and splashing children. They wouldn't let Wireman build the pool until exterior construction was completed on the second tower. For the speculators who were unable to flip their units and were looking for a way out, the missing pool offered an opening.

Wireman gave Caribe owners a chance to buy at Turquoise Place before he offered the luxury units to a broader market. Two brothers who owned a Sea-Doo dealership and had made more than $1 million flipping condos in Caribe signed up for four at Turquoise Place, priced about $1.2 million apiece.

They immediately flipped one for a $25,000 profit to a Mississippi gas station owner, who then paid one of the brothers $80,000 to deliver to him purchase contracts for four more Turquoise Place condos. It was baffling that someone, no matter how wealthy, would pay someone else $80,000 to fetch a folder of paperwork from a real estate office. But that, insisted the brother who pocketed the quick $80,000, was the arrangement. The brothers were unable to unload the other three units, though. When the first tower was finished, they lawyered up.

The brothers were among several buyers who sued to avoid closing.

Retreating buyers alleged flaws and deficiencies that might void their purchase contracts, notably the postponed outdoor swimming pool. The marketing brochure drawings showed refrigerators on the balconies instead of bar sinks, litigants argued. It turned out that the hot tubs on the balconies had to be filled and drained with a hose from inside. Doing so saved Wireman millions on plumbing, they claimed, and now they would have to suck on a garden hose to siphon out their dirty hot tub water in their million-dollar oceanfront pad. Some litigants even measured their units and determined that they were 129 square feet smaller than the 2,430 square feet promised in marketing brochures.

Wireman's team said the buyers were coming up short on square feet because they had measured from the finished walls instead of the actual boundaries between units that were unseen behind the drywall. They argued that the sinks by the barbecues were more useful to a cook than small refrigerators. There was nothing Wireman could do about the pool except build it as soon as tower two was topped out. The developer pulled the plug on towers three and four.

The neighboring homeowners who'd become multimillionaires on paper when Wireman agreed to buy their old houses were never minted. Their houses would sit in the shadows of towers as they had once feared.

That spring, in 2008, with the real estate market in full meltdown, Shallow met Shaul Zislin for a drink to celebrate a deal. They had just unloaded a whole-floor penthouse in a posh new building over the state line in Florida. They were yucking it up and throwing them back at the bar at the Hangout, an eighteen-thousand-square-foot restaurant and music venue that Zislin owned. He had built the Hangout at the Gulf Shores public beach when he realized the market was turning against the sorts of residential towers that he had planned.

Zislin, the south Florida investor, was fortunate that his original plan had become embroiled in city politics. The topic of how his development should mesh with the adjacent public spaces was the subject of several community meetings and much consternation at city hall.

The Gulf Shores City Council paid $180,000 to a consulting firm, which produced a thick plan called Envision Gulf Shores. It recommended moving the beach highway a few blocks north so that the area around the public beach would be more welcoming to pedestrians. It was a sensible recommendation to move a state highway away from the crowded public space. But it was fairly preposterous as well. Even if the political will and many millions of dollars materialized to move the highway, it could take years to come to fruition. The good news for Zislin was that all the study and public hearings had kept him from breaking ground. Had he been able to start building as soon as he bought out the little businesses at the beach, he might well have wound up like Rick Phillips and Larry Wireman, battling failed flippers in court over their deposits.

The rotten real estate market had most people in town pretty down, so the joyous celebration of Shallow and Zislin attracted notice.

"What the hell are you celebrating?" someone down the bar asked.

"We just sold at Capri," Shallow said.

"What'd you get for it?"

"One eight!"

That earned Shallow and Zislin some attaboys and back slaps. The others at the bar were heartened to hear the market had a pulse. No one bothered to ask what they had paid for the eight-bedroom, eight-bathroom penthouse. Had they, beer might have sprayed from their noses.

Shallow and Zislin, fifty-fifty partners in what had been a highly speculative venture, had agreed to pay $3.5 million for the penthouse. They lost $1.7 million. It could have been worse. A lot of people around town didn't have the cash to pay their way out of upside-down real estate deals. Shallow and Zislin had been on a years-long hot streak and could afford their penthouse drubbing.

Shallow had repeated as the world's top-selling RE/MAX agent in 2006 with sales of $186 million. His sales dropped to $77 million in 2007 but were still enough for a third straight year atop the RE/MAX leaderboard.

Shallow saw the crash coming in 2007. He ran into another real estate agent who bragged about owning fourteen condos. Shallow knew the guy earned about $50,000 a year. That might have been enough income to afford a little house in my neighborhood, but one place on the water, let alone fourteen, should have been out of the question. Shallow ran into another acquaintance who told him that he had signed contracts to buy a dozen brand-new houses in a nice golf course community. *You're a framing contractor,* Shallow thought, *you did what?*

It was time to reel in the Dolphin Club. Clients would call hoping to buy. Shallow would talk them into selling instead. Too many people owned too many condos that they clearly could not afford, he told them. Prices had risen well beyond what could be covered renting units to vacationers. The market was about to be flooded. It was time to sell and get to the sidelines. "The whole caper was over," Shallow said.

A wealthy man from Birmingham called him one day wanting to join the club. He'd withdrawn more than $3 million from his IRA and wanted to flip condos with it.

"Bad idea," Shallow said.

"No, seriously. I want to turn it over to you. You handle it," he said. "I've been watching you for five years and following everything. I need to get in."

"Take your money and put it in the bank. Draw a point, half a point, on it. In three years, call me."

"Nah, I'm serious."

"So am I," Shallow said.

Naturally, not everyone listened. One of the Bon Secour Village developers was particularly stubborn. He had bought ten condos in a tower Shallow marketed in 2006. Shallow called him the next year and told him it was time to sell. He consented and Shallow sold them all, producing a net profit of about a million dollars. Shallow advised his client to sit on the cash and wait for the bottom.

The soon-to-be-bankrupt man wouldn't hear it. "I'm going to keep going."

# 16

## STREETS WHERE NOBODY LIVES

The real estate sales commissions that had been powering coastal Alabama's economy dried up. All the buildings and subdivisions that failed to materialize meant a lot of lost paychecks. The suffering extended from framers and drywall installers to furniture store clerks and sod growers. Home equity evaporated, drying up a big source of cash that had fueled the previous years' consumer spending frenzy. As it did nationally, the real estate sector's collapse dragged the local economy into recession.

The city governments had been counting on millions of dollars in development fees and property taxes and were caught overextended. Orange Beach, which used to regularly purchase multimillion-dollar properties such as the island at Perdido Pass and the old marina on Terry Cove, was unable to come up with $120,400 to buy a small parcel that the parks and recreation department wanted for a new office. Even after slashing the municipal budget by about 18 percent, to $42 million, Orange Beach faced a seven-figure shortfall. Hours were cut at the recreation center to save on electricity. Double-sided printing was mandated at city hall. The fire department auctioned off one of its boats.

In Gulf Shores, three dozen city employees, most of them full-time, lost their jobs. They were kept on the payroll through the holidays and compensated for their unused sick days and vacation time. Some received severance. More would have been laid off had not some senior police officers and firefighters volunteered for early retirement to save younger coworkers' positions. Deeper cuts would be needed to balance the books in 2009, when accountants at city hall predicted that the reduced value of taxable property, combined with going cold turkey on development fees, would leave a multimillion-dollar gap in the budget.

The *Register* was also strapped. Craigslist and its free classifieds had come to town and wiped out one of the newspaper's main sources of cash. Meanwhile, the recession greatly reduced the display ads and inserts that businesses bought. On top of it all, the newspaper had begun giving away its stories for free online. That pretty much eliminated the need to pay for a subscription unless you were a coupon clipper or needed to line a lot of birdcages.

The paper added up the savings that could be had by the coupons in that day's edition and printed the sum in the top corner of the front page. It would say something like "$361.90 in today's coupons," in space that was normally reserved for big news or a college football score. It was hard to tell whether that said more about the newspaper or its readers. To save money itself, the *Register* shuttered the small bureau in Foley to which I had been assigned and told me to work from home. The front bedroom of my house, where I set up shop, offered a prime view of my neighborhood going to seed.

Some mornings when I fetched the newspaper from the driveway, I was greeted by neighbors who were already drinking beer. They didn't have much else to do. Work was scarce. Houses that had been packed with construction and storm-cleanup workers were abandoned and left in rough shape, their muddy lawns rutted from serving as spillover parking.

The bushes at the front of the subdivision's entrance wilted to crisps. Some were green only from the weedy vines that had woven up through the dead branches. Landscapers came buzzing through every few days in clouds of dust, racing their mowers over patches of seared centipede grass and dirt. They sculpted the withered shrubs with gas-powered weed whackers. Every so often, a sharp clink punctuated the buzz. It was the sound of the trimmer string striking one of the bottles that had been pitched into the bushes.

I made picking the litter out of Audubon's entryway part of my weekend lawn-mowing routine and got a good sense of my neighbors' tastes. They really seemed to like Wild Irish Rose. It was impossible to tell whether they were polishing off the candy-colored swill when they pulled in or tossing out the empty bottles as they left. Either way, the bottles were always on the driver's side. My friend Robbie, another reporter at the newspaper, noticed a Wild Irish Rose bloom in the bushes during a visit. Robbie knew it wasn't a drink of choice among mortgage payers. "Dude," he said, "homeless people live here now." Robbie was more right than he knew.

By 2009, foreclosures were starting to pile up in Audubon Place. There had been eight when the year began and fourteen by the time it ended. Better than one in every ten of the neighborhood's houses were taken back by lenders. Repo men snatched the luxury vehicles out of the driveway of one neighbor. He'd gone from working something like sixty hours a week installing granite countertops to hardly any at all.

Opioids poisoned the neighborhood. People who were laborers during the housing boom didn't have much trouble convincing pill-mill doctors to prescribe for old aches suffered on the job. Enterprising addicts could fill a prescription in four states on the same day if they hustled along Interstate 10 between Florida and Louisiana.

A young woman who was renting next door to me lost custody of her children and began shuffling in her pajamas to a party house down the street. Sometimes I wouldn't see her for days. I tossed wadded-up slices of bread over the fence to the dog she left tied up in a dusty corner of the yard. She came home once when I was spraying a hose over the fence to fill the dog's empty bowl. She saw me but said nothing and walked inside.

I called an Orange Beach councilwoman, Tracy Holiday, who was involved with animal rescue groups. When she arrived and saw the dog tied up, she called the sheriff's department. A deputy came, took a look over the fence, and said there wasn't much he could do. Some dogs were just outside dogs, he explained, and it didn't appear to be starving. Hadn't I just said I'd been sending food and water over the fence?

When her power was cut off next door, my neighbor opened the windows and decamped for the drug den. She'd left a litter of kittens inside and they shredded the screens. In short order they were flopping out of the window half-wild and almost certainly hungry. The birdbath I kept by the shed became a scene of slaughters. I was carrying groceries inside one evening and a pair of the kittens darted inside underfoot. Herding cats, especially those that have gone feral, is more challenging than it sounds.

Occasionally I'd get a phone call from someone who'd seen the FOR SALE BY OWNER sign. We'd set a time for a showing. Usually a Saturday. I'd cancel my plans and spend the morning spiffing up the house. Then I'd wait. Invariably, the person who'd called would fail to arrive. When I called to see if the showing was still on, I'd get bumped to voice mail or it would just ring and ring.

Another neighbor died from a drug overdose. She was found with a needle stuck in her arm. Her corpse was wheeled out of the house as the afternoon school bus pulled up. Audubon's children were emptied into the scene. I don't remember the woman's name, but I'll never forget her pickup truck. There were big white pit bull silhouettes affixed to the rear window behind both the driver and passenger sides. Between them, in tattoo script, other stickers spelled out, "If you ain't pit, you ain't shit."

One Saturday morning, the neighborhood awoke to the police cordoning off what those of us who lived nearby knew to be a drug den. They were on scene to investigate the death of an eleven-month-old boy. The child's young mother, in the midst of an intoxicated slumber, had rolled onto her baby and smothered him.

One afternoon, I had to interrupt a phone interview that I was conducting in my home office to chase two fighting men from my front yard. They were pulling up the decorative stones from the flower bed and flinging them at each other while they argued over a soured sale of pain pills. One of the men was a neighbor, so I sided with him. After a few minutes, the man we'd run off slunk back and rang my doorbell. He pleaded for a ride. The guy he'd come with had been scared witless and sped away when an old woman who lived where the fracas began brandished a pistol and shot his pickup truck. I told him to leave or I'd go get the gun-wielding granny.

My life had become uncomfortably solitary working in the house where I also lived alone. Most of my friends and the women I dated lived in Mobile, which could be a two-hour drive round trip. It wasn't feasible to get there, or have them come down to the beach, much outside the weekends. One night I was grocery shopping at Winn-Dixie and realized that the cashier was the first person I'd spoken face-to-face with that day. It was time to make some friends in the neighborhood.

I had won credibility with some of the laid-low laborer dudes on the street after one of them saw me in my garage cutting tile with a wet saw. "I didn't think you were the type of guy who could lay tile," he said. He was a spooky redneck. I didn't trust him. But our shared facility with grout was enough of a bond to become buddies. I was part of the gang and joined the guys on a boozy bowling outing. The next thing I knew we were sharing compact discs and lending each other lawn care equipment.

One evening, I was invited to join some of the guys for beers. They had the Braves on and pizza en route. The pizza delivery guy was still parked in the driveway when another car pulled in beside it. The guys had also ordered crack. Even by their hard-partying standards, it seemed aggressive. It was a weekday. And not even dark out yet.

Unlike the real estate agents and construction workers put out of work by the crash, I had plenty on my plate. Writing about the real estate collapse was my primary assignment for the newspaper. As far as juicy stories went, it was like drinking from a fire hose. Lawsuits were flying between failed flippers, lenders, and developers.

A common theme emerged from the cases: just like the people who programmed Wall Street's mortgage-backed security pricing models, no one in south Alabama seemed to have given much thought to what might happen if real estate prices stopped going up.

Early in his first term, in April 2009, President Barack Obama gave a speech at Georgetown University. The subject was the economy. Foreclosures were endemic. Unemployment was at its highest rate in a quarter century. "This recession was not caused by a normal downturn in the business cycle," the president said. "It was caused by a perfect storm of irresponsibility and poor decision-making that stretched from Wall Street to Washington to Main Street."

Home prices actually perked up the month that Obama made that speech. It was the first time they hadn't declined from one month to the next in almost three years. You'd never get the sense in south Alabama that there had been any respite, though. The landscape was scarred by real estate failure.

Neither Bama Bayou's name change nor the pivot from go-karts to water park could save it. Vision Bank, which had lent its developers $21 million, foreclosed on the property over nonpayment and repossessed 144 acres that the developers had bought from Orange Beach. The beleaguered bank credited the developers with $10.3 million for the property and sued them for the remainder. The Bama Bayou developers and other lenders countered with claims that Vision withheld disbursements that would have enabled completion of the entertainment district. Instead work stopped. The husk of a seven-story condo building stood opposite an unfinished grandstand where the dolphin shows would have been. Weeds sprouted head high around the abandoned sales office. Someone scrawled, "No Trespassing Vision Bank," on a sign and hung it at the entrance near the foot of the toll bridge.

It was not the grand welcome that Orange Beach officials had in mind when they teamed up with the developers years earlier. The denuded property bled sediment into a creek and stained the Intracoastal Waterway clay red whenever it rained. Eyesore and environmental catastrophe aside, Orange Beach did pretty well on the deal. Taxpayers earned a $7 million profit flipping the land to the developers.

Those who had bought units in the unfinished condos were wiped out. Among them was Orange Beach mayor Tony Kennon. He was buddies with Dean Young, the hard-assed political operative who'd roiled the 2004 municipal election, and had resigned from the city council amid allegations of sexual harassment made by two women at city hall. Kennon stormed back into office by winning the 2008 mayor's race in a landslide. Before any of that, Kennon was an early Bama Bayou buyer. He and his wife paid more than $200,000 to the developers to help get construction going. They had planned to hold it, to rent it like a hotel room. Unfortunately for them, the developers didn't sell nearly enough of the water park residences to finish construction. The mayor's money was gone.

Bama Bayou's bust was a punishing loss for Park National, too. Vision's bad real estate loans had already cost its Ohio acquirer millions. Now the lender was warring with its top borrower. Tens of millions in additional losses were in play. In court it came out that Vision had lent $83 million to more than a dozen entities related to Joe Raley Builders, the local outfit spearheading Bama Bayou. That amounted to roughly an eighth of all of Vision's $691 million in assets at the time that it was sold to Park National. The Ohio bank's chief executive, C. Daniel DeLawder, assessed the acquisition bluntly at a gathering of investors at New York City's Waldorf Astoria. "Vision Bank has been terrible," he said. "That would be a good way to say it."

All around my neighborhood, developments sat stalled like Bama Bayou, in some early stage of gestation. Thousands of plotted and clear-cut lots were empty. Fancy stone signs heralded subdivisions with names such as Heather Terrace and Iberville Square, but beyond the masonry and azaleas there was usually little more than sidewalks, streetlamps, and maybe an empty model home or two. Locals took to calling such subdivisions pipe farms for the utility stubs that sprouted from the empty lots.

A neighborhood called Fulton Place was laid out on a bucolic, sloping tract a few minutes southeast of my house. Of the 107 homes planned, only 7 were built. Not far away, the Villages of Creekstone was supposed to have 350 houses. Investors from Atlanta clear cut about 190 acres along a pristine back bay, had a truckload of sewer pipe and sixteen palm trees delivered to the site, and then went bust. The palm trees, roots still wrapped, died. The sewer pipe was sold in a bankruptcy auction. Like Bama Bayou, the abandoned building site became a serious source of sediment plumes.

In Andhurst Walk, which was supposed to be filled with high-end houses, I drove along empty curlicues of pavement until I came upon a large and very out-of-place house. There was a FOR SALE sign in the yard, the lawn was clipped, and there were cars in the driveway. I knocked on the door and introduced myself to the man who answered.

His name was Chuck, and he said that he and his wife had bought the lot and built the three-thousand-square-foot house in 2007. They waited for other homes to be built, but more than a year later there had been none. The sign out front promised SECLUDED LIVING FROM THE $190S, but this was not what they had envisioned.

A sick relative needed them back in Pennsylvania, so they listed the house for sale in January 2009. They started at $460,000, but by the time Chuck and I met they had lowered their asking price to $343,000. There had been just one showing in four months.

"Someone comes here and it looks abandoned," he said. He was right about that. A cloud of mosquitoes hummed around us. Distant whistles sounded from the high school sports complex beyond the trees at the back of his lot. We stood there talking about his dilemma and my own, slapping at ourselves to squash the bugs. I caught myself swatting with my notebook. "We're going to lose a lot of money," he said.

Not nearly as much as the developers of his subdivision. Investors from Mississippi were desperately trying to sell everything that didn't belong to Chuck and his wife. The developers needed $4.8 million to pay back what they'd borrowed to buy the property, but they couldn't get anything close to that.

Chuck had a lot more money at stake than me, not to mention a serious family matter from which his mortgage predicament was keeping him. My worries were minuscule compared with his. All things being equal, though, I wondered which was worse: trying to sell a house on an established street being overrun by opioids or on an empty one being grown over by centipede grass.

At what was to become Alabama's biggest residential building, construction ground nearly to a stop.

The rise of Brett/Robinson's 1.9-million-square-foot Phoenix West II was stalled. Only about half of the condo tower's 358 units had sold. Gene Brett, one of the company's principals, went to the Orange Beach City Council to ask a favor.

The building was five stories short of its targeted thirty-one. Brett/Robinson didn't finance its towers. Instead of accepting letters of credit, the firm required preconstruction buyers to pay in installments, a fifth of the sales price at a time. The flow of cash, instead of borrowed money, funded construction of the seventeen towers the company had erected along Alabama's beaches. The building wasn't in danger of being repossessed, but the top floors couldn't be built until more condos were sold. "The only thing we can do to finish that building is to sell it," Brett said.

Brett/Robinson was doing all it could, he said. Open houses were hosted seven days a week. The firm started a video blog for publicity. A camera would follow the seventy-three-year-old as he ambled around the construction site in a hard hat, joshing with workers and coaxing compliments out of buyers. Prices were slashed. Instead of pumping concrete up the tower, the firm switched to the cheaper but more cumbersome method of hoisting it up by the bucketful.

The massive project had gotten off to a rough start when Hurricane Katrina knocked out the facility in Mississippi that had been forming the tower's twenty-two hundred concrete pilings. Each concrete stick was seventy-five feet long and it took a while to line up another place from which to procure them. Delay caused Brett/Robinson to miss the market on its biggest building yet. "We're fighting for our lives on the building there," Brett told the council members. His request was simple yet extraordinary, and also a little weird. He wanted permission to hang a three-hundred-square-foot banner from the unfinished skyscraper to advertise that there were units for sale.

Big signs advertising auctions and the availability of repossessed properties went up all over Pleasure Island. Regions Bank pounded one into Rick Phillips's property along Perdido Pass that was big enough to be seen from both the beach highway and the boat channel.

In Gulf Shores, the auction of sixty-two units at his San Carlos tower attracted a big crowd. There was free seafood and beer. More than 250 people, Bob Shallow included, showed up. Shallow waved his paddle and took down the first condo that hit the block, a furnished four-bedroom unit that cost him $480,000.

Condos that the developer had sold for more than $1 million before they existed couldn't crack $500,000 now that they did. The smaller units that originally sold for $475,000 fetched as little as $240,000. The results were bad, but at least there were bidders.

When Wachovia foreclosed on a $20 million loan the Bon Secour Village developers took on to buy about nine hundred acres along the Intracoastal Waterway, the bank scheduled a sale by public outcry.

It took place on a broiling Tuesday in September. It was a more sober affair than the San Carlos auction. There was no shrimp, no Corona, and no one came to bid.

A lawyer for the lender read aloud the metes and bounds for seven separate parcels that constituted the foreclosed land. He rambled on loudly to fulfill a legal duty but spoke to no one in particular. Timber trucks rumbled through the square every so often and drowned him out.

A few jurors nibbled snacks under a shade tree beyond earshot. A couple of courthouse employees smoked cigarettes against a wall. Another of the lender's lawyers and I were the only ones there for the sale.

When the auctioneer finished reading the legal descriptions, he looked at me and then at the other lawyer. With no bids, he said, the land was awarded to an entity called REDUS Alabama LLC, in which Wachovia's new owner, Wells Fargo, was housing repossessed properties. The developers would be credited with $10 million, or about half of what they owed.

Then the auctioneer slid the papers from which he'd been reading into a folder, put the bundle under his arm, and walked away with the other lawyer.

# 17

## BUYER'S REMORSE

After Hurricane Ivan, a developer from Atlanta flew to town in a private jet to court the owners of a storm-damaged condominium complex in Orange Beach. He hired the same architect who had designed Turquoise Place and had him draw up a twenty-six-story glass-wrapped tower with 128 units to replace the wrecked low-rise, Sapphire Beach.

He offered the owners of the damaged Sapphire Beach condos a deal: They could hand their keys to him and walk away with about a million dollars in cash, or they could wait for a luxurious unit in the new tower. About half of the owners took the money. The others opted for condominiums in the new building, which they'd come to regret.

Two years after inking the Sapphire Beach deal, the developer from Atlanta went broke. His Riverbrooke Capital Partners filed for bankruptcy protection in 2007, claiming debts of $135.3 million and less than $3 million in assets. Riverbrooke wasn't selling many houses, according to business records filed with bankruptcy court. But it threw off cash to its owners nonetheless. It paid for cars for the two owners. They each drew $25,000 a month in salary. The flights into Gulf Shores' dinky municipal airport cost nearly $3,000, compared to the couple hundred dollars it would have cost for a ticket to Pensacola International Airport nearby.

The company controlled a knot of limited liability companies with hands in more than a dozen developments across the Southeast. Riverbrooke's boondoggles included the empty Villages of Creekstone subdivision, which was not far from where I lived and spoiling Wolf Bay with plumes of runoff.

In an expensive area northeast of Atlanta, Riverbrooke built four houses atop a dump before bolting. The empty houses were cordoned, and sternly worded NO SMOKING signs were posted after explosive amounts of landfill gas were detected. In Orange Beach, those who signed on for the Sapphire Beach redux not only lost their condominiums but found themselves on the hook with Riverbrooke's lenders as well. By early 2010, what had been one of the most expensive land purchases ever in Alabama—$126,000 per linear foot of shoreline—wound up in the possession of the Alabama Department of Revenue over about $61,000 in unpaid property taxes.

"All I wanted was my condo," said a Mississippi man who signed on to the redevelopment pact. In a deposition taken during the fallout, he told lawyers that he thought he had a claim on the surfside land in case anything went wrong with the high-flying developer from Atlanta. Instead, the arrangement set up the Mississippian to be a debtor when the developer went under. "If I would have ever thought we would be sitting in here today, I wouldn't have held out for the big condo," he said. "I would have just, you know, took the money when I could have took it."

It was easy to feel for people who were screwed in situations like that. But they were the exception. Few of the litigants in the condo cases were sympathetic characters.

Take, for instance, the Sea-Doo dealer who wanted out of his Turquoise Place sales contracts. He made a fortune flipping before he and his brother got caught holding more than $3 million worth of condos in the declining market. By all accounts, Turquoise Place was meticulously designed and magnificently appointed. It was true that not having an outdoor pool for a year or so would be a bummer and that the lack of such an amenity might dampen rental demand. But it was hard to argue the condos weren't what buyers had bargained for. The brothers had been repeat buyers in Wireman's towers. They had owned five condos at Caribe at one time or another and sold all but one, piling up more than $1 million in profit. They flipped units in other towers as well.

When pressed by Wireman's lawyer during a March 2009 deposition, one brother could think of only once, on a vacant lot, when they had ever lost money speculating on real estate. He swore under oath that he and his brother had the cash to pay for the Turquoise Place condos. He was just so miffed about the missing swimming pool, not to mention the other deviations from the sales brochure, that he didn't want the condos. He went so far as to write letters to the Alabama Office of the Attorney General and the U.S. Department of Housing and Urban Development urging investigation into what he alleged had been violations of the Interstate Land Sales Full Disclosure Act. "My rights were violated," he kept insisting during the deposition.

The Sea-Doo dealer swore repeatedly but not very convincingly that the market collapse and his inability to flip the three condos—which were listed for sale at that very moment—had nothing to do with his desire to extricate himself from the deals. He claimed to not understand exactly what was meant by the term "flipping," even though doing so had made him wealthy. Wireman's lawyer wasn't buying it.

"You've been, as we've discussed, a fairly active guy in the real estate market over the last fifteen years. It's no secret, would you agree, that the real estate market has been in a mess for the last couple or three years?"

"No question about it."

"Isn't that what this lawsuit is about?"

"Absolutely not."

The lawsuit, the Sea-Doo dealer insisted, was about looking over the balcony of a $1.2 million condominium to the beach below and seeing a sandpit where the pool ought to be. From a balcony that was supposed to have a refrigerator but didn't. A balcony with a store-bought hot tub that had to be filled with a garden hose.

Another backpedaling buyer was a competitive weight lifter who offered himself as an expert witness to bolster his grievances against Turquoise

Place as they related to the resort's fitness center. He argued that the gym at Turquoise Place was not that great. It wasn't necessarily better than the one at Caribe, where he and his wife already owned a condo. They wanted out of Turquoise Place. When they agreed to buy there, they did so under the impression that it would be "as fine as Trump Tower." The one in Chicago. Wireman's team countered that while the gym might disappoint a professional weight lifter, the expensively outfitted fitness center was sufficient for run-of-the-mill beachgoers. The developer enlisted an appraiser who had been to both the tower in Chicago that carried Donald Trump's name and Turquoise Place. He testified that Turquoise Place was indeed just as nice as, if not nicer than, Trump's place on the Chicago River.

To a person, the Turquoise Place buyers testified that the collapsing market and their inability to flip the units for a profit had nothing to do with their refusal to honor the purchase contracts they'd signed. But it was pretty obvious that if the market had remained as frenzied as it was in 2005, there wouldn't be so many lawsuits. As one litigating buyer wrote in an email to another, Turquoise Place's "quality and workmanship are second to none. Views are awesome. If condo market hadn't fallen so bad, we would be tickled to death with these condos!"

Then again, as arbitrators noted in their rulings, Wireman and his sales agents, mainly his wife, had repeatedly told buyers that the first tower was sold out when it was not. Wireman had secured deposits for only as many as the bank required for the construction loan. Dozens of condos had yet to sell in the first tower when Wireman started shopping those in the second. The developer had fostered expectations that simply getting one's hands on a folder full of condominium documents was a fail-proof way to pocket tens, and often hundreds, of thousands of dollars. When the market turned and buyers couldn't do that, it should have been no surprise that they and their lawyers would be sizing up the building with tape measures and parsing the fine print on marketing brochures, one arbitrator wrote.

The rulings were mixed. Some buyers were let off the hook, usually when the focus of their claim was the developer fibbing about demand. Other cases went Wireman's way and buyers such as the weight lifter were held to the term sheets they'd signed. The arbitrator in that case paraphrased

Coleridge in his decision. "In Xanadu did Kubla Khan a stately pleasure-dome decree," he wrote. Regardless of what the weight lifter and his wife had envisioned, it was clearly unrealistic. They had bargained for a luxurious condominium and the developer had delivered.

A popular strategy for wriggling out of purchase contracts was to admit to being infected with condo fever and then to blame the condition on sales agents and developers. These buyers claimed, usually with compelling evidence, that they were goaded into deals with assurances that they would be able to sell to someone else for a big gain and never have to actually pay for anything. But it turned out that many failed flippers were no neophytes. They were almost always more experienced in real estate deals than they let on.

A lawyer portrayed a Georgia couple as elderly and duped when they sued the sales agent and developer who'd gotten them to buy a $669,900 condo at the mouth of Bon Secour River. Sure, they were getting up there in age, but she had a doctorate and had been a public school superintendent. He had been a real estate agent for a decade. They had two other investment condos on the beach. They were no rubes. Yet they said they had relied upon a sales agent's promises that there was someone lined up to buy the condo from them for $100,000 more than they'd paid and that under no circumstances would they have to actually buy the condo.

Developers of that building, Sunset Bay at Bon Secour Island Villas, faced a revolt when they tried to get buyers to close on the units. The litigious buyers included a man who owned a busy gas station and car wash in Foley, the namesake of a big furniture store, and a couple who owned a popular country restaurant.

The woman who owned the restaurant had a hard time articulating why she had agreed to pay $749,900 for a yet-to-be-built condominium after intercepting a phone message a real estate agent had left for her sister.

"I don't know if it's one of them caught-up-in-the-moment things," she told lawyers in a deposition. "Everybody is buying, buying, buying. You know what I'm saying?"

She insisted to the lawyers that she was not a flipper. Though she admitted that her aim was to sell the condo to someone else for more than she had paid. In other words, to flip it. At that moment, she had the condo listed for $50,000 less than she had agreed to pay. She was desperate to get out from some of the real estate she and her sod-farming husband had bought in the frothy years. They were underwater on a $2 million house on Ono Island. A condominium in Palm Beach, Florida, had become a real money pit. They also had a getaway in Pigeon Forge, Tennessee, an Appalachian vacation town where Dolly Parton has her Dollywood theme park.

The restaurant owner didn't do much research when she made her investment. She was told that it would be very nice, with wood finishes, and that she would be able to pass it on to someone else for a fat profit. That was all she needed to hear. She drove out to the property once with her husband. The condo site was still just saw grass and pine. There were some nice houses nearby. She kept the sales contracts she'd signed and other documents related to her $749,900 purchase in a bag next to her desk. She never read them. When it came time to close on the condo, she went to her bank, which had provided the letter of credit for the down payment. She asked for a loan and the bank said no. That's how she ended up in court.

Years ago, she had been in a similar situation. She had sold a house out along a dirt road where her family had some land and the buyer backed out of the deal the very day she was moving out. She was angry and refused to return the balking buyer's $500 deposit. They duked it out in small claims at the satellite courthouse in Foley. She prevailed and got to keep the $500. Yet she struggled to see how that related to her present predicament.

The most surprising of the buyers to cry foul at Sunset Bay was Daniel Sizemore, the founder and CEO of Vision Bank. If anyone knew the rules and risks of real estate speculation, he did.

Sizemore had spent a lifetime as a loan officer and bank executive, yet he downplayed his sophistication during a deposition in his suit to get out of buying a $759,900 condo at Sunset Bay. Sizemore had founded three different banks, including Vision, a publicly traded company, yet he swore he'd never had an email account. He owned a computer, but he said he had no idea how to use it. It was hard to tell if he was putting on when he said he couldn't remember the addresses of his homes or if he simply had too many to keep track.

Sizemore owned two condos at Caribe, another in a building across Perdido Pass, a Gulf-front lot in Gulf Shores, a house on the Fort Morgan peninsula, a place at a marina on the Florida Panhandle, and a pair of houses in Port St. Joe, Florida. He had recently cleared $25,000 flipping a Lighthouse condominium and also had a $175,000 share in the Orange Beach land deal that his buddy Jim Brown got the mayor-on-the-take to facilitate. Sizemore and some others who were cloaked in limited liability companies made $1 million flipping land out on Fort Morgan to the Bama Bayou developers, who were Sizemore's biggest borrowers at Vision Bank. Sizemore had even flipped Vision to Park National as the market crested. If he had waited another month or two to sell the bank, all the bad loans on Vision's books would have been his problem.

At Sunset Bay it was he, the banker argued, who was hoodwinked. The pool was barely bigger than a hot tub, and the balcony was too small for a table and chairs. Also, the building wasn't even close to being sold out, as he had been led to believe. Since real estate deals aren't reported to the county until the transactions are closed, there was no way to know that the developers had held back sixteen of the forty units, hoping for higher prices than the initial presales.

Even worse, a lot of the condos that had been sold turned out to have been purchased by the developer, his ex-wife, and the sales agent. Sizemore hired his former Vision board member Buddy Brackin to try to get him out of the deal.

Lawyers gathered other buyers, such as the older couple from Georgia, who also alleged they were misled about demand at Sunset Bay. One lawyer even pursued claims under the Racketeer Influenced and Corrupt Organizations Act, which was written to combat organized crime. He argued that the developer, sales agent, mortgage broker, and an appraiser were all in cahoots. Using the RICO Act didn't work, but Sunset Bay sank nonetheless. In November, twenty-five of the building's forty condos were auctioned off on the courthouse steps.

Bob Shallow was there and bought each one of them. He had struck a deal the night before with the Mississippi bank that had repossessed the property. He'd said he'd buy all twenty-five condos, but he needed boat slips with which to pair them. Shallow agreed to pay $4,000 per slip and went to the courthouse auction to win.

The development's embattled sales agent and her husband were there as well. Shallow leaned over and told them that whatever they bid, he'd offer a dollar more. He won the condos with a bid of $3,550,001.00.

He elected himself the owners' association president and got to work fixing up the building. The elevators didn't work. There was no propane for heat or cooking. He bought two more foreclosed units a month later. It took him a while, and he had to finance a few buyers himself, but Shallow eventually sold each of his twenty-seven Sunset Bay units for a profit.

# 18

## THE SPILL

On a Friday morning in June 2010, I walked outside to grab the newspaper and noticed an acrid smell. I looked up over the hedge, hoping to find someone tarring the roof on the abandoned house next door. Nobody was there. Inside, my phone rang.

The odor was emanating from the Gulf of Mexico, six miles to the south, where huge rafts of goop from BP's Deepwater Horizon oil spill were about to splash ashore. From the balcony atop a condo tower in Gulf Shores, a thirteen-year-old girl from Baton Rouge spotted a rust-colored shadow on the horizon. It was the width of a three-lane highway and seemed to be slithering toward shore.

"Mom, is that the oil?" she said.

Her mother stepped onto the balcony and squinted out at the Gulf. Then she walked back inside and called the newspaper.

I arrived at the state park beach next to her condominium just before the oil did. It didn't appear that the people on the beach knew what was coming. It was less crowded than usual in the middle of a June Friday on account of the oil spill's threat, but there were plenty of people in the water when the slick hit the surf. Unwitting swimmers stumbled ashore splotched with crude. Children on the beach poked the sunbaked goop with sticks and scooped it into water bottles. It looked like pudding but was thicker and as tacky as roof tar. People sniffed at it. It had been baking in the sun for weeks and was odorless; the scent I had picked up at home was on the wind, originating offshore where freshly spewed crude hadn't yet had the fragrance cooked from it.

It would be an unforgettable beach vacation for these kids. Not long after the oil washed ashore, a bus pulled up and cleanup workers wearing rubber boots and neon vests filed out. It was like in a movie when government spooks sweep into a scene to clear away signs of an alien landing. The workers shoveled the oil into clear plastic bags and got on their hands and knees to pick little spatters of it from the sand as though they were gathering forensic evidence. Panicked city officials were next to arrive.

Though the real estate market's collapse had destroyed wealth and erased a lot of jobs, Alabama's beaches were buoyed by strong tourism spending. Gulf Shores and Orange Beach even benefited from the recession as the gloomy economic climate prompted many to scale back from summer vacations abroad in favor of a week at the beach. Everyone in town had been living on pins and needles since the Deepwater Horizon drilling rig exploded and sank south of the Alabama-Mississippi state line. The longer BP's well spewed crude, the more likely it was that Alabama's beaches would endure an ecological nightmare and an economic disaster.

With an ever-larger glob of oil lurking offshore, Gulf Shores leaders rolled the dice, letting the inaugural Hangout Music Festival take place as planned at the city beach. A shift in the wind was all it would take to drive the crude ashore while the beach was packed with concertgoers. The winds cooperated, though, and the three-day music festival was a hit despite some fuss at city hall over one performer's cussing. The festival had been dreamed up and bankrolled by Shaul Zislin to promote the big restaurant he'd built instead of condominiums. He'd spent $3 million to bookend the public beach with stages, buy dozens of palm trees, and hire acts such as the Roots, Alison Krauss, and John Legend.

Tens of thousands of people came to the beach on what was usually a slow weekend. Once the party was over, though, reality set in. Fishing grounds were closed. Vacationers canceled condo reservations. City officials hired pilots to fly over the Gulf to scout for incoming oil.

The day before the oil made landfall, Orange Beach's fire chief spotted an island of sludge lingering off the coast during one of the flights. The next morning, it was closer to shore and a couple of boats were dispatched in an attempt to corral the slick with an oil-absorbent boom. The open ocean's undulation made that impossible. The blob got away before a better-equipped cleanup vessel could reach the scene.

By July, all thirty-two miles of beach between Mobile Bay and the Florida Panhandle had been fouled. An iridescent sheen had slipped past the oil-absorbent barricades strung across inlets and was tainting the back bays where dolphins and osprey fed. Federal biologists took the extraordinary step of digging up sea turtle nests and shipping the Ping-Pong-ball-sized eggs in a specially outfitted FedEx truck to Florida's Atlantic coast, where they were reburied out of harm's way. The cleanup workers started wearing Tyvek suits and driving tractors. Dish soap was set out at showers along boardwalks. Waiters, hotel clerks, and beach attendants lost their jobs. The for-hire fishing crews who normally chased cobia and red snapper resorted to scouting for crude as part of the cleanup effort. Shrimp boats dragged boom through the water instead of nets. The breeze carried a whiff of WD-40.

BP and the Environmental Protection Agency held a forum to solicit ideas on how to clean up the historic spill. Salesmen hawking pressure washers, specialty soaps, and absorbent fabrics descended upon the convention center in Mobile and turned it into a sort of miracle-fix trade show.

Meandering around the convention center was like stepping through one late-night infomercial after another. One man buttonholed me and insisted that a degreaser he had developed was the answer. He called his product SW1000 and said that if it was diluted with water and sprayed onto oil-soaked marsh, the crude would slide right off blades of riparian grasses and whatever else it might stick to up in the bays and bayous. "For a million-gallon spill, I would need ten thousand gallons of my product to take care of it," he said. To demonstrate the safety of his concoction, he squirted a glob into his palm and slathered it onto his face like sunscreen. See, he said, nontoxic.

State securities regulators had to run off a man who came from Chicago touting a bacterial compound that he said would make the oil disappear. He was attempting to raise $600 million from local investors for his solution when Alabama securities fraud investigators sent him a cease-and-desist notice.

One morning, Mac McAleer, the former Krispy Kreme Doughnuts CEO, summoned me to LuLu's, the Jimmy Buffett–themed restaurant he'd built on the Intracoastal Waterway for Lucy Buffett, the singer's sister. McAleer was excited. He had figured out a way to contain the blowout in the Gulf and wanted me to write an article about his invention so that it might catch the eye of those directing the spill response. When I arrived at LuLu's, he showed me a drawing of a big floating ring. Boats could drag it out above the out-of-control well and long drapes hanging from its underside would funnel the gushing crude up into the big round corral at the surface. The doughnut-mogul-turned-developer had dreamed up a giant doughnut.

Nerves were raw around town and conspiracy theories ran wild. I spent one night speeding around in the dark on a boat with a manic local who promised he could show me BP's cleanup crews dumping banned chemicals into the Gulf. I didn't see anything suspicious but did get seasick and miss a night of sleep. Distraught adults wept in public meetings and cursed the BP employees who had been dispatched to reassure them. One particularly perturbed fishing captain was about to shove off for a day's work in the accidental oil patch when he sent his crew on a last minute errand at the marina. The deckhands hadn't made it far when they heard the pop. Their captain had shot himself dead.

The city councils went from debating building setbacks to arguing about topics well beyond their expertise, such as whether the air was safe to breathe. In August, business owners and laid-off workers opened their mailboxes to the letters from a company that BP had hired to disburse the first wave of restitution payments. The envelopes contained letters describing enclosed checks, but there weren't any checks. The company had accidentally sent them without payments.

The *Register* was fraying as well. The recession arrived just as its business model was collapsing. Furloughs were followed by layoffs. It was time to think about a new job.

My search was accelerated one afternoon after the paper's executive editor called to gauge my interest in moving to Mobile to report on that city's government. It was a nice assignment, but I was stuck with a house by the beach and didn't want to spend hours each day commuting to and from the downtown newsroom.

I told him that if the paper put me up in a studio apartment during the week, or paid me a few hundred dollars more a month so that I could rent a garage apartment or some other place to sleep on that side of the bay, I'd do it. He said he'd think about it.

A couple of days later he called back and said he had a better idea: he had explained my situation to a buddy of his who was a Baldwin County judge. The judge suggested to the newspaper's editor that I file for bankruptcy protection in order to dump my mortgage debt.

"Do you have a car payment?" asked my boss's boss's boss. "You can probably get rid of that, too."

I am grateful to him and the other editors at the paper, such as Dewey English, who gave me a job after college and treated me so well. I'd run through a wall for them if they asked and never hesitated to work days on end in disaster zones or put myself in all sorts of uncomfortable situations to get stories. But I wasn't going to file for bankruptcy protection so that I could switch beats.

Had I wanted to walk away from the house, I would have done so years earlier. That night I polished my résumé and emailed stories I'd written to editors at bigger newspapers. Finding a new writing job in the midst of a recession and the disintegration of the newspaper industry wasn't even the hard part. I had to figure out what to do about the house. I focused my job search on the South, figuring that a day's drive was, for a while at least, about as far away as I could stray from my underwater home.

Though Washington policy makers had bailed out banks to keep them lending, pushed interest rates to historic lows, and initiated programs for borrowers in danger of losing their homes, there weren't many options for someone in my situation, which was getting worse with each new foreclosure on Audubon Drive.

By the summer of 2010, there had been seventeen foreclosures, including the abandoned house next door. About a year earlier, a bashful couple with two small children moved in. They added a lot of trash to the empty swimming pool, though I never actually noticed them in the backyard. In fact, I rarely saw them at all.

Whenever they pulled their beat-up minivan into the driveway, they hopped out and rushed into the shingle-shedding house. A few times I knocked on the door to ask if it was all right if I mowed their weedy front lawn or cut back our shared hedge. They were home, but no one would ever answer the door. Only once did any of them speak to me. I was in the front yard and waved when they pulled into their driveway. As they walked toward the house, their daughter, a toddler, yelled over the hedge, "Turn it down, neighbor!" Her mother shushed her and hurried the child inside. I had gotten so used to living without neighbors—conscious ones, at least—that I had developed a habit of playing music at unneighborly volumes. The little girl called me out.

The family vanished a few months after they arrived. Citi, which had bought the firm that had bought the loan that Vision Bank had made to the long-gone couple who bought the house, foreclosed in February.

The New York bank bought the house from itself on the courthouse steps for $80,100. That was a little more than half of what the couple had paid for the house around the time we bought ours and a lot less than I would need to clear my debt on a smaller, albeit much better kept, house. A man stopped by after the auction, changed the locks, and stuck a FOR SALE sign in the yard. A few months later, the house became the possession of Freddie Mac, which unloaded it to an Indiana woman for $44,900.

Distressed sales such as courthouse auctions don't factor into appraisals. I wished they did. Instead, it was the second, even lower sales that were used as comparable transactions to establish the value of my home. A September appraisal of my house came back at $76,000, down about a third from two years earlier.

Though the situation with my house was worsening, my job search yielded an offer to work in the Houston office of *The Wall Street Journal.* I owed something approaching $60,000 more than what I could hope to fetch for my house given all the competition from foreclosures. My only option if I wanted to take the job at the *Journal* was to rent out the house until the market improved.

Determined to lower the payments, I drove to the bank where I had taken out the mortgage five years earlier and asked for the banker who had made my loan. I was told he no longer worked there and was handed a 1-800 number. I spoke to one call-center worker after another, on hold for hours, restarting the conversation with each transfer or disconnection. The bank required a comical amount of faxed correspondence. I spent a lot of time in line at the Office Depot service desk to send documents that I was pretty sure no one would actually ever receive.

The lawyers, real estate agents, and mortgage brokers I consulted shook their heads when I explained my situation. A few bank employees told me, candidly, to skip a payment or two and feign distress to draw the bank to the negotiating table. I did that once and was inundated with threatening calls.

Renting the house presented another obstacle. Though my ex-wife hadn't been involved with the property for years, her name remained on the deed. To enroll it in a rental program with a local property manager, I needed her signature. And I would need it going forward for all sorts of things, such as on leases and consenting to repairs. She had a more nihilistic view of the situation, though, and declined to go along. It was hard to blame her, but it added to the complexity of my dilemma. In order to move on with my life, I had to do something absurd. To rent out my house, I had to buy it from us, repaying the existing mortgage to sever her ties to the property.

It was a stroke of luck that our original mortgage broker had, unbeknownst to me, put us into a second loan that needed to be refinanced after five years. According to an appraisal that the bank had ordered, the property wasn't worth enough to clear the first loan, let alone the second mortgage. Thankfully, my first mortgage was from the same bank, which gave me some negotiating leverage. It wasn't just one loan that would sour for Regions if I walked, it would be two.

I'd been a faithful bill payer for years, and the bank opted to refinance rather than fight with me. There was a new federal program that allowed the bank to finance my house for more than it would appraise if I could come up with about $15,000 to cover closing costs and make up the difference between what I owed and the $122,500 the bank was willing to lend me anew. I drained my recession-battered 401(k) and did it.

I was buying my first home a second time, which meant I didn't qualify as a first-time home buyer. I also paid a big tax penalty for withdrawing my retirement fund. And since the loan amount was still higher than the property's appraised value, part of the financing was made at 10.05 percent, which was closer at the time to a credit card rate than a mortgage. The bank sprang that detail on me at the closing table.

It dimmed the prospect of ever breaking even as a landlord, but I had no choice if I wanted to move on in my career. Plus, I'd already moved to Texas. The house was still an anchor, but I'd bought myself a longer chain.

# PART III

# 19

## FOR RENT

Though it sure felt like it, south Alabama was not the epicenter of the housing bust. Among the contenders for that distinction were south Florida, where empty condos pushed the foreclosure rate to almost 20 percent, and Las Vegas, where the foreclosure rate reached nearly 10 percent. Atlanta was walloped as well. But Phoenix, where home prices fell by more than half, stands apart for what rose from the wreckage: the Wall Street landlord.

In the boom years, speculators ran amok in the desert around the Arizona capital. Builders held lotteries to winnow the field of people who wanted to buy yet-to-be-built tract homes at the edge of Phoenix's stucco sprawl. A lot of the buyers had no intention of ever moving in. They just wanted to flip the finished houses to someone else for a quick buck. When home prices fell and they couldn't sell them for more than they paid, a lot of them walked away.

Unlike Alabama, Arizona allows mortgage borrowers to bail on home loans without worrying about the lender coming after them for the difference between what they owe and whatever the house fetches at auction. The jilted lender gets only the house. Walking away stains a borrower's credit, of course. But the borrower can leave the keys on the counter and disappear without worrying about getting tangled up in court with the lender wanting more. The flood of voluntary foreclosures further depressed prices around Phoenix.

The median home price plummeted from about $262,000 in 2006 to $122,000 in 2011. In some places, such as Tolleson, an edge suburb of curvilinear streets and faux adobe, prices fell by two-thirds. In a zip code near the city center, they fell by 87 percent. Nearly a home's entire value. Even in the nicest parts of Greater Phoenix, home prices dropped by 40 percent.

Geoff Jacobs was running a real estate development company in Phoenix when the market crashed. His firm, Empire Group, had obligations to investors and payroll to fulfill but nothing to build, potentially for years. Jacobs had to figure out how to put his employees and his investors' money to work.

Jacobs liked to emphasize Phoenix's rapid population growth whenever he met with investors. He'd explain how the constant flow of new arrivals to the valley around the city meant demand for the subdivisions and shopping centers that Empire built. "We add the population of Kansas City every five years," Jacobs would say.

The forces driving the migration to Phoenix were intact despite the housing market's collapse. It was still warm and sunny year-round. The cost of living was still relatively low. It was cheaper for northerners to retire in the Sonoran Desert than in Florida and remained a destination for families and businesses unable to afford California. Midwesterners, like some of my friends from high school in Ohio, escaped dreary winters by enrolling at Arizona State University and never left. People were still coming to Phoenix. They just might not be able, or desire, to buy houses as they once had. They would have to live somewhere. So would all the people who lost their primary residences to foreclosure.

The repossessed houses being sold at auction around Phoenix became too cheap to ignore. They could be bought at auction for half what it would take to build something comparable. Jacobs figured that his employees, who had built and sold thousands of houses around the valley, could just as easily buy foreclosed homes, fix them up, and lease them out—at least until prices recovered and they could sell them. Rents were rising, moving in the opposite direction of home prices. Jacobs took the rental idea to Empire's investors in 2009 and came away with $150 million to buy houses.

The night before auctions, Jacobs and his team would study the docket, whittling the list to about a dozen houses that they thought would make good rentals. Then they decided the most that they'd be willing to pay for each of their targets. For the next two years or so, as the foreclosure rate in Phoenix reached 5 percent, Jacobs and his team left auctions with almost every house they'd circled. They bought more than a thousand of them, spruced them up with about $7,000 a pop, and usually had tenants moved in within a week or two.

One day in early 2012, Jacobs was practicing his stroke at a driving range when he got a call from an Empire employee who'd been sent to an auction. It was procedure to call if bidding for any of the firm's auction targets approached the maximum set at the previous night's prep sessions.

"I'm at this house," he said. "Our bid was $85,000 and we're at $85,000."

"Okay," Jacobs said. "I'll go to $87,000."

The price jumped to $90,000. Then $95,000. The home wound up selling for about $100,000. Jacobs was bewildered. Who was this aggressive bidder who had arrived on the auction scene? By the end of the day, he had a name. The bidder was from an outfit called Invitation Homes.

The summer before, in 2011, a team of housing analysts at Morgan Stanley sent the investment bank's clients a report that would become wildly influential. It was titled "A Rentership Society." In it, as well as in subsequent papers, the analysts forecast a surge in the number of renters and a potentially massive opportunity for investors to convert the glut of repossessed homes into rental properties.

There were more than 1.6 million foreclosed homes on the market around the country and judging by the hundreds of billions of dollars in delinquent mortgages out there, more were on the way. In each foreclosed home, the analysts saw both a potential rental property and a new renter hitting the street whose needs—room for children, access to good schools—were unlikely to be met by an apartment.

The analysts noted the bursts of household formation that usually follow recessions, during which people tend to delay things like marriage, having children, moving out of their parents' homes, and even divorce. Banks were stunned by losses and facing the wrath of lawmakers. They were being as tightfisted with home loans as they had been lavish with them before the crash. Billowing student debt was making it as difficult as ever to save for down payments, which were back in style among lenders.

Attitudes toward renting were changing, too. Homeownership had resulted in financial pain and sacrifice for millions of Americans. The argument that paying rent was wasteful had lost resonance. The economy's shift from manufacturing to service and information jobs has meant fewer workers tethered to particular towns for their entire careers. That had boosted the option value of renting, the analysts said. Being able to move for employment without worrying about selling a house and paying sales commissions and other fees was more important than ever. A big rental investor who was an early acolyte of the rentership society once asked me, "Is renting a home really that much different from renting the money to buy one?"

For many it may not be, especially if they have to put their life's savings at risk.

Though home prices had come down, other ownership costs were up. Hurricanes along the East and Gulf Coasts and wildfires out west were pushing homeowner's insurance premiums higher in some of the most populated parts of the country. Cash-strapped municipalities were raising property tax rates to counteract the negative effects that lower property values were having on revenue.

Homeownership, long upheld as the American dream, was in crisis, the Morgan Stanley analysts wrote. One in five homeowners either was no longer willing or able to make mortgage payments or had lost every penny of home equity. If you counted only people with a mortgage, it was roughly one in three. "That dream," the analysts wrote, "has become more of a nightmare."

The first great hauls from the housing bust came when contrarian fund managers, such as John Paulson and Michael Burry, and traders at Goldman Sachs constructed complex wagers against subprime mortgages. The Morgan Stanley analysts said the next fortunes could be minted scooping up repossessed homes and renting them out. They estimated that even in the worst-case scenario—one in which home values never recovered and not a penny could be borrowed to amplify returns—the yield from renting homes bought cheaply enough on the courthouse steps or from desperate banks would be much higher than almost any other investment given how low interest rates were being held. The opportunity as they saw it was nearly boundless, measured in trillions of dollars. They deemed it Housing 2.0.

There were doubters. Mostly apartment owners. They were in the business of managing large numbers of residences, and it was hard enough when they were all under one roof. There were good reasons no one had ever attempted to manage huge pools of rental homes, skeptics argued.

If ever there was a time to try, though, it was now. Apple released its iPhone in 2007 and the iPad in 2010, launching a new era of mobile computing. These devices as well as advances in cloud computing enabled investors to conduct an unprecedented land grab and profitably manage thousands of far-flung properties.

The phones at Morgan Stanley were flooded by inquisitive investment fund managers. Ben Bernanke, who helmed the Federal Reserve during the crisis, endorsed the idea in early 2012 while speaking at a National Association of Home Builders conference in Orlando, Florida. "It could make sense in some markets to turn some of the foreclosed homes into rental properties," Bernanke said. By then, more than $1 billion had been raised by investors for the purpose of doing just that. Some of the biggest names in finance were hoarding houses.

An investment banker introduced Blackstone Group, the world's largest real estate investor, to a group of Arizona men with a fast-growing rental-home business. They had been buying mobile home parks around Phoenix when home prices crashed and decided to trade up to single-family houses. Their business was called the Treehouse Group and led by Dallas Tanner, a fourth-generation Phoenician about my age who had just completed his graduate degree at Arizona State. Treehouse accumulated eleven hundred rental homes with investments from the country club set, but Tanner and his partners wanted to expand to other cities. They went looking for an investor to pair with, someone with deeper pockets than the doctors and dentists who had so far been funding their splurge.

Treehouse had bought a few houses in Atlanta and California but needed many more properties in each market to make managing them cost-effective. Treehouse enlisted a young investment banker named Rich Ford to find a match on Wall Street. Ford approached Carl Icahn, the corporate raider and activist investor, and pitched the Carlyle Group, a $200 billion Washington, D.C., firm that had gained prominence privatizing government businesses and carving out unloved divisions from big corporations. Blackstone took a meeting.

Jonathan Gray, the New York firm's real estate chief, was mulling a move into single-family real estate, and his team was vetting rental operators for potential partnerships. Gray began his career on Wall Street with Blackstone in the early 1990s straight out of college. Blackstone was just starting out in real estate investing when he joined, sifting through the wreckage of the savings and loan bust for bargains. The firm's first find was a bunch of garden apartments in Arkansas and East Texas. They were nearly full of paying tenants but could be had for so little that Blackstone reaped a 62 percent annual return. From then on, Blackstone was hooked on property. By the time the housing market cratered in 2007, Gray had taken the reins of Blackstone's real estate investing business and built it into a behemoth.

He engineered the firm's $25 billion takeover of Hilton Worldwide, which would eventually earn the firm more than $14 billion in profit, and its $39 billion purchase of Sam Zell's office property empire, which Blackstone dismantled and sold in pieces for a $7 billion gain. Blackstone owned high-profile properties all over the world. For a few years, the firm even owned one of the most notable buildings in coastal Alabama: the outlet mall up the road from my house in Foley.

Gray himself had become a billionaire, one of the rare ones who earn their fortune working for someone else. Profiles mentioned his cheap wristwatch, his lack of an advanced business degree, and that he had met his wife in a poetry class, as if to belie his staggering wealth and the shrewdness with which he was investing ever larger sums at Blackstone. He was also said to walk to work.

Gray had made the firm's real estate investing business the envy of Wall Street and put himself into position to succeed Blackstone's co-founder Stephen Schwarzman as CEO. Cashing in on the historic crash in home prices and forging into single-family homes, the final frontier for institutional real estate investing, would be the cherry on top.

Wall Street firms were suffering from panicked investors withdrawing money from investment pools such as hedge funds. There had been no run on the bank at Blackstone, though. The firm's private-equity funds lock up investors' money for a decade or more. Private-equity investments such as office towers, apartment complexes, and entire companies can't be liquidated like stocks and bonds to accommodate withdrawals.

Blackstone's leaders had also been spooked by surging real estate prices and developers who seemed to be ignoring the laws of supply and demand. Condo developers from the Gulf Coast courted Blackstone's dealmakers, but when they got a look at the sales contracts, they learned that buildings purported to be sold out had really just been reserved by parties related to the developer and a few speculators aiming to flip. There was no reason to assume real buyers would ever materialize. Blackstone decided to sit out the most frenzied moments of the residential real estate mania. Because of its restraint and decade-long grip on its investors' cash, the firm had billions of dollars from pensions, sovereign wealth funds, and rich families with which to go bargain hunting when the bubble burst.

In 2012, Gray was back home in Chicago visiting family for Thanksgiving when he and his father hopped in the car and went for an after-dinner spin to do some due diligence. Gray wanted to see for himself what sorts of foreclosures were out there. He had a list of addresses and asking prices. He was shocked by how little the repossessed homes cost. He snapped a picture of one house, tapped out a message beneath the photo, and texted it to Dallas Tanner back in Arizona: "Guess how much we can buy that one for?"

At Blackstone's Park Avenue offices, the firm's brass weighed a big rental-home investment. Blackstone's billionaire chief executive was on board. "Oh my goodness, this could be huge," Schwarzman said. "Nobody is going to be able to borrow. They're going to need housing."

The only issue was that the Treehouse guys were looking for $150 million. That wasn't big enough for Blackstone to bother. One of Gray's lieutenants told them that they'd need to boost their ambitions at least tenfold.

The first property that Treehouse bought with Blackstone's money was a three-bedroom, two-bathroom tract house in Tolleson, outside Phoenix. It had been built by D. R. Horton in 2006, along with a few hundred look-alike beige houses. A local man had agreed to pay the builder $209,120 for the house on spec. Six years later, Treehouse, soon to be renamed Invitation Homes, bought the house at a foreclosure auction for not quite half the original price. That was the start of a $10 billion home-buying spree.

Other big investment firms followed suit. Wall Street cash flooded into foreclosure auctions in Atlanta, Las Vegas, Northern California, Phoenix, big cities in Texas, and all throughout Florida. At an auction in Sacramento, a house flipper named Ryan Heck was bewildered by a bidder who bought every house that hit the block.

"Dollar over," he kept saying. "Dollar over. Dollar over. Dollar over. Dollar. Over."

He'd say it until the other bidders gave up. Neither Heck nor the other regulars at that particular auction recognized the dollar-over guy. It turned out he was with an out-of-town concern called Treehouse and had instructions to buy everything that cost less than what it would cost to build a similar house. Every house auctioned that day fit the bill.

Heck wasn't sure what to do. Right after college, he and his father made some money engineering cables out of telecommunications systems and selling the surplus wires to scrappers in China. When the housing market collapsed, Heck started buying foreclosed homes, fixing them up, and selling them. It was a rush showing up at an auction clenching $500,000 in cashier's checks and leaving with a house or two. He had bought properties in Sacramento, Seattle, and Reno, Nevada, when Invitation Homes and other well-funded operations started crashing auctions.

Sometimes Heck could peek over another bidder's shoulder at their iPad, see the top price they were allowed to pay for a particular home, and run the dollar-over routine on them. Even cheating a little, he couldn't really compete. He had a handful of cashier's checks. The new guys had duffel bags full.

Heck tried to raise money from big investors, as Tanner and Treehouse had. He called Blackstone. He was in his mid-twenties, though, someone who a few years earlier aspired to be a professional snowboarder and had just a few dozen flips and rental homes on his résumé. His pitch for a $100 million foreclosure fund fell flat. Unable to beat the bulk buyers, Heck joined one called American Homes 4 Rent.

In May 2011, self-store magnate B. Wayne Hughes boarded a plane and flew with one of his deputies to Las Vegas to buy foreclosed houses. A few weeks later, they went to Phoenix to buy some there.

Hughes had risen from a *Grapes of Wrath* upbringing to become a billionaire by basically inventing the self-storage industry. He was early to notice that Americans were accumulating more stuff than their houses could hold. And also that many of them would rather rent extra space in which to stow it than part with Grandma's old sofa or whatever else they were hoarding. Hughes and a partner pooled $50,000 and in 1972 opened a self-storage facility in El Cajon, California. Four decades later, his Public Storage had thousands of locations marked by the company's bright orange signs and a stock market value in excess of $20 billion.

The housing bust was a boost for the storage business. People downsizing from houses to apartments or moving back in with Mom and Dad needed somewhere to stash their extra stuff. Hughes realized a lot of people were going to need a place to go, too. He believed he could do for rental homes what he had done for the then scattershot and loosely managed storage business: consolidate, centralize operations, use computers to do the jobs of people whenever possible, and establish more aggressive market rates. Rental homes were just storage for people, he would say. The key was picking the right people to store.

Before they went looking for houses, Hughes and his lieutenants decided what types of tenants they wanted. Then they sought out houses that would attract them. Families with school-age children were their prize. They were likely to stay in houses longer than singles, willing to swallow annual rent increases if it meant not uprooting their children from schools and neighborhood friends. Tenants who stayed for years on end meant lower turnover costs and fewer months during which no one was paying rent.

Hughes excluded from his house hunt anything smaller than three bedrooms and two bathrooms. He shopped in highly rated school districts with little crime and in neighborhoods close to transit corridors and public amenities. Newer cookie-cutter homes were ideal because they would need fewer big-ticket repairs such as new roofs and air conditioners and maintenance would be less expensive than in older, more heterogeneous houses.

The first house that Hughes bought in Las Vegas rented for $1,050. That was what other landlords in the area charged for three-bedroom houses with nice yards. It was a steal. Apartments nearby with only two bedrooms were renting for $1,400 a month. That was all the evidence Hughes needed that rents could be pushed higher. He and his lieutenants had bought about a hundred houses and were tinkering with their business model when a man from Alaska's state oil fund called their offices in Southern California.

Jay Willoughby was the chief investment officer of the Alaska Permanent Fund, which invests the royalties that oil companies pay to the state and disburses annual dividend checks to residents, usually between $800 and $2,100 a head. By 2012, the payments were under pressure. Alaska's revenue shrank because of the recession and the advent of shale drilling, which had enabled U.S. energy producers to extract huge deposits of oil much closer to drivers than the tundra. Things were getting so tight in Alaska that the state even cut back on snow plowing. The best way to keep the royalty payments and state budget from shrinking too much was to get a better return on the fund's $40 billion. That was Willoughby's job.

The rental-home idea piqued Willoughby's interest. A lot of money could be put to work mopping up the mortgage meltdown. He had interviewed something like thirty potential partners in search of a way to invest in single-family homes when he heard that the people behind Public Storage were buying houses. Willoughby called David Singelyn, the Public Storage executive Hughes had tapped to lead the rental-home venture, and a lawyer who worked for Hughes.

"Hey," Willoughby said, "I understand you guys are in this business. We're thinking about it and we'd like to talk."

Hughes's lieutenants denied buying houses. Before he hung up, though, Alaska's investment chief made a final overture.

"Well, you know we have $400 million or so," Willoughby said. "In theory, if this were to work out right, we'd be interested in investing."

"We're not doing it," the lawyer said. "But how much do you charge for your capital?"

"We don't charge anything."

"Why don't you come down to Southern California," the lawyer said.

# 20

## MEET YOUR NEW LANDLORD

As Wall Street forged into landlording, so did I. My first tenant was a single mother with a young child. She paid $650 a month and agreed to keep up the yard with the mower and trimmers that I left behind. Once the property management company took its 15 percent cut, I was left with enough to cover about half of my monthly expenses. That was a lot of money to lose every month, but it was a big relief to have the refinancing squared away and someone living in the house so that it wasn't sitting empty.

I convinced myself that the situation wasn't that bad, that a lot of people had it much worse. Many did, of course. I was thankful not to be weighed down by more daunting mortgage debt and that I was able to move for a new job. It was easy to see how people could get stuck. For all the damage that little house in Alabama was doing to my finances, it hadn't derailed my career. In fact, in the perverse way that bad news is good business for newspapers, the whole real estate fiasco had helped me out of my jam. The stories I wrote about the collapse, as well as the oil spill, were what earned me a better job.

Houston was a good landing spot. It was a culturally rich metropolis riding high on the shale-drilling boom. As far as big cities go, it was relatively inexpensive. I found a nice apartment overlooking a swimming pool in a hip, leafy neighborhood a few minutes' drive to my office downtown. My monthly losses in Alabama were a small price to pay to be there and out of Audubon Place, never mind the chance to work for the newspaper I fetched from my grandfather's driveway when I was young. I knew people who spent more money playing golf, gambling on football, and on graduate school. Though unprofitable, landlording from afar started out smoothly and allowed me to get on with my life. Then the rent checks stopped coming.

My tenant had invited relatives to move in, and they refused to leave. I hesitated to evict them around the holidays, hoping that her ability—or perhaps willingness—to pay rent might change in the new year. It did not. On a lark, I performed one of my old daily reporting duties and checked the Baldwin County jail's booking website. There I saw my tenant, in a fresh mug shot. She had been booked on a charge of felony theft. Her relatives who had been staying at my place had been in and out of jail as well, locked up over charges such as narcotics and running from the cops. It seemed unlikely that rent was forthcoming. They left only after I filed eviction paperwork in court and they learned that sheriff's deputies would be by to see them out.

Another single mom wanted out of her lease after she got a look at the diverse student body at the Foley schools for which my home was zoned. The schools in neighboring Gulf Shores were in the same district, funded equally, but almost entirely white. She wanted to move and enroll her child there.

Another renter asked permission to break her lease so that she could take a better job out of state. Knowing what it was like to be trapped, I agreed to let her out as long as she left the place clean so that I could get it back on the rental market as soon as possible.

Apparently, there was a misunderstanding. She didn't clean up. She cleaned the place out. She took the microwave, washer and dryer, yard tools, and just about everything else that wasn't nailed down. She even swiped the smoke detectors, which were hardwired to the house and out of reach without the ladder. She took that, too.

On the plus side, I was able to nudge the rent higher guilt-free with each new tenant. It never took more than a day or so to find a renter, although the frequent turnover entailed cleaning expenses, lost rent, and an aggravating routine with customer service representatives at the local utilities. A respite from major hurricanes reduced my insurance premium, and the property tax bill dwindled along with the value of the property, which county assessors appraised in 2011 at less than $60,000. That wasn't even half of what I had paid for the house. In good months, my loss got to be less than $300. When rent went unpaid or costly repairs popped up, my monthly loss could have a comma.

A few of the homes in my neighborhood were bought at the bottom by investors and turned into rentals. But it was nothing like what was going on in places such as Atlanta and Phoenix, where Wall Street was gobbling up houses. The foreclosure auctions I attended on courthouse steps in south Alabama were lonely affairs. It'd be me squinting and sweating through my suit, maybe another silent onlooker, and some lawyer representing the likes of RCH IV-WB LLC or some other alphabet soup murmuring in the midday sun. They felt like pauper funerals. Auctions in the places where Wall Street was putting down roots were Roman orgies by comparison.

Investors circled the first Tuesday of each month on their calendars and booked flights to be in Atlanta. That's the day when every county in Georgia held foreclosure auctions. The foreclosure rate reached 3 percent around Atlanta, which meant that on one day each month thousands of homes were available for dirt cheap around the Deep South's economic engine.

Ryan Heck, the house flipper who joined American Homes 4 Rent rather than compete with the big companies for foreclosures, was part of a team that would fly into Atlanta for what was known among investors as Super Tuesday. Heck and others of B. Wayne Hughes's bidders would gather at a Sheraton Hotel along the interstate north of the city on the evening before Super Tuesday and divvy up $20 million or so of cashier's checks. Sometimes American Homes would ship the money to buyers' homes, with orders to lock away what was effectively millions in cash until it was time to splash it on the courthouse steps. Other times one of the bidders would retrieve a stash from American Homes' headquarters in Agoura Hills, California, and carry it aboard a flight to Atlanta. On Super Tuesday mornings, the bidders would fan out to different counties to buy houses, a few million dollars' worth of cashier's checks in hand.

Their instructions were strict. Nothing older than twenty years or so. Nothing too rural. Nothing smaller than three bedrooms and two baths. Nothing without a garage. Nothing that cost less than $100,000. Nothing that would rent for less than $1,000 a month.

At auction, they were likely to encounter competitors from any number of well-funded home-buying operations. A *Who's Who* of high finance had caught foreclosure fever.

KKR, the corporate buyout firm made famous by the book *Barbarians at the Gate,* and BlackRock, the massive money manager, invested. Warren Buffett, the revered billionaire from Nebraska, bought houses. So did mortgage-backed securities pioneer Lewis Ranieri. Oliver Chang, the lead byline on the influential Morgan Stanley reports, quit his housing research job and began buying houses with the financial support of the Carlyle Group, bond-investing powerhouse PIMCO, and others. New York hedge fund giant Och-Ziff Capital Management put money behind a restaurateur in Northern California named Gregor Watson, who was buying foreclosures. Cerberus Capital Management—in the news for its disastrous buyout of Chrysler, which ended with the automaker's bankruptcy—gorged on nonperforming home loans. Geoff Jacobs, who launched an early rental operation in Phoenix, partnered with Progress Residential, a multibillion-dollar endeavor started by Donald Mullen, a former Goldman Sachs mortgage chief who had overseen the firm's lucrative "big short" of mortgage-backed securities. Hotelier Barry Sternlicht, who became a real estate tycoon buying repossessed apartment buildings from the government after the savings and loan crisis, and Donald Trump confidant Tom Barrack, who followed a similar path to moguldom, each built up national home-rental operations. Blackstone's Invitation Homes was buying as much as $150 million worth of houses a week.

These bulk buyers competed for properties mainly with one another. Typical home buyers were sidelined. Many Americans' credit had been torpedoed by foreclosure and short sales, in which they sold their homes for less than they owed in deals with their lenders. Mortgage underwriters required 20 percent down payments, which eliminated another swath of Americans from qualifying for home loans: those with good credit but little cash. There were also millions of underwater homeowners like me. We had more than enough mortgage debt.

Bulk home buying wasn't for the weak kneed. Buyers couldn't see inside before they bid at foreclosure auctions. Sometimes interiors were like new. Occasionally there were nice surprises, like marble countertops. Often there was a mess. Just clearing out the junk left by a hoarder could add 10 percent to renovation costs. There were wild stories. A corpse in the Carolinas. Basement marijauna farms. A turnover crew that renovated the wrong house in California, surprising a family just back from vacation with a new kitchen and news that their possessions were in a landfill. The first house Gregor Watson bought with Wall Street money was half missing.

It was on a hill in Oakland, California. Watson's inspector went by and it looked good from the street. He couldn't see around back because of a fence and some overgrown ivy. When he looked through a small pane in the front door, he glimpsed a magnificent view. He had no idea that was because the back half of the house had tumbled down a cliff when a water main burst beneath the street. The owner had bolted with the insurance money and so the property was foreclosed and auctioned off. Watson feared he was finished as a real estate investor. He was lying on his kitchen floor when he told his wife as much. He dialed his financial backers in New York and tried to soften the bad news with humor.

"The good news is we have a great view," Watson said. "The bad news is that we have half a house."

The hedge fund guys didn't laugh, but they let him keep buying houses. It took six months, but he got a refund for the half house.

Investors concentrated their buying around big Sun Belt cities to which people were moving, such as Phoenix and Houston. They targeted good school districts, and when they found zip codes that checked all their boxes, they bought as many houses as they could. Density was critical. There had to be enough homes in each place to make managing them efficient enough to justify the expense of setting up shop. For the most aggressive buyers, like Blackstone's Invitation Homes and American Homes

4 Rent, that meant accumulating several hundred—even better, several thousand—properties in certain markets. Their buying helped set a floor for prices in some of the worst-hit parts of the country. Unfortunately for me, south Alabama didn't check Wall Street's boxes and property values there continued to fall.

Toward the end of 2011, the *Journal* moved me to New York City to write about Wall Street financiers. I was even farther away from the house and could only imagine what was going on in Alabama.

One of the big stories I had followed in the *Register* was about Joan Teeters, an evangelical woman who had run house-flipping commercials on late-night television during the boom. Federal investigators caught up with her and a web of co-conspirators and straw buyers and sent them to prison. They had committed millions of dollars' worth of mortgage fraud, stiffing home sellers all over Gulf Shores and Foley as well as Fannie Mae and the FDIC.

The real estate news back in Alabama was consistently bleak. Banks weren't bulldozing incomplete condominiums and torching them as they had in the 1980s during the savings and loan debacle, but fire sales of bank-owned properties occurred with regularity.

Bad debt swamped Park National, which had bought Vision Bank and its trove of questionable real estate loans along the Gulf Coast. The Ohio bank had to set aside $66 million for losses in 2011 and was jettisoning repossessed properties in Florida and Alabama left and right. In a September 2011 auction, Park National unloaded more than one hundred properties that Vision had lent against. They included foreclosed houses near mine and condos within the flipper hives along the waterfront, including Bella Luna and Caribe. A few weeks later, Park National held another multimillion-dollar housecleaning in Orange Beach. Bob Shallow stopped by and picked up a couple of Gulf-front lots for $1.5 million.

Park National eventually dumped Vision Bank. An Arkansas holding company that operates as Centennial Bank paid $27.9 million for Vision's seventeen branches, its roughly $500 million in deposits, and the $354 million of loans on which borrowers were still making payments. Centennial made Park National keep more than $100 million of Vision's nonperforming loans as well as another $56 million that its examiners deemed suspect.

The purchase price for Vision Bank was just a sixth of the roughly $170 million that Park National had paid for the lender five years earlier. But just getting rid of Vision had the effect on Park National's balance sheet of a $60 million gain. Two months after the sale to Centennial was finalized, Park National repaid the $100 million it had received in the government's TARP bailout.

The Ohio bank still had to deal with more than $150 million worth of bad loans that Centennial wouldn't touch. Park National tucked those into a subsidiary called SE Properties Holdings and went about auctioning off repossessed properties and suing borrowers who'd defaulted. In Louisiana court, SE Properties pursued the investors whom Jim Brown and Ken Wall had ripped off in order to bribe the mayor. The bank sold off several cottages out on the Fort Morgan peninsula built but not sold by its best customer, Joe Raley Builders.

Litigation between Raley, Vision, and others over the failed Bama Bayou development got nasty. The builder and other investors claimed the bank pulled their funding even though they were current on payments, dooming the project. Scott Raley blamed the bailout for the bank pulling the plug. "If you're in the boardroom, are you going to bet on Bama Bayou or bet on $100 million from the government?" There were allegations in the civil case of fraud and claims of cash-in-envelope bribery between the bank's employees and the builder. As the parties slung mud in Mobile's federal court, weeds grew high among the husks of unfinished buildings and the partly built dolphin-show stadium.

Across the toll bridge from Bama Bayou, local investors bought the banknote for about half the residences at the Wharf, from which flippers had fled when the market turned. The investors auctioned the condos off individually for far less than they were originally priced when preconstruction buyers had to be turned away. Those same investors paid $4.5 million for most of the bank-owned Bon Secour Village property. The failed town founders had paid $20 million for it a few years earlier.

In New York, a colleague and I learned that American Roads, the company that owned the Foley Beach Express toll bridge, was preparing to file for bankruptcy protection. It was barbelled by real estate busts. The traffic projections that Macquarie had used to convince investors that there would be enough toll revenue to cover debt payments proved tragically optimistic. Traffic was a trickle compared with the Australian bank's forecasts.

The bank and its consultants had told the New York private-equity firm that bought American Roads as well as debt investors and a bond insurance company to expect 10 million cars to cross the bridge in 2012. Really, though, just 2.3 million trips were recorded. Worse yet for American Roads, interest rate swaps attached to the debt financing backfired. The swaps were meant to protect against rising interest rates. When rates were cut in response to the housing crash, a bill came due from the bank with which Macquarie had wagered. The wrong-way bet added $334 million to American Roads' debt. In 2012, the toll road company faced debt payments of $35 million against $14.2 million in pretax earnings. The next July, the company filed for bankruptcy protection.

Alinda surrendered the bridge to Syncora Guarantee, which had insured the American Roads' bonds against default. Syncora sued Macquarie over the inflated traffic projections. My colleague and I wrote a front-page article about the episode, and several other toll-road deals around the country that were crumbling because boom-era housing and traffic predictions failed to materialize. The *Journal* hired a photographer to illustrate the story and he sent back some grim photos of Bama Bayou, overgrown and deserted at the foot of the bankrupt bridge.

I knew less about what was going on at my own house. The few clues I received didn't paint a pretty picture. A curious line item on a repair invoice following my first tenant's particularly destructive tenure read: "pressure washed garage floor due to fish odor." Citations from the neighborhood homeowners' association alerted me to mysterious heaps of vegetation piled out front and a boat in the driveway that was taller than the house.

In one letter to homeowners, the neighborhood association threatened to close the communal playground because of the used condoms, cigarette lighters, and graffiti turning up. Another letter I received in New York called for volunteers to help repair a breach in the perimeter fence that residents of a nearby trailer park were using as a shortcut to the dollar store.

*What trailer park?* I wondered. *What dollar store?*

After about a year in Texas the *Journal* moved me to New York, where one of the assignments that I drew was writing about Blackstone. For obvious reasons, I was especially interested in Invitation Homes, the firm's massive rental bet.

One night around the holidays in late 2013, Blackstone's executives hosted a private dinner with reporters at Manhattan's Smith & Wollensky steakhouse. I was seated next to Stephen Schwarzman, the firm's cofounder and CEO, and spoke with him about the tens of thousands of houses the firm had bought and turned into rentals. I joked with the billionaire about being a tiny competitor of his. He made the bull case for owning rental homes. Then Schwarzman pointed up, leaned over, and said, "Don't sell your house."

*Steve,* I thought, *that won't be a problem.*

A few months later, I opened a letter and learned that county tax assessors had valued my property at $52,200, less than half of what I owed the bank and less than half what my insurance company deemed the house to be worth in the event it burned down.

Seven years after the U.S. housing market collapsed, at a time when millions of others had put the economic calamity behind them, I was still stuck. The house I owned would be twice as valuable on fire than on the market.

# 21

## JOANIE

The flood of Wall Street cash meant nothing for me, but it lifted a lot of other landlords. Consider Bruce McNeilage.

He had an epiphany about rental houses in 1998, while attending his father's funeral in Dearborn Heights, Michigan. McNeilage met a woman there named Joanie, whom he judged to be about sixty-five. Joanie lived in the neighborhood. McNeilage asked her how long she'd lived there.

"Thirty years," she said.

McNeilage, a financial planner with such matters top of mind, remarked that it must be nice to have the mortgage paid off, to own the house free and clear. Living the American dream, he said.

"No, no," she said. She rented the house from a Mr. So-and-So. "A very nice man."

*She hadn't paid off her own mortgage, she'd paid off Mr. So-and-So's mortgage!*

"What made him a nice guy?"

Mostly it was that he was attentive, she said. Seven years earlier, he even gave the place a paint job and replaced the carpet.

That was twenty-three years into Joanie's tenure in the rental house. *If that's nice,* McNeilage thought, *I can be nice times ten.* Mr. So-and-So owned houses all over the neighborhood, each filled with Joanies who were paying his bills, taking care of the properties as if they were their own, and asking for little more than fresh carpet every couple of decades. McNeilage did the math and realized there was a lot of money to be made housing the Joanies of the world. He decided then that he was going to buy rental homes.

He saved his money and bought a few houses to rent around Fort Lauderdale, Florida, where he was living. The results were mixed. After a few years, he moved to Nashville. Houses were much cheaper in middle Tennessee, which meant McNeilage's money could go further than it had in Florida. He settled about a half hour south of Nashville in Spring Hill, a house-sprouting swath of countryside where General Motors had a giant factory.

Spring Hill was an ideal place to own rentals. There were a lot of big employers around on account of the GM plant and Nissan, which has its North American headquarters in one direction and an assembly line in the other. Spring Hill's schools share a district and funding with Nashville's wealthy southside suburbs, where country music stars and corporate executives live. Spring Hill was pretty much the cheapest place to live in Tennessee's top school district.

Once he had mortgages on seven houses, McNeilage couldn't borrow any more. So he went to see a wealthy friend. He hoped to add five houses to his stable and asked his buddy if he could borrow the money.

"Fuck it," his rich buddy said. "Do fifty."

McNeilage began building houses to lease all over Spring Hill. Most of his tenants paid between $1,595 and $1,795 a month to live in houses that were indistinguishable from those that were owner occupied. Some people paid as much as $3,500 for his really big houses. His rent roll included doctors, a guy who played for the Tennessee Titans, and a lot of regular working people. Some of his tenants never renewed their lease after their first and stayed in his houses on a month-to-month basis, paying premium rents for years on end.

The housing crash didn't hurt McNeilage. Far from it. Demand for rentals grew when the housing market seized up. He got some competition from a local builder who had to lease dozens of his unsold spec homes when sales sputtered, but McNeilage's tenants tended to stay put. Besides, there were always others lined up, eager to enroll their children in the good schools.

Spring Hill's economy snapped back from the recession. When GM went bankrupt in 2009, the automaker dialed down the plant to produce just components. The facility was back to making cars by 2012. The ramp-up attracted autoworkers from Michigan and Ohio. Many rented because they were saddled with underwater homes back north. American Homes 4 Rent, armed with more than $600 million from Alaska's state oil fund, bulked up in middle Tennessee by buying out local landlords.

The builder who had leased out the homes that he couldn't unload when the market crashed sold fifty of them to American Homes in 2012. Not long after the company bought out his rival, McNeilage tracked down American Homes 4 Rent's CEO at an industry conference. He introduced himself. "You bought out my competitor," he said.

"So?"

"Now I want to buy you out."

The executive scoffed.

"Or you can buy me out," McNeilage said.

He handed his business card to the executive, who turned and handed it to another man. He put it in his pocket. A few weeks later, the company paid McNeilage nearly $10 million for his forty-two houses, tenants included. The California company wanted more around Nashville to achieve economies of scale, so it enlisted brokers to scoop up houses on the open market.

McNeilage had turned his attention to Atlanta a few years earlier. As the foreclosure crisis unfolded, he convinced his grade school buddy Chris Zachary to join his rental-home gambit. McNeilage and Zachary had collaborated on moneymaking schemes as teens. They mowed lawns, shoveled snow, and collected beer cans outside Detroit's Pontiac Silverdome during rock concerts. Now, as adults of some means, McNeilage convinced Zachary that they should buy as many houses as they could while prices were low.

"It'll never be this bad again," McNeilage said. "We'll sit back sometime and talk about how we got rich to our grandkids."

They put $350,000 together, named their company Kinloch Partners after the elementary school in Michigan where they met, and McNeilage headed to Atlanta to buy houses.

Greater Atlanta was a wasteland of abandoned and bank-owned homes. Loose lending by the likes of Countrywide and rampant speculation had emptied neighborhoods. Prices had plummeted. McNeilage paid as little as $38,000 for houses that cost $200,000 a couple of years earlier. Bank of America, pitiable acquirer of Countrywide, was selling entire streets full.

Model homes in particular could be bought for very little. The garages, used as sales offices, held scenes frozen in time. There'd be a desk, a cheap radio, stacks of marketing brochures, a congealed cup of coffee, maybe some petrified open house popcorn, and a newspaper sports section from 2008. It was as if the market imploded one day while the salespeople were at lunch.

Before he left Tennessee, McNeilage hired a man named Ruben Martinez, a handyman and fellow Michigan native, to help him get the houses in shape to rent. Martinez was basically homeless, sleeping on a relative's couch in Tennessee, when he answered a Craigslist ad McNeilage had posted seeking a super for a small apartment building he owned. Instead, he took Martinez to Atlanta for $250 a day to help him flip foreclosures. They didn't even learn each other's last names until after they had already left for Georgia.

McNeilage settled into a routine of three days in Nashville and four in Atlanta, where he and Martinez operated out of pickup trucks and $35-a-night hotel rooms. They rented a storage space to stockpile microwaves, rolls of carpet, and scratch-and-dent water heaters. Eventually McNeilage bought a big house for Martinez and his crew to live in, and he stayed there whenever his wife and infant son weren't visiting. When they were in town, McNeilage would get a motel room and swaddle the baby in a pulled-out dresser drawer.

No one ever complained when he and his guys worked on houses after dark, sometimes by the high beams of their pickups. Often there were no neighbors to complain. If a family was living next door, they were usually glad to see someone tending to a vacant house, no matter the hour. To curry favor, McNeilage and his crew would cut the overgrown lawns of other empty houses, plant flowers, and spread fresh mulch in the beds in subdivision entryways. He'd tell the neighbors, many packed into houses like after World War II, that they were welcome to park in his driveway at night. That helped his houses appear to be occupied.

Neighbors were a good source of leads, too. McNeilage would ask if they were interested in selling or if they knew anyone looking for a rental. Occasionally, they'd respond with a story about a pending foreclosure down the street. Just as the Morgan Stanley analysts had predicted, many foreclosures created not just a potential rental home but also a renter. McNeilage would offer to rent the about-to-be-ousted people the house he had bought and rehabbed down the street. An easy move. Then he would buy their old house from the foreclosing lender, fix it up, and rent it to someone else.

In Spring Hill, his aim was to have tenants stay in his homes for as long as possible. In Atlanta, though, McNeilage aspired to see his tenants only once: when they signed the lease.

To accomplish this, he had to sell the occupied rental house to another investor before it was time to collect the second month's rent. McNeilage got to where he could buy a house from a bank on a Monday, have it leased by Saturday as Martinez and his crew were wrapping up the rehab, and sell it the next week to a big investor for nearly twice what he had paid. When McNeilage arrived in Atlanta, he told Martinez they might be there six months. Six years later, in 2016, they were still going strong.

Despite the Federal Reserve holding interest rates at historic lows and the Treasury Department injecting hundreds of billions of dollars into the lending system, the national homeownership rate kept declining. Part of the problem was people like me, who couldn't sell their house to buy a new one, as well as those—me again—who didn't have enough cash for the more robust down payments that lenders demanded. Banks were not without blame. The infusion of taxpayers' billions might have saved many of them from going under, but it didn't really get them lending again.

Even Ben Bernanke, who was rolling in six-figure speaking fees and a healthy book advance after steering the Fed through the crisis, was denied trying to refinance a mortgage. Banks, Bernanke quipped, "may have gone a little bit too far."

Some of the largest rental investors decided that renting was more than a stopgap until home prices bounced back. These investors wagered that if big enough, and run with corporate efficiency, pools of suburban rental homes could be organized as dividend-paying public companies just as financiers had done with apartments, office towers, shopping malls, and storage units. They began to absorb rivals and expanded their buying from the courthouse steps, where the action was waning, out into the open market, where prices were still pretty low and they didn't have much competition from regular house hunters.

American Homes 4 Rent had about eighteen thousand houses when it offered shares in an IPO. Issuing stock gave the company a currency with which to acquire rivals much larger than Bruce McNeilage. In 2014, American Homes used its shares to add thirteen hundred homes. Two years later, American Homes issued more than half a billion dollars' worth of new shares to acquire a nine-thousand-house rival. The company added thousands more houses one at a time at auctions and on the open market. By the end of 2016, American Homes owned about forty-eight thousand houses. No single-family landlord had ever come close to managing so many.

Others were gaining. Real estate moguls Barry Sternlicht and Tom Barrack merged their rental homes into a single thirty-thousand-home company called Starwood Waypoint Homes. Combining cut down on overhead expenses, boosted economies of scale, and meant larger pools of collateral against which money could be borrowed to buy more houses.

Like everyone else at the depths of the mortgage meltdown, rental investors, even those with credit as sterling as Blackstone and B. Wayne Hughes, had trouble borrowing money to buy houses. In 2013, though, Blackstone and investment bankers at Deutsche Bank figured out a way to borrow against the houses that Invitation Homes already owned. Instead of a bond backed by home loans, they created a security underpinned by lease payments from a group of rental homes. The first rent-backed bond that Invitation Homes sold pooled about thirty-two hundred of its houses as collateral, mostly in Phoenix and Southern California. The deal enabled the company to lay off risk to investors and raised $479 million to prolong its house hunt.

The bonds were a hit with investors. Other large landlords followed with their own rent-backed bonds. They didn't usually pay much more than 4 percent, but with the Federal Reserve holding short-term interest rates near zero, hedge funds, insurance companies, and the like ate them up. By 2017, Invitation, American Homes, Starwood, Progress, and a few others had sold more than $16 billion worth of rent bonds.

These companies presented a persuasive case for a permanent suburban rental class. Rents were rising amid growing demand from people who couldn't or wouldn't buy yet needed room for a family and wanted access to good schools. Home prices had risen above their precrash highs in many markets. Not only did that make the rental companies' collateral more valuable, it pushed homeownership beyond the reach of many.

Before prices collapsed, the pace of household formation had been split pretty evenly between renters and those who owned their residence. Between the beginning of 2007 and early 2017, though, roughly twenty-four new renter households were started for every one that owned its home. Many of the new tenants were toward the higher end of the income spectrum for renters, too. A decade earlier, these people would have probably bought homes.

That January, Donald Mullen, whose Progress Residential had accumulated about twenty thousand houses, was the featured speaker on a conference call hosted by a firm that analyzes real estate investments. Mullen was in the midst of raising a $1 billion private-equity fund so that Progress could keep buying houses.

If anyone knew a thing or two about cynical bets on middle-class liquidity, it was Mullen. He'd helped oversee Goldman Sachs's fruitful wager against the housing market a decade earlier. Progress aimed to provide an "aspirational living experience" to tenants who were typically about thirty-eight years old and married, with a child or two, annual income of about $88,000, less-than-stellar FICO credit scores around 665, and a hobbling $45,000 of debt. If they wanted to live the middle-class lifestyle to which they were accustomed, they'd have to rent. "Our residents are quite a ways away from being able to purchase a home," Mullen said.

As Mullen described his firm and the finer points of large-scale landlording, one of the analysts hosting the call interrupted with big news. Invitation Homes had disclosed in filings associated with its forthcoming IPO that Fannie Mae had agreed to guarantee up to $1 billion of its debt. That meant that Fannie, still a ward of the state, effectively put taxpayers on the hook for any losses that investors might suffer on a roughly billion-dollar rental bond that Invitation assembled.

It was a leg up for one of Mullen's competitors, but an important endorsement for the big-time rental-home business. Five years earlier, Fannie's regulator, the Federal Housing Finance Agency, had blocked Freddie Mac from backstopping debt issued by investors who were buying houses in bulk. Times had changed, and so had the minds of housing regulators. The guarantee of Invitation Homes' debt signaled that homeownership might no longer be a government priority. Mullen sounded giddy.

"This is a great outcome," he said. "Not just because it obviously will reduce the cost of our financing, but it puts a further stamp of approval on this industry."

# 22

## FOR SALE

Landlording was going so well for others that sometimes I wondered if I should double down. I could buy another house in Audubon Place while borrowing costs and prices were low, rent it out, and use the profits to average out the loss I was taking at my old house, where my expenses were too high to ever profit. That seemed easier than selling or refinancing the house I already owned.

Periodically, I would check in with real estate agents in south Alabama to see what they thought my house might fetch. Home prices along Alabama's beaches were rising from the bottom, albeit slower than in many other parts of the country, and I had chipped away at my debt with each monthly payment. The agents never responded with a number that was worth the trouble or expense of ousting my tenant and testing the market.

I also kept in touch with the woman who'd steered me through the refinancing episode when I had to get my ex-wife's name off the deed so that I could move to Texas for work. The lady at the bank was diligent, friendly, and probably about as helpful as she could have been. Once or twice a year, I'd pester her about refinancing. My calls were prompted by unnerving developments at the house, like a pricey repair or some fuss with the tenants. Sometimes I picked up the phone after reading a blood-boiling news article.

An inquiry in 2014 was triggered by a story written by one of my former colleagues at the *Register*. It was about Rick Phillips, the developer who had gone bankrupt in spectacular fashion a few years earlier. Phillips was offering preconstruction condo units in a twenty-three-story tower that he wanted to build in Orange Beach. Phillips had his office furniture and far-flung real estate liquidated by a bankruptcy trustee in a piffling attempt to satisfy $124 million of debt he'd racked up trying to build towers during the boom. If he was back in the condo game, surely I must be close to emerging from underwater. Alas, I was not.

The next spring, in 2015, my colleagues at the *Journal* wrote a couple of stories about how enough time had passed since the crash that foreclosures were falling off the credit reports of hundreds of thousands of people who lost homes or whose house flips flopped at the onset of the crash. With the blemishes gone from their credit reports, they were again able to buy homes. It was flabbergasting to think that the couple who abandoned the house next to me and let it fester might be house hunting while I was still digging out.

Same for all the speculators on the beach and in the deserted subdivisions who fled when they couldn't flip and tipped the market into free fall.

When the mortgage broker returned my call, I would make the case that if the bank would refinance my house at the prevailing interest rates, which were a lot lower than what I was paying, it would relieve my financial burden and increase the likelihood that I could—and would—continue to make payments. Who was I kidding?

I had never missed a payment or even been late except the time I intentionally held a check back a few days to get the bank's attention. Regions Bank had no reason to believe that I'd suddenly stop paying. I was a reporter for a national news outlet. All anyone had to do was google my name and they'd see that I was employed and know where to find me. It was a bit like the situation with the neglected dog in my zombie neighbor's backyard. As long as I was tossing bread over the fence and filling its bowl from my garden hose, the dog wasn't in immediate danger of dying and the sheriff's deputy saw no reason to act.

The mortgage broker would politely tell me that the bank was not interested in refinancing the debt. "I have not found an appetite to reduce your interest rate," she began one email. She'd attempt to soften the blow by applauding my stick-it-out attitude. She might as well have called me a sucker. I had lived in the South long enough to know that "Bless your heart" is not meant to be nearly as sympathetic as it sounds.

By 2017, the flood of foreclosures in Audubon Place had subsided and houses were cracking the $100,000 mark again. They lagged the broader market, to be sure; national home prices had exceeded their precrash highs in the third quarter of 2016 and I was still way off from what I had paid back in 2005. Still, it was encouraging to see the return of prices befitting a home after years in which houses in Audubon Place cost about the same as a really nice car. For the first time in a decade, I might have a chance to sell my house without having to come up with tens of thousands of dollars to pitch into a deal.

I'd been consulting for a few months with a real estate agent named Eric Nelson. He said he was confident he could sell the house for about what I owed so long as I could get my tenants out and tidy up the place during the spring selling season. That was a problem. Summer would be nearly over before my tenants' lease was up.

I was weighing whether to make them an offer to move out early when a woman from the property management firm called to tell me that my tenants wanted to move down the street to an almost identical house with cut-rate rent. It was troubling to think that the rents in Audubon Place might be going down, but the cheap house seemed like an anomaly. The square-foot price for sales in the neighborhood was still climbing. I told the property manager to let my tenants out of their lease without penalty on the condition that they leave the place as clean as possible and be out by midnight on March 31.

I called Nelson to tell him that I was headed his way and walked over to my boss's office to let her know that I needed to take a week off work to tend to personal business in Alabama.

I arrived at the house in the early morning hours of April 1, 2017, for the first time since 2010 when I left to take a job in Texas. Audubon Place was asleep. The lights were on inside my house, however, and there was a huge pickup truck emblazoned with the University of Alabama football insignia parked in the front yard.

I pulled into the driveway next to the truck, wondering if perhaps my tenants had not yet left. I walked around the side of the house and peeked inside the kitchen window. It seemed empty inside, but I couldn't be sure. The Roman shade that I had hung above the sink as a new homeowner twelve years earlier was lowered and I couldn't see much. I went back to the front door and pressed the doorbell. There was no sound. I added "new doorbell" to the to-do list I was compiling in my head and wrapped my knuckles on the door a few times. If anyone was in there, they didn't have a dog. After a few breaths, I slid the key into the lock and opened the door.

The house was in better shape than I had expected, though it had changed enough that it no longer felt entirely mine. The front door was painted the same slate blue, but the first room beyond it was a new yellowy white. Small trees and shrubs I'd planted, which couldn't have walked off by themselves, were gone, roots and all. There was no trace of the raised garden bed nor the slate step stones that had been arranged around it. The walls of the walk-in closet off the master bedroom were scuffed from furniture being crammed in for a makeshift third bedroom. I'd forgotten the washer and dryer had been stolen and regretted packing light. On the bright side, two cypress saplings the size of pencils when I planted them in 2006 now towered above the house.

The pickup truck in the yard was gone when I woke up. It turned out to belong to one of my neighbors. Three couples, each with at least one child, shared the three-bedroom cottage. The house that had once spilled wild kittens was now bursting with people. Judging from the magnetic signs stuck to each of their automobiles, they worked for a company cleaning condominiums and vacation homes down at the beach.

For three days and nights I painted, planted bushes, and repaired leaky faucets. I made so many trips to Lowe's for mulch and electrical outlets that one of the cashiers expressed interest in renting the place if I couldn't sell it. I rattled the windows with music as I worked and slept a few hours each night in a sleeping bag on the floor of my old bedroom. On the second day, my real estate agent, Eric Nelson, surprised me, dressed to help in the yard. I had made good progress and didn't want to take him away from marketing the house to spread mulch. Nelson's gesture was uplifting, though. He was as serious about selling the house as I was.

Audubon Place had perked up since 2010. Older couples seeking bargain retirement homes near the beach had moved in and tidied up several of the neighborhood's problem properties. The trash-strewn pool next door had been filled in and sodded over. It made a nice little patch of grass surrounded by cement, like a rug in the middle of a room. Yet hints of the seedy days remained.

One evening, I emptied the attic. The power tools and other home-repair gear that I had stashed up there for such an occasion were long gone, replaced by the junk of tenants past. As I toted abandoned possessions to the curb, a neighbor came by and asked if my renters had left behind anything good. There were Halloween decorations, art supplies, baby photos, trade school brochures, sheet music for a late Rolling Stones album, a pair of blocky and barely worn black shoes that looked like a young man's hasty purchase ahead of a court appearance, a Nintendo, a few dirty movies.

"Any pills?" he asked.

In the conversation that followed, I learned that my house had been a place to score painkillers.

There was a downpour the next morning. The rain made a pond of my yard. The grass seed I'd spread the night before floated on top. I worried the rain would wash the fresh coat of picnic-table red from the shed. I was painting my old home office at the front of the house when a garbage truck pulled up. A man in a slicker clinging to the back sized up the mound of renovation debris and my renters' old stuff and waved the driver on.

There wouldn't be another garbage pickup for a week. I didn't want showings to start with a soggy, days-old heap of trash. The woman who ran the homeowners' association would have a field day fining me for a mess like that. I dropped my paintbrush and raced outside.

I was dripping wet, barefoot and shirtless, paint splotched, and waving my arms as if the garbage truck were the last raft off a sinking ship. By some miracle, the driver not only saw me but stopped. The man on the back said he didn't think I'd paid my bill because there wasn't a county-issued bin at the curb. I told him about my renters' habit of leaving with everything that wasn't tied down and promised that I was current on the garbage bill. He waved to the driver to back up.

As we flung the bags and boxes into the truck, he looked at the FOR SALE sign and asked if I was open to a rent-to-own arrangement. I was not. But it was another in a string of inquiries that suggested strong demand for a little house like mine. There weren't many move-in-ready houses around that could be bought for less than $120,000. Tourism had come roaring back and lots of hospitality and service workers were looking for places to live.

The day before the downpour, a boy had walked over while I was planting shrubs in front of the house and asked if I had sold it yet. I told him that I hadn't and he took down the Realtor's phone number from the yard sign. The boy lived down the street and said his aunt sent him. Before I'd finished working and before we'd even put any pictures of the place online, Nelson called to say he'd received an offer. It was a lowball bid from an out-of-towner who was coming to take a job at a big youth sports complex being built along the Foley Beach Express. I turned it down, but the interest was exciting. I'd never received an offer in any amount.

Before I left to return to New York, I walked around back and took in the yard as the sun set one last time. Despite all the trouble the house had caused, there were things about it that I would miss. The way the low afternoon sun passed through the trees and cast the house in soft green light. The chatty songbirds that took turns splashing in the birdbath. The occasional whinny from the farmhouse over the fence. The fading smell of a steamy coastal day coming to an end, like an oven after the food has been removed.

I spent the long drive to New York making calculations in my head. What was the lowest offer I could accept? How long could I afford to leave the house vacant and on the market? If it didn't sell soon, I'd have to rent it again, postponing escape for at least another year. I should have jotted down the phone number of the thoughtful garbageman. He seemed like a solid tenant.

I needn't have worried. Within a week, a retired couple from Minnesota agreed to pay $112,000. They waived an inspection and my agent volunteered to cut his commission to help make the deal happen. The appraisal hit the mark, no termites turned up, and closing was scheduled for May.

Everything was going smoothly until I called Regions Bank to request the precise amounts needed to pay off my loans. The bank wouldn't tell me. I was directed to a toll-free line where I was bounced around a call center like a basketball that had rolled through a puddle of muck. It was as if the lender had never dealt with someone selling their house. Eventually someone told me that I had to make the request in writing, via fax, and could expect an answer to be mailed to me a week or two later. That was preposterous. The whole deal could fall apart on that timeline. I shuddered at the thought of having my escape from a ten-year ordeal depend on a fax to a bank processing center in Mississippi being answered. I raised hell with every bank employee I could get on the phone. Eventually the mortgage broker back in Alabama produced the numbers. After fees and sales commissions were subtracted from the $112,000 that the Minnesota couple had agreed to pay, I owed Regions $34.28.

The buyers signed the papers in Alabama and they were sent overnight to me in New York. The envelope arrived the next day at my office in midtown Manhattan and I found a banker at a nearby branch to notarize the documents as I signed each one. Then I slid them into a mailer, enclosed a check for $34.28, and dropped it into a FedEx box on the corner.

From the original purchase in late 2005 to the sale in May 2017, I lost $25,500. My losses as a landlord? The best I can tell from tax returns and other records, it was something north of $35,000. It would be much more if the lost gains on my 401(k), the tax penalties for withdrawing retirement funds early, and incalculable opportunity costs were factored in. Whatever the grand sum, it didn't matter. I was free.

# 23

## WALKING AWAY

My ex-wife may have been right. I probably should have walked away from the house, ignored the mortgages, and dared the bank to come after us. Perhaps my lender would have been content with the house. And if it hadn't been and the bank had taken me to court for more, I probably could have gotten free for less than the $60,000-plus that I frittered away hanging on. The saga could have ended much sooner, even after tacking on the inevitable drag on my credit. It takes only seven years for a foreclosure to fall off a credit report. It took me ten to sell the place.

After I sold it, my editor at *The Wall Street Journal*, Jamie Heller, asked me to write an essay for the paper about my decade tethered to an underwater house. After reading an early draft, she suggested I add a bit about why I hadn't just walked away. I couldn't come up with a good reason. Even now, with more time to reflect, I have a hard time explaining why I didn't give it up somewhere along the line.

Stubbornness was a factor. Pride, too. As a reporter for the *Register*, I got an intimate look at an all-time case of mass rapacity. I knew which side of history I wanted to be on. It certainly wasn't over with the flippers who pushed home prices up for financial gain and then bolted at the first sign that their wagers wouldn't pay. Or with the slobs next door who bailed on their house without bothering to take out the trash. That's not to say that I found honor in bleeding out financially or believe there's reward in the afterlife for those who pay all of their bills.

Thanks again to my newspaper job, I knew enough about what was happening at the county courthouse to believe that there was a fair chance I could wind up lugging around a big monetary judgment if I walked away. If I was going to be shackled to debt, I preferred it associated with something in which I could live or rent out, not a court order.

The longer I stuck with it, the more I locked myself in. When I was unable to sell the house in 2007, I had no idea prices would take so long to reach bottom. Nor could I have fathomed the eventual depth of my money pit. The longer I waited, the greater the consequences of walking away became.

I had shown my hand to the bank during efforts to refinance when I moved away for the new job. Regions Bank, where I also had bank accounts, knew where to find me and that there were paychecks to pursue. When I became a landlord, I added commitment to my tenants. My house was their home, and if I stopped paying, they would suffer. Once I had stuck with it for a few years, it seemed a waste to walk away. I became resigned to see it through.

I wasn't alone. Millions of Americans kept paying on underwater home loans. At work at the *Journal,* I came across a hedge fund firm called Fir Tree that had reaped more than a billion dollars in profit betting that people would pay their mortgages even after their homes were no longer worth what they owed.

Fir Tree's fund managers were among the investors who bet before the bust that home prices would fall and mortgage-backed securities would lose value. As Fir Tree cashed in on its contrarian wagers, employees at the multibillion-dollar firm looked for ways to keep playing the crash.

Panicked investors were dumping bonds made up of second mortgages, which have secondary claims to houses that are also collateral for first mortgages. If a property has lost value when a borrower defaults, there may be nothing left to repay the second mortgage once the first mortgage is satisfied. Considering that more than twelve million U.S. homes were worth less than their debt, there was a good chance that a lot of second-lien mortgages were out of the money. Investors feared a deluge of defaults among homeowners like me who had paid peak prices before the bust or borrowed against properties at inflated values.

In March 2010, Moody's, the credit-rating firm, lowered its grades on second-lien mortgage bonds that were sold in the years running up to the crash because the underlying second mortgages were "almost universally" underwater. The downgrade prompted a sell-off that gained steam as home prices fell. For many underwater homeowners it made economic sense to walk away from the bad debt, which often amounted to six figures. Academics and lawyers laid out persuasive cases for walking away, especially when not doing so imperiled borrowers' long-term financial health.

Fir Tree planted itself on the other end of the trade, buying up billions of dollars' worth of jettisoned second-lien bonds for pennies on the dollar. The firm's executives reasoned that a lot of people would not walk away, that they were paying for shelter above all, and that the present value of their house wasn't terribly important.

If someone didn't need to move and could afford the monthly payments, what did it matter if the collateral value of the home was less at the moment than what was owed? Americans have a habit of doing whatever they could to pay on their debts regardless if their creditor had any claim to collateral. Every year they make trillions of dollars of credit card payments even though the consequences of not doing so are fairly minor. It was hard to imagine people packing up and moving their families, volunteering for foreclosure, or negotiating short sales just because their second mortgages had weaker or even no claim to collateral.

Second-mortgage bonds had already suffered a lot of defaults, of course. A rash of them had prompted the credit downgrades in the first place. But Fir Tree executives bet there wouldn't be nearly as many defaults as the bonds' fire-sale prices implied. They also suspected that many of the soured loans were not up to snuff and that the firm could pry restitution from the banks that stuffed bad loans into the bonds.

To pursue such compensation, Fir Tree needed 25 percent or more of each bond and had to prove specific instances of shoddy underwriting. By 2013, Fir Tree had spent about a billion dollars buying second-lien mortgage bonds with a face value of roughly $9 billion. Only Fannie and Freddie owned more.

With enough mortgage bonds in hand, Fir Tree gained access to the individual loan files that underpinned the securities. The firm hired people from a defunct mortgage underwriter to pore over the troves of loan documents associated with its bonds in search of missing documents, misstatements, and outright whoppers. The former mortgage underwriters knew from experience where to look and found plenty amiss.

There was a self-employed cement pumper with a surprising stated monthly income of $11,000, which turned out to be less than $4,000 when the borrower later filed for Chapter 7 bankruptcy protection. On another loan application, a transportation company safety officer claimed to make $156,000 a year. That raised red flags. The employer later verified that the borrower's actual annual salary was less than $24,000. A self-employed window washer was said on a mortgage application to earn $78,528 but came clean in a subsequent bankruptcy filing by reporting income of $12,907. A golf ball salesman's six-figure salary was marked up by a factor of five.

Fir Tree forced banks to pony up for spurious loans like those. In all, about half of the $2.6 billion in profit that Fir Tree collected from its second-mortgage scheme was redress for unsound home loans.

The remainder of the firm's profit, more than a billion dollars, came from people like me. As we made our mortgage payments each month on our underwater houses, the bonds in which the loans were bundled paid interest and their value rose. Fir Tree had been right about borrowers.

"People don't walk away," said Brent White, a University of Arizona law professor who advocated to little avail that strategic default was nothing with which to be ashamed. "They'll say, 'I made a promise to pay this mortgage and I'm going to keep this promise and it's immoral not to.'"

In academic papers and other forums at the depths of the crisis, the Arizona professor made the case for walking away. He argued that lenders, the government, and other institutions puffed up the consequences of strategic default and cultivated anticipatory shame among homeowners.

A bank would default rather than throw good money after bad. In fact, they often did. White used an example from 2009, when Morgan Stanley handed over five San Francisco office buildings to creditors rather than repay more than a billion dollars it had borrowed to buy the properties. Morgan Stanley's traders and investment bankers were raking in billions for the bank. It had the wherewithal to keep paying. But the office buildings weren't worth nearly what the bank had paid before the crash. Morgan Stanley decided that defaulting was the right thing to do for the firm and its investors. There was no moral dilemma at the firm over dumping a regrettable real estate purchase as there was raging in millions of underwater households.

"The problem is the asymmetry of norms," White said. The parties on each end of a home loan couldn't be more different. Banks are amoral. They are beholden to act in the interest of shareholders and profit. People, usually, are moral. They value promise keeping and fear the public shame of not being able to hold up their end of a bargain. "It's like playing a game of poker and the rules are different," he said.

In a 2010 paper, White studied the personal accounts of 356 people who chose to strategically default. He was met with a deluge of correspondence after he was quoted in newspaper articles suggesting that strategic default was something that severely underwater homeowners should consider. In these narratives, the professor found no "triumph of rationality over emotion." In fact, emotion was usually the driving force behind decisions to default.

"Many strategic defaulters feel great anxiety about their financial situation, are overwhelmed by a sense of hopelessness, and are angry that their lenders and the government have refused to help," White wrote.

The defaulters with whom he corresponded almost always expressed guilt or shame. White argued that if their actions had been rational, they would have walked away a lot sooner than they did. Most people he heard from didn't default until their house had lost half or more of its value and after they had made extensive efforts to work out deals with their lenders. Rational actors would have walked away long before they raided their retirement accounts or racked up credit card debt to stay current on underwater mortgages. That's the kind of stuff White's subjects were doing. He described a bunch of people who were at wits' end when they walked away. White titled the paper "Take This House and Shove It."

(Other economic researchers who disagreed with White and called strategic default a menace nonetheless agreed with his findings that morality and emotion were at play. A group of them surveyed two thousand Americans in late 2008 and 2009 and 81 percent said they believed that strategic default was immoral.)

Jeff and Shannon McLaughlin agonized over selling their underwater house outside Orlando for less than they owed. Even after they'd decided to move ahead with a short sale, they had trouble bringing themselves to skip a payment to beckon their lender to the table. He would say, "This is the month." And then he'd send a payment. That happened a few times. Finally, the real estate agent the couple was working with called and chewed him out for prolonging things.

During the early years of their marriage, the McLaughlins scrimped to save. They lived in a $450-a-month place best described as a barn. By 2005, with home prices around Orlando rising beyond their reach, they decided to buy. They were panicked about missing their chance to become homeowners. They put offers on nine houses before an above-asking-price bid of $185,900 got them a three-bedroom house about an hour's drive north of the city. The house had sold for $140,000 a year earlier.

The McLaughlins put $30,000 toward the closing costs and down payment and took out a second mortgage to cover the remainder of the down payment so that they wouldn't have to buy mortgage-default insurance.

When the market crashed, the neighborhood deteriorated. It wasn't just vacants and drugs. There were also black bears, whose path from the woods to the subdivision's trash cans happened to be in the McLaughlins' backyard. He became president of the homeowners' association and tried to turn things around, but the neighborhood was too far gone for much more than short-lived cosmetic improvements. The couple decided it was no longer safe for their young children. They had to move.

They had paid off their $26,000 second mortgage and were scratching away at their larger loan's principal but still owed $135,000. Home prices in the neighborhood had plunged below $100,000.

The bank agreed to forgive the difference if they came up with a few thousand dollars. So in 2012 they went to the bank with a few thousand dollars. An investor paid $95,000 for the house. The family moved into a vacation condo that Jeff's grandparents were no longer using on the other side of the city. Their savings, more than $60,000, were gone, their credit was wrecked, and it was tight in the condo with three children. But at least there were no troublesome neighbors or bears.

In 2011, White, the University of Arizona professor, wrote a short book aimed at helping underwater homeowners like me and the McLaughlins work out whether strategic default was right for us. I read it retrospectively and still wasn't sure I'd made the correct decision.

My case for walking away was that I was terribly underwater. I also could have avoided draining my 401(k) on the cusp of a historic stock market rally. Plus, I needed to move away for a better job far more than I needed access to credit.

My credit score didn't really matter to me; I didn't even know what it was. I had had my fill of homeownership. My student loan rates were locked in. And where I wound up, in New York City, I didn't need a car. The only significant expense for which I might need to borrow would have to do with the house in Alabama. I lived in mild fear of receiving word that the air conditioner had died or that the roof needed to be replaced. I daydreamed about a tree falling on the place and smashing it to pieces, but the fantasy ended abruptly when the wind deductible came to mind.

What appropriately gave me pause about walking away, according to White's guide, was that my house was in one of the thirty-nine states that allow lenders to pursue deficiency judgments. White specifically mentions Alabama as a state where homeowners should think twice about walking away for how easily lenders can win judgments against borrowers who owe more than their repossessed homes bring in a sale. Another deterrent was that the bank would know my default was calculated. Going from current on payments straight to 180 days delinquent on my mortgage while continuing to pay other bills would be an obvious sign that I was acting strategically rather than out of serious distress.

Tax law afforded me small inducements either way. As a landlord, I could deduct 4 percent of the value of the house each year, which took some of the sting out of sticking it out. Meanwhile, the Mortgage Forgiveness Debt Relief Act of 2007 exempted forgiven debt from taxation and made walking away less costly if the bank happened to stand down or agree to a short sale.

Bankruptcy law offered avenues to shed or reduce my debt. But I wasn't bankrupt as I understood the term. I could pay my bills. My house just wasn't worth what I owed. I would have entertained a short sale, but in all those years with the FOR SALE sign in my front yard, no one ever put forth a credible offer of any amount.

White estimated that only about 3 percent of borrowers who could afford their mortgage payments made a strategic decision to default. Most people were like me and muddled on.

In Mission Viejo, California, Cristie Connors and her husband were floored when the house across the street sold for $525,000. Their house was smaller and they had paid $715,000. It was 2009 and they were way underwater. California law allowed them to drop the keys in the mailbox and move out without worrying about the bank coming after them. It was tempting.

"We looked at each other and said, 'Are we crazy not to walk away? Where would we live?'" Connors said. A bookkeeper, Connors crunched the numbers and decided that renting wasn't worth it once the mortgage-interest tax deduction for their California-sized loan was considered. "It didn't make sense to put our family through the stress of moving."

When her husband landed a job in San Jose, they rented out their underwater house. They had some problem renters and lost money at first but were fortunate in 2013 when their adjustable-rate mortgage reset to 3.25 percent, half the interest that they had been paying. With much lower payments, their rental home began to earn money instead of burn it. They sold it in April 2018 for $800,000, which was enough to cover the note, pay sales fees, and make up some of the losses from their earlier years as landlords. That freed them to buy a house in Northern California and also to invest with friends in some rental homes southeast of Los Angeles in Riverside, where prices hadn't fully recovered.

Jeff Moon, who had been city administrator in Orange Beach for much of my time as a reporter there, was underwater when he had to move for a new job running the day-to-day of an Atlanta suburb. Moon found a steady renter, but he collected much less each month than his mortgage payments. He and his wife lost about $1,000 a month hanging on to their Orange Beach house. Moon never considered walking away, though. That would have been a bad look for someone whose job is managing public finances, he said. The tax break from renting helped him withstand the losses. After eight years, the price rebounded and he sold.

Al Wojtowicz, a financial adviser in Illinois, got into an argument with a friend who walked away from an underwater home even though he could afford the payments. Wojtowicz had a few friends who did that.

He and his wife were in the same predicament. The value of their town house outside of Chicago had fallen to about half of the $300,000 they had paid months before the crash. They were down six figures and the builder had gone belly-up before finishing the neighborhood. Yet they were gainfully employed—she's a physical therapist—and the town house was big enough for the family even after their second child was born.

The couple reworked the terms of their loan through the government's Home Affordable Refinance Program to pay down their principal debt more aggressively. A new builder arrived to finish the neighborhood. They used gains from savvy stock investments to pay the $30,000 of mortgage debt that wasn't covered when they sold their home in 2014. Credit intact, they bought a bigger house before prices popped and in time for the arrival of their third child.

"It exacerbated the problem when people walked away," Wojtowicz said. "I don't think it would have been as bad as it was if people wouldn't have done that."

# 24

## FROM THREE HOUSES TO FOUR

Stefania Albanesi was working as a researcher at the Federal Reserve Bank of New York, poring over credit data, when she made a surprising discovery. She was studying borrower files from between 2005 and 2009 and noticed that mortgage defaults among those with low, or subprime, credit scores had risen proportionally with their historical rate. That was odd.

It was 2013, a year or two removed from the worst of the so-called subprime crisis, and here it appeared that the explosion in foreclosures involved people with good credit. There was no disproportionate increase in loans to subprime borrowers during the housing boom reflected in the data. Nor was there evidence of an inordinate number of people taking on a mortgage for the first time. That betrayed the narrative that the housing market collapsed because a lot of people who were not worthy had become homeowners. Albanesi had been studying the effects of a 2005 bankruptcy law when she arrived at these findings. They were too interesting to set aside. She decided she'd present them at a briefing that researchers were to give to William Dudley, who was president of the New York Fed.

Albanesi practiced her delivery on colleagues in the research department. They were skeptical. What she was telling them didn't jibe with the prevailing wisdom about the crash. It was irrefutable that securities tied to subprime mortgages sank investors, like the bankrupt Bear Stearns hedge funds that were the housing crash's keeled-over canary. There were flocks of marginal home buyers out on the street following foreclosures and new billionaires on Wall Street who had been minted specifically by betting against subprime mortgages. Albanesi's fellow researchers asked if she was sure of her analysis. She was sure.

She found a more receptive audience in Dudley. A former chief economist at Goldman Sachs, Dudley told Albanesi that he had been skeptical that subprime mortgages alone took down the housing market. There were a lot of sketchy and fraudulent loans, to be sure, but not enough to account for all the foreclosures. He encouraged her to keep digging.

A few years later, the National Bureau of Economic Research published a paper by Alabanesi and professors from Boston and Switzerland. The three of them had analyzed millions of anonymous credit files that the New York Fed obtained from a credit-reporting firm. The files contained hundreds of bits of information about each unnamed borrower, including bankruptcies, foreclosures, loan balances, late payments, zip codes, and credit scores. It was collected between 1999 and 2013, during the run-up and through the worst of the housing collapse.

Albanesi and her coauthors discredited the notion that the crash had been spurred by a subprime lending boom. The amount of credit extended to subprime borrowers had stayed pretty constant over the years and even suffered somewhat as home prices pushed beyond the reach of many would-be buyers. Before prices fell, borrowers with the lowest credit scores accounted for about 70 percent of defaults. But once home prices began their descent, the share of defaults among the least creditworthy borrowers shrank to 35 percent. It was those with good credit scores who accounted for the bulge of borrowing before the crash and they again who were responsible for the rise in defaults. Albanesi and her coauthors attributed this to real estate investors, such as the condo flippers and subdivision speculators that had swarmed coastal Alabama.

To identify these investors among the millions of credit files, the economists looked for borrowers with multiple first-lien mortgages. They found a big rise in people with average to good credit scores adding second, third, and fourth first mortgages. This group that had been deemed little risk to default did so at uncharacteristic rates once its speculative bets began to sour. "The rise in mortgage delinquencies is virtually exclusively accounted for by real estate investors," the economists wrote in their paper.

The work of Albanesi and her partners was the first that I had come across to describe the foreclosure crisis as I had seen it play out in south Alabama. I was writing about failed flippers and wiped-out developers for the *Register* long before my neighbors' cars started getting repossessed and foreclosures plagued Audubon Place. The suffering among lower-earning households began when the construction boom came to a halt and big employers, including real estate firms and city governments, shed jobs. The guy across the street who woke up one morning to find the repo man had snatched the shiny truck he'd leased in palmier times had been nearly idled at work. He had gone from working sixty hours a week installing granite countertops in waterfront towers and golf course subdivisions to having most days off to putz around and get wrecked. I wrote to Albanesi and scheduled a trip to see her at the University of Pittsburgh, where she was teaching economics.

Albanesi, a native of northern Italy, kept a small, sparse office in a tower at the downtown campus. One of my two seating options when I arrived was a beanbag chair. She was working on a follow-up to the 2017 paper that challenged the notion that subprime borrowers were to blame for the crash.

Between 2009 and 2010, nearly two-thirds of all foreclosures came from people whom she and her research partners had identified as real estate investors from the multiple first mortgages they held. Albanesi drilled deeper into these real estate investors and studied their behavior during the years in which the housing bubble inflated. They tended to be aged between forty and sixty-nine in the early aughts. But starting in 2004, their ranks swelled with younger investors, people in their twenties and thirties who were taking on additional mortgages to make speculative home purchases. The data suggested that once someone got a taste for owning more than one home, the likelihood increased that they would buy more.

"If you only have one first mortgage, the probability that you get a second is 4 percent," Albanesi said. "If you have two, the probability that you get a third is about 10 percent. And if you have three, the probability that you get a fourth is about 25 percent."

The restaurant owner back in Foley who'd found herself owning houses from Palm Beach to Pigeon Forge came to mind. So did the Sea-Doo dealer who loaded up on million-dollar units at Caribe and Turquoise Place and the Bon Secour Village developers who had accumulated enough condominium units along Alabama's beaches to house a small army.

The surge of people going from two first mortgages to three and from three firsts to four crested in 2005 and 2006. As soon as home prices declined, investors shed mortgages at unprecedented rates. Albanesi assembled those findings into a 2019 paper.

She charted the foreclosure rates in various cities over time for investors and then for those of non-investors, or people who lived in the homes they had borrowed to buy. She pulled up the Miami chart on her computer screen. South Florida hosted a condo-flipping game that made south Alabama's seem bush league.

"You can see that foreclosures for non-investors peaked right at the end of the recession, but for investors you see they peak about a year earlier," Albanesi said, tracing the arcs on her screen. The first bump was the people who bought houses as investments. The echo was the people who bought houses for shelter. "This is consistent with what you saw on the Gulf Coast, that investors start defaulting first," she said.

It makes sense that investors would be quick to abandon a bad bet. Someone with four first mortgages can lose three houses to foreclosure and still have one left in which to live. Those with just one house didn't have that luxury. By the time the recession struck and the lower earners and least creditworthy got behind on their payments, banks were already plagued by problem loans from the well-off borrowers who were not supposed to default. It was easy to see how a bank choking on defaults would be less able and willing to be flexible with a second wave of distressed borrowers, Albanesi said.

The regulatory response to the crash didn't consider two classes of borrowers, she said. Credit for housing became less available to the people who needed it most—aspiring homeowners with lower incomes—while still allowing well-to-do borrowers to leverage speculative housing bets in a manner unfathomable in any other asset class.

Albanesi said government regulators' response should have been the other way around. So long as they can afford the payments, why not let lower-earning Americans borrow as much as they need to buy homes? On the other hand, if investors want to treat tract houses and waterfront condominiums like stocks and bonds, they should probably use their own money to do so. The average joe can't borrow money to buy stocks, but as long as he's got a pretty good track record of paying his cell phone bill, he can buy houses almost entirely with borrowed money. It's easy for real estate investors to go overboard when the personal risks are so low and the potential rewards so high. If housing bets go errant, it's lenders and neighbors who pay the price.

"Investors generate this extra amplification of shocks in the housing market that then affects the other segment of the market, people who just want to have a home," Albanesi said. "We should have different treatment of these different classes of borrowers."

Other economists have come to similar conclusions. Economists from Duke, Dartmouth, and MIT published a paper in late 2018 that also laid blame for the mortgage meltdown's severity on an explosion of defaults among prime borrowers. "The great misnomer of the 2008 crisis is that it was not a subprime crisis but rather a middle-class crisis," they wrote.

They found that the default rate of borrowers at the upper end of the spectrum, those with FICO credit scores above 720, jumped from roughly zero to 5 percent. The subprime default rate doubled, but the increase wasn't nearly as steep as it was among prime borrowers. Worse yet for unsuspecting lenders and mortgage-backed security investors, the mortgages that prime borrowers stopped paying on were usually much larger than those of subprime borrowers, which meant bigger losses. The more volatile the prices were in a particular market, the more defaults there were. That suggested the presence of speculators concerned with asset value, not shelter.

One of the authors was Antoinette Schoar, who teaches finance at the MIT Sloan School of Management. In April 2019, MIT held a daylong conference near my office in Manhattan on the impact of the crisis and the future of finance. Schoar presented her research there.

"The strain on the financial system came from the large mortgages and the unexpected defaults came from the prime sector at rates that we hadn't seen before," Schoar said. She clicked the screens in the room to a chart showing good-credit borrowers' share of delinquent mortgages rising from 29 percent in 2003 to 61 percent three years later. Then she showed another illustrating a decline in homeownership among lower-income households. The slide began in the early aughts when home prices shot up and became less affordable. When home prices fell, these people's rate of ownership plunged disproportionately to those of better-off borrowers. Subprime borrowers were priced out in the boom, and then after the bust, when home prices might have been within reach for lower earners, they were shunned by lenders.

"The fact that we still haven't fully internalized this diagnosis of the crisis to me is very concerning," Schoar said. "We designed a system where we're forcing the poorest part of the population to be procyclical in their home buying. They can't buy when prices are low because constraints are very high. We see that disproportionately it's not as restrictive to the richer part of the population. To me, this is a very concerning side effect of what has happened in the aftermath of the financial crisis."

A few hours later, MIT alum John Thain, who sold Merrill Lynch to Bank of America when he couldn't save it, held court and told about the time he realized that the computer models used to value mortgage-backed securities couldn't factor in falling home prices.

# 25

## COMPANY TOWN

It wasn't just tighter lending standards that made homeownership so challenging for a lot of regular Americans after the crash. There was a formidable new competitor for houses in many of the most attractive suburban neighborhoods.

In April 2017, a real estate agent named Don Nugent listed a three-bedroom, two-bathroom home for sale in Spring Hill, Tennessee. It sat on a cul-de-sac at the northern edge of town. The house was built in 1997 and had a gable roof, an attached two-car garage, and his and hers sinks in the master bathroom. The owners bought it four years earlier for $160,000. They needed to move to another state and wanted a quick sale. That wouldn't be a problem.

The market in Spring Hill was red-hot. The economy around Nashville was one of the fastest growing in the country. Job seekers were streaming into middle Tennessee, and the good schools, relatively affordable housing, and a new third shift at the GM plant led many to settle in Spring Hill. Builders raced to plat new subdivisions, but after being idled during the crash, they were well behind the influx of people. Houses sold hours after hitting the market.

Nugent hardly had time to pound the sign into the yard before he started fielding offers. The sellers had four to weigh within a few hours. The high bid of $208,000 came from a couple with a child looking for their first house. American Homes 4 Rent matched their offer, all cash.

Unlike the family, American Homes didn't need to borrow a penny to buy the house. That erased the risk of a low appraisal or some lending hang-up derailing the sale. American Homes would do its own inspections, saving the seller time and big expenses. The company wouldn't fuss over scuffed floors or ugly paint since it would be renovating the house, using the same paint colors, flooring, and appliances as those in its hundreds of other houses around Spring Hill. The California company could close sales as soon as the seller desired.

Nugent had sold other houses to American Homes, which was founded by self-storage magnate B. Wayne Hughes and financed with Alaskan oil money. The sales agent lamented steering this latest house from a family that seemed to really want it. But it was his duty to get the best deal possible for the sellers. For clients in a rush to sell, the company's offer was too good to pass up.

Twelve hours after the sixteen-hundred-square-foot house hit the market, American Homes signed a contract to buy it. The house was the seventh that the company had bought on that short, curbless street and one of twenty-six hundred or so it had accumulated around Nashville. About a month later, the house was back on the market. This time it was for rent, for $1,575 a month.

The family whom American Homes beat out for the house was precisely the type of tenant that the company was hoping would lease it: parents who, for the sake of their children's education and social lives, were likely to rent for years without interruption.

"We decided the most stable tenant would be the family," Hughes told the oil fund trustees on a trip to Juneau to update them on their rental gambit.

"Some of you have had children, I'm sure," Hughes said. "They don't ever want to move."

Bruce McNeilage, who sold his rental houses around Nashville to American Homes, sent me an email after I had written a story for the *Journal* about real estate moguls Barry Sternlicht and Tom Barrack merging their rental-home companies. McNeilage told me about his deal with American Homes and said that I ought to come to Spring Hill. Sternlicht, Barrack, and other money-is-no-object out-of-towners had bought a lot of houses there, he said.

Before I booked a trip, I did a little digging. I looked at every deed that had been filed in Spring Hill since 2010, when financiers began scooping up houses, searching for buyers with names like AH4R-TN 3 LLC, CSH 2016-2 Borrower LLC, and other mouthfuls with which they held properties. Once I had the corporate buyers' names, I checked tax rolls for any houses that escaped notice in the deed files.

This turned up nearly seven hundred houses that had been bought by entities affiliated with four big landlords: American Homes 4 Rent, the Sternlicht-Barrack combination called Starwood Waypoint, a company called Streetlane Homes that California-based foreclosure buyer Gregor Watson helped launch, and the former Goldman Sachs mortgage chief's Progress Residential. In six years they had bought about 5 percent of all the houses in Spring Hill. Local real estate agents estimated the big companies controlled three-quarters or more of all the houses in the area that were for lease. There was no way to be sure of the total number of rental houses. The notion that houses in town would be bought to be rented out was new enough to Spring Hill that neither city hall nor county officials counted rentals.

Spring Hill was farmland in the 1980s when General Motors chose a swath of rolling pasture south of Nashville for a factory to build its now defunct Saturn line. When the plant opened in 1990, Spring Hill's population was about fifteen hundred. By 2017, the rural homesteads where GM filmed its folksy Saturn commercials had been covered over in a maze of subdivisions in which more than thirty-six thousand people lived.

Weeks after American Homes snapped up Don Nugent's gable-roofed listing, the company's CEO, David Singelyn, sat in a hotel conference room in Manhattan pitching money managers at a real estate investing conference. Singelyn said that the average household income declared by those applying to rent from American Homes had climbed to $91,000, from $86,000 a year earlier. He offered that as evidence that rents had room to rise.

"This is a choice they make to rent and their wherewithal to pay rent today as well as pay rent in the future, with increases, is sufficient," he said. "It's just up to us to educate tenants on a new way, that there will be annual rent increases."

Renters in Spring Hill were getting the lesson. The shift from a landlord they might bump into at the supermarket to a New York Stock Exchange–listed corporation with tens of thousands of houses and quarterly numbers to make was jarring for Bruce McNeilage's former tenants. It was particularly painful to those whom he'd let rent month to month. American Homes raised their rent by hundreds of dollars a month with little notice. Others were thwacked when their leases came up for renewal. American Homes had bought out McNeilage's largest competitor, so there wasn't much that disgruntled tenants could do but pay up if they wanted to rent in Spring Hill and keep their kids in its top-rated schools.

When I visited, McNeilage took me to a Cracker Barrel to meet Bruce Hull, Spring Hill's vice mayor. Hull owned a local home inspection business and had been hired to comb over the first few dozen houses that American Homes bought when it came to town five years earlier. "The rent is crazy," Hull said. "It hasn't been that long since you could get a three bedroom, two bath for $1,000 a month."

That $1,000-a-month house of yore was renting for closer to $1,800, which was roughly a third more than it would cost an individual with a typical mortgage to own those same properties given prevailing borrowing, insurance, and tax rates. The problem with buying a house in Spring Hill, though, was that you had to beat the big rental companies, and it wasn't just all-cash offers that gave them the edge.

Concerns such as American Homes 4 Rent and Progress Residential employ the latest in machine learning. A company called Entera Technology trained computers to pinpoint the types of houses for which Wall Street's landlords were looking. Entera's algorithms zeroed in on available properties in bulk buyers' preferred school districts and sorted them not just by easily quantifiable characteristics like the number of bedrooms or distance to downtowns but also by more qualitative traits such as sunny kitchens.

Entera was started by a computer scientist named Martin Kay, who built data platforms for customers that included ConocoPhillips and the U.S. Department of Energy before he got into housing. Kay sold a technology business before the crash, and when home prices hit bottom he used some of the proceeds to buy dirt-cheap houses around Dallas, San Antonio, and Houston, where he lived.

Kay wrote programs to mine the mountains of home listings for the sorts of houses that would attract the type of tenant he sought. Like other investors, he was looking for family-sized houses in good school districts. Rivals noticed his knack for getting to plum rental properties first and asked Kay to help them sift through the tens of thousands of properties available for sale in the Sun Belt markets where they were buying.

Entera's software works like a dating app. Rather than making romantic connections, it's programmed to pair investors with their ideal rental properties. Entera's computers scour the multiple listing services that Realtors compile, foreclosure auctions, online sales platforms, and lists of nonperforming bank loans and gather hundreds of data points for each single-family property that emerges for sale around cities such as Nashville, Charlotte, and Phoenix. Then the computers screen for characteristics that each investor desires, including proximity to schools and shopping, the year of construction, property taxes, and insurance costs. Some want houses within a certain distance to a Starbucks, a sure sign of disposable income and measure of neighborhood affluence. Other investors have well-lit cooking spaces on their wish lists.

Teaching a computer to figure out how far away each house is from the nearest Starbucks was easy. Getting one to spot sunny kitchens was more of an undertaking. Kay and his colleagues first taught a computer what a kitchen looked like by feeding it tens of thousands of images of kitchens and telling it, "This is a kitchen, this is a kitchen, this is a kitchen." They gave similar lessons on brightness, pointing out windows and light fixtures. They also had to address obstructions to sunlight, like big trees or buildings next door. Once the computer got the picture, it pored over listing photos, written property descriptions, public records, and satellite imagery, looking for sunny kitchens.

Kay and his partners decided to focus on helping better-funded investors find houses rather than enlarging their own pool of homes. Their specialty was data science, after all, not collecting rent. Whenever Entera needed money to train its algorithms on a new market or add employees, Kay would sell some of the Texas houses that he'd bought on the cheap. By 2018, Entera's algorithms had unearthed tens of thousands of houses that wound up in the portfolios of American Homes 4 Rent, Invitation Homes, and others.

Entera wasn't alone in the race to apply computing power to Wall Street's shopping spree. Progress's Don Mullen boasted that the technology his firm used could identify prospective rental properties within minutes of being listed for sale. In Manhattan, a firm called Amherst Residential, which buys and manages pools of rental houses on behalf of investors, adapted software it had used to value mortgage-backed securities to instead churn out acquisition leads, estimate renovation costs, and predict rental yields. By 2018, Amherst had invested nine figures in its technology and had used the software to buy thousands of houses.

Besides instantaneous alerts that a house it might want had hit the market, Amherst's software had gotten really good at estimating renovation costs. Artificial intelligence constantly refined the predictive model to account for the results of completed jobs on similar houses. Amherst's computers had gotten so good at budgeting rehabs that they were pinning cost estimates to within 5 percent or so of actual costs. That was down significantly from a few years earlier when Amherst routinely overran renovation budgets by 20 percent, executives said when I visited their office for a demonstration of the $100 million house-hunting machine they had built. They would need a lot of help from technology if they were to achieve their long-term goal of a system that managed a million rental homes.

That's a long way from the twenty thousand–odd houses Amherst leased out under its Main Street Renewal brand. Institutional investors altogether hadn't yet amassed three hundred thousand houses, by the firm's estimates. But with something like sixteen million single-family rentals in the United States, there was a lot of consolidation to undertake of the predominantly mom-and-pop business. Plus, the way demographic and economic trends pointed, it looked as if demand for rentals would surpass the supply of houses available to lease.

In 2017, the big investors that Amherst tracked bought more houses than they had the year before for the first time since 2013, when they acquired about seventy-nine thousand properties predominantly on the courthouse steps. Now they were plucking houses off the broader market, doubling down on an already $60 billion bet that the suburban rental class is here to stay. It's a wager that the crisis was so traumatic for people like me, and so destructive to our finances, that we'll be renters forever, that soaring home prices and a load of student debt, $1.6 trillion and counting, will force much of the younger generations to rent.

Investors around the world were getting comfortable with the idea that clusters of suburban homes could be managed efficiently enough to be profitable and were lined up at rental managers' doors in hopes of emulating the success of early investors such as Alaska's oil fund, which banked a $300 million profit in 2016 selling American Homes 4 Rent stock.

Money flowed from all corners. At a time when not many other investments delivered much of a yield, rental houses cranked out cash. Bond-buying insurance companies, hedge funds, pension plans, sovereign wealth funds, stock market investors, community banks, and even Chinese millionaires wanted a piece of the action.

Jordan Kavana, a Florida real estate investor who bought foreclosed homes and nonperforming loans after the crash, wrangled millionaires in China and pooled their cash to buy and build rental homes in the Southeast. A Canadian investment firm called Tricon Capital Group teamed with a Texas pension plan and a Singaporean fund to acquire about $2 billion worth of rental homes. Bruce McNeilage showed me emails he was getting from community banks around Atlanta offering promotional borrowing rates to rental investors. "Right now there's more money than deals," McNeilage said. "I've got to find houses."

With as much money as they could spend and state-of-the-art house-hunting technology, the biggest investors didn't give would-be buyers like Aaron Waldie much of a chance. Even though Waldie and his wife possessed upper-crust credit scores and had plenty of cash to put down after profitably selling their house in California, they were outgunned in Spring Hill when they moved for his new job in the finance department of a local hospital.

The Waldies put down a handful of above-asking price offers and were outbid each time. When they found themselves negotiating to participate in a bidding war for a house they'd not actually seen, they pulled back, resigned to rent. They moved into a house that Starwood Waypoint owned in the next town over. It was their first rental since right after college, two decades earlier. The couple had no complaints about their corporate landlord or the house, but they were paying a lot more than they would if they'd been able to buy the same sort of property.

They were among the millions of fresh renters who had pushed the U.S. homeownership rate to its lowest level in a half century. Rental investors wagered that the sharp rise in homeownership leading up to the crash was an aberration and that the much lower postcrash rates were more in line with historical norms. They were also betting on new attitudes toward homeownership, that owning a home was no longer such a critical piece of the American dream and that more people would be content to rent.

"It's much easier to follow your dreams if you're renting than if you're dealing with the boat anchor of ownership," a top executive at one big landlord told me. "People are realizing that houses are not necessarily the best places to store wealth," said another. Investors like these insist the stigma of being a tenant has waned.

Dallas Tanner, the Invitation Homes founder and chief executive, is young enough to be counted among the millennial generation that his company courts. He likens attitudes toward renting homes to those of leasing a car. "Fifteen years ago, it was a little bit taboo to tell somebody you leased a vehicle. Nobody wanted to talk about whether they leased versus owned," he said. "Nobody cares today."

I get the appeal of renting. With a little less luck, the crash in home prices could have sunk my career as well as my bank balance. I'll think twice about trading my ability to move on short notice for homeownership or committing my savings to shelter.

On the other hand, many Americans save money only unintentionally, when they make their mortgage payments each month and accrue equity in their homes. If homeownership falls out of fashion for even a generation, there could be dire economic consequences unless renters become diligent savers and prudent investors. If that happened on a grand scale, it would be as momentous a shift in American behavior as abandoning homeownership en masse.

Though the personal saving rate has risen since the recession, people are still socking away significantly less than they did in the sixties and seventies. They're not investing more. Goldman Sachs analysts crunched the numbers and found that while the wealthiest 1 percent of Americans have bought $1.2 trillion in stocks and mutual funds since 1990, the remaining 99% of us were net sellers, to the tune of $1 trillion.

Relying on homeownership as the main way to build wealth went awry in a major way a decade ago, though, and there's no reason to believe it couldn't happen again. Even without last decade's crisis, the home-as-piggy-bank arrangement has produced wildly different results. The successive houses in which I was raised around Cleveland were by no means bad investments, but if my parents had bought when they did in Denver or Seattle, I'd feel a lot better about their retirement. My own story would have been a lot different had a newspaper editor in Nashville rather than Mobile responded to the writing samples I mailed out after college. In place of proper retirement plans and pension systems, many Americans leave a lot of their financial prospects to real estate happenstance.

Counting on rising home prices to fund retirements also requires incomes to climb in step so that the next generation can afford to buy out aging sellers sitting on loads of home equity. It's a system that's become severely strained amid surging home prices and stagnant wages. Census data show that median household income in the United States was about $63,179 in 2018, up 5 percent, or about $3,100, from 1999 when adjusted for inflation. Over that same period, the inflation-adjusted price of homes rose by more than a third, according to the Bank for International Settlements. Millions of millennials buried in student debt and priced out of ownership spell big trouble for the baby boomers who staked their late-in-life financial health on someone coming along to pay a big price for their McMansions.

It's possible that the big rental investors underestimate how deeply ingrained homeownership is among American aspiration. Plenty of people probably feel like Walt Whitman when he wrote a few years before the Civil War that "a man is not a whole and complete man unless he owns a house and the ground it stands on."

When I was reporting for the *Journal* on Wall Street's infatuation with Spring Hill, I spoke with one of McNeilage's former tenants who seemed like an ideal subject for the story. For years his rent was stable. Then American Homes became his landlord and boosted it 35 percent over three years. He and his wife wrote to the company and called its local office repeatedly to appeal for more modest increases. There was no response. They had reluctantly signed their latest lease just before we spoke. They wanted one more year at least, so that their eldest child could graduate from the same high school at which she had started. Not long after they signed, American Homes responded to their earlier pleas and knocked $20 off the monthly rent.

"Hilarious, I know," he wrote to me. He wasn't sure his family could afford further increases no matter how badly they wanted their younger children to remain in their schools. "We're almost priced out at this point. We're going to have to make some hard choices next year."

Then he apologized and said that I couldn't use his name in the story. He held out hope that he could convince American Homes to hold the rent steady when his lease came up for renewal and he didn't want to rankle anyone at the company. He also said, without elaborating, that he didn't want his employer to know that he was renting.

Each December, single-family rental investors flock to Scottsdale, Arizona, for a conference. At the 2018 conference, the landlords ranged from the leaders of American Homes 4 Rent and Invitation Homes, which had absorbed the houses of Sternlicht and Barrack to give it some eighty-two thousand rentals, down to smaller competitors such as Bruce McNeilage and Jordan Kavana.

They were met at the chic conference hotel by hundreds of representatives from companies that wanted to lend them money, mow their lawns, and sell them houses. Home Depot and Lowe's sent their remodeling arms. There was a start-up from Los Angeles called Rently selling smartphone-enabled dead bolts that landlords and house flippers use to facilitate self-showings. There were firms that bundle loans to landlords into bonds and others that specialize in lending to flippers. Panel discussions included a Federal Reserve economist, hammer-wielding HGTV-style fix-and-flippers, and executives from high-tech flipping firms, including Opendoor Labs and Offerpad, which use sophisticated technology to ferret out houses to buy, spiff up, and quickly resell—often to rental investors.

Martin Kay was there touting Entera's algorithms. Ryan Heck, who had been an auction buyer for American Homes 4 Rent, was drumming up business for an Uber-esque firm that linked up landlords with lawn care providers. One band of entrepreneur dudes milled about in suits cut from a fabric emblazoned with green elephants. The getup was part Hermès, part clown, and put to mind pajamas. But it did the trick when it came to attracting notice. I made a point to go by their booth in the exhibition hall to see what they were up to, which was hawking a subscription furnace-filter service.

Interest in becoming a landlord had swept the country. In 2018, investors—a mix of landlords large and small, as well as old-fashioned speculators and algorithmic flippers—bought better than one of every ten houses sold in the U.S., according to property data firm CoreLogic. There were talks at the conference on how to manage a hundred house flips a year and debates about whether it made economic sense to build brand-new houses for the purpose of renting them, given all the competition for existing homes that was pushing prices to historic highs. Salesmen sent by home builders mingled and invited rental investors to make offers on their unsold inventory or join them in developing subdivisions.

The biggest landlords got together the night before for a meeting of the National Rental Home Council, the lobbying group they had formed. They invited John Burns, the well-regarded real estate consultant from California, to discuss their prospects. His message was that their immediate future was bright. Though the employment picture was rosy, affordability was severely strained for aspiring homeowners, particularly in many of the metro areas where big landlords owned houses. Few builders were producing new houses for under $400,000. Meanwhile, not a third of renters could afford the median-priced existing home, which cost about $267,000. Rents were rising and mortgages were difficult to come by for people with spotty credit. President Donald Trump's 2017 tax bill eliminated benefits of homeownership for many Americans by lifting the standard deduction above what most homeowners would get if they itemized deductions, such as mortgage interest, and limiting the amount of property taxes that can be written off.

The conference got underway the next morning with a panel of A-list landlords, including American Homes 4 Rent's David Singelyn, Dallas Tanner from Invitation Homes, and Kevin Baldridge, who was president of Tricon American Homes, the rental-home arm of Toronto's Tricon Capital Group, which was buying houses in partnership with a Singaporean fund and a Texas schoolteachers' retirement plan. Baldridge, who had run a big California apartment company before moving into single-family homes, served as president of the landlords' nascent lobbying group. He ended the talk urging the landlords in the audience to consider joining their Nation Rental Home Council.

"We get our narrative out," Baldridge said. "In the very beginning we were landlords that were coming in and buying homes from everybody and evicting people and that was not the case and now we get to tell what we're doing in the communities."

That was true. Most of the houses these investors bought were already empty, sold willingly by the lawful owner whether it was a bank, tax collector, or regular person. They were often cast as villains. The mega-landlords were a strange new thing to emerge from a bout of national trauma, and they weirded out a lot of people. Wall Street eating the suburbs, reaching its tentacles into home equity, the bastion of middle-class wealth. Weren't these the same types of people whose mortgage-debt bender had helped cause the collapse? In most cases, they were not the same exact people who gorged on mortgage-backed securities. The big rental company executives' jobs were simply to turn money into more money, to create yield for investors, and here a once-in-a-lifetime way to do so had presented itself.

Rental executives tend to be proud of cleaning up neighborhoods that were beset by foreclosures. They set floors for plummeting prices in the places where they bought, made homeowners' associations and local governments' whole, and provided nice places to live in safe neighborhoods with good schools that families might not otherwise be able to afford. Rental executives were highly attuned to their reviews on consumer websites and believed, with mounting evidence in support, that the nicer they made their homes and the happier their tenants were, the more money they would make. Baldridge has online reviews of Tricon American Homes sent to his inbox daily, insists that employees refer to customers not as tenants but as residents and established a fund to help renters with sudden money problems stay in their houses. A four-person panel, which includes two former Tricon tenants, vets the requests for rent assistance and doles out the cash.

With hundreds of thousands of houses, though, it was hard to keep everyone content. There were a lot of roofs that could leak, millions of potentially drippy faucets, and countless opportunities for vermin to result in problematic Yelp reviews. A disgruntled tenant of one big company became known among reporters for the spider infestation in her rental home, for which she sought publicity and vengeance.

The National Rental Home Council had shown impressive flex in California, Baldridge said. A lobbying firm it hired in Sacramento opened doors and helped it defeat legislation that would have allowed cities throughout the state to establish rent control.

"Had it won, it would have allowed every city to interpret what it wants for rent control," he said. "Not only would it open up rent control, but every city would have its nuance. To try to operate in that environment would have been crazy. What happens in California then goes all over the country, so we really wanted to take a stand there. American Homes 4 Rent and Invitation Homes played a part in pushing that back."

Another legislative proposal that the mega-landlords viewed as problematic would have added weeks to the eviction process. Unscrupulous landlords were using a loophole, not accepting payments on weekends, to make rent payments technically late and trigger eviction for tenants they wanted out. The practice was happening enough that there was widespread support in the statehouse to end it. Adding a couple of weeks to evictions cut into the rent that houses could be earning. That was something the National Rental Home Council couldn't stomach. Baldridge told how the lobbying firm got the group a meeting with the bill's authors and pitched a compromise: Don't add days to the three-day grace period, but don't count weekends and holidays against it either. The lawmakers went along with that.

The group even swayed the governor, Baldridge said. Another bill would have forced owners of more than one hundred rental units to report a lot of additional information to California regulators. It was going to be onerous and expensive for big landlords. The National Rental Home Council lobbied lawmakers to no avail. The proposal passed the legislature and was sent on to the governor's office, where the rental companies found a more sympathetic ear. The bill was vetoed.

"We all have our day job, but we're going to get bigger and we're going to be a bigger target," Baldridge said. "Unless we really start advocating, we're going to constantly have someone gnawing at us."

Before the meeting adjourned, Singelyn, the American Homes 4 Rent boss, piped up and said it wasn't just statehouse stuff with which the group could help members. Assistance could be much more local, down to homeowners' associations. "It's the blocking and tackling as well as at the HOA level that may impact you," he said.

Imagining these guys in loafers tangling with the uncompromising, lien-wielding woman back in Alabama who ruled the Audubon Place Homeowners Association with an iron fist was funny. I had never been much of a match for Mow-Your-Lawn Mary and usually just dug around for my checkbook whenever she busted my tenants for a visible trash bin or for parking on the sidewalk.

I skipped the cocktail parties on the conference's first night and drove west of Phoenix to Tolleson, the edge suburb where Blackstone began its rental gambit. There was no quick way to cut across the valley. I plugged along a mix of clogged interstates and stop-and-start thoroughfares for more than an hour, passing cotton fields, a jail, an Amazon warehouse, the county bus barn, and vast parking lots where delivery trucks parked overnight. There was a shopping center with competing title pawns just before I reached the subdivision with Blackstone's first house.

I caught the neighborhood on what appeared to be bulk trash pickup night. The broken furniture and remodeling debris piled at the ends of driveways gave the neighborhood a housing-bust vibe. This was probably what it looked like at the depths, with all the gutted foreclosures. Swap out the taupe-painted cinder-block fences with slatted wood, switch the tile roofs to tar shingles, and cover the stucco with vinyl siding and it would look a lot like Audubon Place. This neighborhood on the outskirts of Phoenix and mine back in Alabama had much in common: oleander, a communal playground, narrow side yards, and working-class residents.

Blackstone's first house was near one of the neighborhood's many culs-de-sac. It had three bedrooms, two baths, and a yard full of parking-lot gravel. It rented for about $1,200 a month. The house next door, which looked just like Blackstone's, was also a rental, owned by someone's individual retirement account. Blackstone's Invitation Homes owned another house a few doors down. So did American Homes 4 Rent, Progress Residential, and other firms. More than 40 of the subdivision's 520 houses were owned by either Invitation or three of its rivals, according to tax records.

A block away, there was a house for sale that had been bought by an algorithm and could be opened for a showing by anyone with a smartphone. It was listed for sale by Offerpad, a local start-up launched by one of the founders of Invitation Homes and a prolific local real estate agent named Brian Bair.

Offerpad originated with Bair's habit of recommending upgrades and renovations to clients whose homes he was trying to sell. The company uses computers to find houses it can make over with its in-house rehab crews and sell for a profit. Offerpad was racing to perfect programmatic house flipping against stiff competition. Opendoor, a flush San Francisco start-up, uses artificial intelligence to conduct a high-volume, low-margin operation. Zillow Group, the giant sales-lead generator, had branched into speculation.

Although each had expanded to other Sun Belt cities, the Valley of the Sun was where they were really duking it out. Phoenix, with homogeneous and fairly new houses out to the horizon, was an ideal place to finesse their algorithms. In 2018, the three firms bought nearly five thousand houses around Phoenix, roughly one in every twenty existing homes that were sold in one of the country's busiest sales markets.

I thought about downloading the Offerpad app and using it to open up the empty house so I could take a peek at the company's handiwork. The yard was groomed better than those around it. I decided not to be a lookie-loo, though. I had a pretty good idea what the house would be like inside. There certainly wasn't a plate of cookies waiting.

A couple of months after the conference, I was passing through Nashville and arranged to see Bruce McNeilage. He was building a lot of houses to rent in the southern suburbs and he wanted to show them to me.

I met him at Spring Hill's city hall. The building is cross shaped and sits atop a hill behind a Home Depot. We hopped into the pickup truck that functions as a mobile office from which McNeilage manages a growing number of rentals. He practically lived out of the truck as he hopscotched between the four states where his firm owned properties. Dry-cleaned dress shirts and blazers hung in the backseat, which was piled with tools and paperwork.

Since selling his houses around Spring Hill to American Homes 4 Rent, he had flipped about four hundred around Nashville and Atlanta to institutional investors. There was insatiable appetite on Wall Street for his house-and-tenant packages, though he kept some for himself.

In 2016, he flirted with a transition to television. Unlike HGTV, which pumped out eye candy for the kitchen-island obsessed, McNeilage wanted to convey the gritty side of landlording. He made a promo reel for a quasi reality show called *Mr. Bruce Needs His Money.* It opens with McNeilage in a well-appointed living room. "My name is Bruce McNeilage and I'm the toughest landlord in America," he says over a hard-rocking guitar riff.

Then it's McNeilage amid remodeling debris, arguing with ne'er-do-well tenants and banging on doors, wanting to know about the rent. He packs a pistol and wears cuff links that read "buy" on one wrist and "sell" on the other. He kicks in a front door while holding a phone to his ear. We meet his wife, Melanie, who appears apprehensive. "He tries to comfort me by telling me that he's always got a gun on his hip, but so do a lot of other people," she says.

Then the music turns twangy and McNeilage's grade school buddy and business partner, Chris Zachary, is introduced. Zachary handles the books and keeps a distance from the day-to-day unpleasantness in which McNeilage appears to revel.

"He has no interest in pressing the flesh, or getting to know the middle class," McNeilage says. "He wants that all on my shoulders. So that's really what I specialize in."

"Bruce loves conflict," Zachary says. "He tends to escalate it until it kind of reaches a crescendo."

To drive home the point, the video cuts to McNeilage nose to nose with a tenant. "I'm going to call the police," the man says, swinging the door shut. McNeilage is left facing a door pasted with utility shutoff notices. As McNeilage storms away, the off-camera tenant mutters, "Mr. Bruce is an asshole," in a tone that makes it sound like the men probably get along most days. At another house, McNeilage whips a flimsy FOR RENT sign from his pickup and stabs it into the yard as a tenant looks on with befuddlement.

"Don't look confused," McNeilage barks. "Look for boxes to put your shit in!"

McNeilage's wife says she wishes her husband would just sell his houses and spend more time at home helping her raise their children. McNeilage is on speakerphone. He's on the road and called to let her know that he'd be away for another day. "Living the dream, honey, living the dream," he says.

After a bit more heavy metal and banging on doors, the promo reel ends with a monologue. "If I don't get paid, people's problems become my problems. If I've got to step on some toes and rattle some cages, I'm going to do it. Because it's my money and you bet your ass I'm gonna get it." A pistol is cocked close up and McNeilage strides with it holstered to his hip down a street lined with uncut grass and utility stubs.

McNeilage, gregarious and sensitive to the plight of others, isn't really the way he played his character. He was hamming it up. Much of the confrontation was staged. Reality or not, it seemed to me like a sure hit. McNeilage's wife put her foot down, though. Instead of a show, he expanded his rental business into new markets.

The Michigan native who had had so much success renting out houses in the automaking hub of Nashville went to South Carolina and built houses around Spartanburg and Greenville that are driving distance to a BMW manufacturing plant. He also bought houses outside Columbia, South Carolina, and Raleigh, North Carolina, and kept at it in Atlanta.

We had seen each other a few months earlier in Scottsdale at the rental investor conference. He had spoken on panels, extolling the benefits of building houses to rent. He'd been doing that since before the financial crisis. Now others were building rentals and he had experience to share.

Today's relatively affluent tenants preferred to move into brand-new houses, to the point that they would pay $150 or so more each month for a new four-bedroom house than they would for one that was, as McNeilage put it, used. Plus, the finishes could be customized to resist wear and tear, and a lot of big-ticket items, such as appliances and the house itself, were covered by warranties. Maintenance costs on new construction were hardly anything the first few years.

McNeilage told the other landlords that he likes to spend money at the outset making his houses more durable and desirable. Take shower doors. The $300 cost is a lot cheaper than repairing water damage later, he said. For paint, he sang the praises of a Sherwin-Williams color called Mindful Gray, which he bought in five-gallon buckets. "If you're doing tan, you're not doing the right thing anymore," he said. "People like gray."

McNeilage had been invited by bankers to Bentonville, Arkansas, to explore a rental play catering to those who worked at Walmart headquarters and the account representatives stationed in town to tend to the giant retailer. He was wooed by a builder with unsold homes in Texas.

The returns were still great around Nashville, though. The housing market was as hot as ever, and a brand-new outer beltway had opened an additional layer of countryside to suburban development south of the city, a swath of space to build the cheapest houses in the best school system in the state. We were headed there.

First, though, we drove through a subdivision in Spring Hill where he, Invitation Homes, American Homes 4 Rent, and other investors were all building houses. McNeilage was eager to show me that he had avoided the lots with power transmission lines running through the backyards. He felt parents would pick his houses over his rivals' when they saw the electric lines strung behind their homes. For about $1,600 a month, his tenants would be able to live in houses clad in cement siding and brick and outfitted with granite countertops and recessed lights. He pointed out where slabs would be poured if it ever stopped raining for a few days. As we left Spring Hill, we splashed past creeks and culverts overflowing from a days-long deluge.

We headed west on the new highway to a fast-developing corner of the county where he had built a subdivision next to an elementary school. Parents could watch their children walk down a grassy hill to school while they sipped coffee in their kitchens. The houses went for about $1,800 a month. McNeilage was having no problem filling them.

We walked up to an empty one for a look. At the door, he kicked off his loafers. As I folded over to untie my shoes, I realized why landlords favored slip-ons. The house smelled of fresh Mindful Gray and had all sorts of upgrades: dark hardwood floors, powerful ceiling fans, tile trim in the bathrooms, a kitchen full of granite and stainless steel. There wasn't anything to suggest the house was a rental. McNeilage went around and collected the warranty paperwork from inside the appliances for his files. As he showed me around the thirty-house neighborhood, he kept his eye peeled for infractions. He made voice memos about trash cans left in a driveway and a firepit that was too close to the side of one of his houses and then stopped to call the builder about rainwater that was pooling in one yard.

"If you come in here and notice this is a rental home, I haven't done my job," he said.

The neighborhood had recently been appraised for more than $10 million, bringing to $34 million the value of the rental homes owned by him and his childhood buddy. McNeilage wanted to get to $100 million and was in various stages of planning for more than a hundred new rental houses in middle Tennessee and other southeastern cities.

As we drove back toward Spring Hill, I asked McNeilage to tell me more about Joanie, the tenant-for-life he'd met at his father's funeral who didn't ask for much other than a fresh coat of paint and new carpet every couple of decades. McNeilage had told an abbreviated version of his landlord origin story onstage in Scottsdale and I wanted to hear more about his muse.

"I still remember what she looked like," he said.

"What'd she look like?"

McNeilage gazed ahead at the wet, empty highway, quiet for a moment. Then he turned to me and grinned a little.

"Like a nice sixty-five-year-old woman with seven-year-old carpet."

# 26

## CUT DOWN

I'd been back in Alabama before meeting up with McNeilage. Between all the painting and the trips to Lowe's, I hadn't had much chance to look around or see anyone when I went to sell the house two years earlier. My good-bye felt unfinished.

I rented a small cottage on stilts across the street from the public beach in Gulf Shores. It stood out on Airbnb among the tower condos furnished with wicker and palm-print upholstery. The owners were young acolytes of Chip and Joanna Gaines, the handsome HGTV couple that beautifies beat-up properties in mid-Texas modern. The beach cottage had a barn door hung across the utility closet, shiplap in the bathroom, and Chip's biography on the bookshelf. A forgettable inspirational saying was spelled out on a menu board on the kitchen counter and a decorative pillow was embroidered with "namaste in bed." Every so often a battery-powered air freshener on a shelf hissed and the place was infused with a fresh whiff of Glade. The owners displayed a "before" picture of the place that showed how miserable and beat-up it was when they bought it. I could practically smell the mustiness in the old photo.

One of the people I really wanted to catch up with was Bob Shallow. He was one of the top sales agents in the world several years running when I'd seen him last. If there was anyone who would give the unvarnished version of what had gone on since I'd moved away, it was Shallow.

When I met him at his office in Orange Beach, he looked me over, complimented my shoes, and asked what I was up to. I told him.

"What are you making?" he asked.

Before I could come up with a way not to tell him my salary, he guessed.

He was close. A little high.

Then he told me what his daughter earned in commercial real estate up north. It was much more than he had guessed for me.

Shallow was getting back into the development game. There was a low-rise complex in Gulf Shores and a taller building in Orange Beach on some surfside property that he'd bought at the bottom. It wasn't the way it was back in 2005. Buyers were less interested in flipping units before they were built. Now, the people in the market for condos were interested in rental income. They were aiming to gross $40,000 or so a year renting to summer beachgoers and monthly to snowbirds in the off-season, while keeping a few weeks open for their own families to gather. These buyers were happy to cover expenses and claim the depreciation on their taxes.

"It's better than a bass boat," Shallow said. "You get to come play with it, use it. But if they all made money, shit, I'd own two thousand of them."

When the market crashed, Shallow had felt compelled to buy foreclosed condos in large part to keep the agents and others he employed working. In that regard, he was a lot like Geoff Jacobs, the Phoenix developer who resorted to renting out foreclosures to sustain his business through the downturn.

"The worst thing in the real estate world is a stagnant market," Shallow said. "You gotta jump in there and buy to stimulate the market." He had scooped up more than sixty condominiums on the courthouse steps when BP's oil splashed ashore in 2010. The environmental disaster added a layer of complexity, but he was proud to have turned away BP's settlement money. Eventually he sold every one of the condos. "Did not lose on one deal," he said. "Made money on every one."

Some of Shallow's clients didn't listen when he said to sell. Among them was one of the Bon Secour Village developers. As prices tumbled he invited Shallow to a party to celebrate a rebound in the market, as if good vibes were all that were needed to turn things around. Shallow swung by.

"Everybody was, 'Oh, isn't it great the market's back?' I'm going, 'Yup. I think it's great.'"

Soon after, the host sought bankruptcy protection with nine figures of debt tied to real estate, including the failed Bon Secour Village.

The thousand-acre development was supposed to ape an ancient harbor town, but Bon Secour Village was mostly woods. The colonnaded and empty sales office had gone from looking like an unfinished bank branch to an abandoned bank branch.

Down the Intracoastal Waterway, beneath the bankrupt toll bridge, nature had reclaimed Bama Bayou's unfinished condo tower and dolphin-show stadium. It had been so long since construction stopped, pine trees sprouted to the condo building's second story.

It wasn't all gloomy scenes like that, though. Builders had swept in and filled with houses the subdivisions that were just street signs and utility stubs when I'd left.

Checkers founder Jim Mattei had his plans for a dozen towers along the Intracoastal Waterway back on the drawing board and was awaiting the state's decision about a new bridge that would connect the property to the beach.

The Alabama Gulf Coast Zoo was moving off Pleasure Island to a hundred acres out of harm's way. Footage from its evacuation ahead of Hurricane Ivan became the basis for an Animal Planet show called "The Little Zoo that Could" and brought the menagerie a measure of fame. It sold $30 million worth of bonds to move north of the Intracoastal Waterway.

The state park had replaced the dumpy motel that was wrecked in Hurricane Ivan with a hotel that outclassed the private resorts. The public beach in Gulf Shores never was developed with high-rise condominiums. Instead it got a tasteful makeover that swapped ugly gazebos and a lot of asphalt for more sand and huge taut sails that are part shade, part public art.

The Hangout was the main attraction. Shaul Zislin's plan B became a popular restaurant and hosts a big music festival on the beach each spring. Cardi B, the risque chanteuse, headlined in 2019. The geezers at Gulf Shores city hall must've gasped when she strutted on stage in a sequined bodysuit cursing like a sailor. But no one complained about all the cash the concert brought to town. Zislin built another restaurant in Orange Beach, fashioned from shipping containers on Perdido Pass, where Rick Phillips and his partners tried to build a tower before they went bust. Zislin once owned a piece of the property. He bought it from a desperate seller for $875,000 and flipped it during the frenzy for $3.1 million to another developer, who sold it to Phillips and his partners for even more. Zislin bought it from the bank after the bust—as well as all the other land along the pass that Phillips had cobbled together—for $2.5 million.

In a twist that I did not anticipate, people couldn't wait to tell me how great the oil spill had been. BP showered Alabama's beaches, really the whole state, with cash to compensate for the lost summer of 2010, when its Macondo well deep in the Gulf blew out and spattered the beaches with crude. Real estate agents who had listings when the oil washed ashore were paid for lost commissions. That was a huge boost considering nothing had been selling before the spill. The oil company also paid for ads promoting Alabama's beaches on national television, suggesting the area to more vacation planners than ever. Alabama even got spill money to shore up Medicaid and renovate the gubernatorial beach mansion in Gulf Shores.

Condo developer Brett/Robinson coaxed BP into forking over $37.2 million so that it could finish the hulking, half-built Phoenix West II tower that had stalled out in Orange Beach when the market crashed. The developer argued that the spill spooked buyers that might have otherwise bought condos in the building. Larry Wireman, the rival developer who battled fleeing buyers at his luxurious Turquoise Place towers, cried foul over the aid to his competitor.

Wireman agreed to meet me at a fancy restaurant on the grounds of his Caribe Resort. It was brunch and I was a little late because I failed to account for the traffic jams generated on Sunday mornings by the Catholic church on the beach highway. Turquoise Place loomed to my right as I inched along. The towers were built right up against the road, glistening higher than I could see from behind the wheel. They were so big that they blocked out the satellite radio's reception.

When I arrived at the dockside restaurant, Wireman asked if I still had any buddies at the *Register.* His newspaper had arrived hours late that morning and he wanted me to convey his displeasure if I knew anyone.

In fact, I had dined the night before along Mobile Bay with Dewey English, the editor who had hired me fresh out of college sixteen years earlier. No one else was left. In the face of brutal cost cuts, English was heroically and somewhat defiantly running coastal Alabama's main news operation with a staff so small that it would have been strained to operate a Pizza Hut. But I didn't want to get into all of that with Wireman.

Without a Sunday paper, the developer had spent the morning watching cable news. He was fired up. We made three passes through the buffet and he shared his feelings on immigrants and abortion. I couldn't find much opening to ask him about condominiums, the corruption case that brought down the mayor and had come so close to ensnaring him, or generally how he'd been the last few years. Wireman said he'd finally put to bed the last of the Turquoise Place litigation and was considering another Caribe tower. He was in an escalating dispute with city hall over the waterfront property and $400,000 that he had paid in exchange for the special zoning to accommodate Turquoise Place. The city hadn't built the firehouse, fishing pier, bathrooms, or boardwalk for which the cash was intended. The property, a strip along the Gulf and a big tract across the street on Cotton Bayou, had been just sitting there for years. Wireman wanted his cash and the property back. Before we could ponder a fourth helping, his wife called and he excused himself. Months later he sued Orange Beach alleging "coercive exaction."

On my way out of town, I popped into Steve Russo's store. The former Orange Beach mayor had been released from prison in 2015, having served about eight years of his original ten-year sentence for being corrupted by developers. On appeal he had gotten campaign finance related counts overturned and time knocked off his sentence.

SE Properties Holdings, the entity that Vision Bank's Ohio buyer sicced on borrowers who defaulted on real estate loans, didn't wait for his release to try to collect on his debts. The debt collectors wanted Russo to pay $853,131.49 for the eight-bedroom beach house in Gulf Shores that had already cost him nearly a decade of freedom. His co-conspirators served much shorter prison sentences. They also used bankruptcy court to wriggle from the six-figure debt generated when the government sold the spec house for a lot less than they'd borrowed to buy the property and build it. The only one left for the bank to pursue was Russo, fresh from an eight-year stay in the clink, where canned mackerel had been his currency.

After years in bankruptcy court, Russo agreed to repay $300,000. Despite it all, the former mayor looked good. He was trim, tanned, and relaxed. Customers who came into the store, including a police officer, still called him sir, just as they had when he ran the city.

The defense attorneys insisted back in 2006 that he not testify in his own defense. The prosecutors hadn't proved anything to merit the charges, they told him. There was nothing to rebut. "Not a day goes by that I don't regret listening to them and not getting up and telling my side of the story," Russo said.

Larry Sutley, the former city attorney, was released from federal prison in late 2010 and pardoned by the state in 2015. He returned to his small law office, where he represents rural utilities and individuals.

The big beach house that got the mayor and him in trouble was standing just as it was when it was auctioned off by U.S. marshals in 2007. Unbeknownst to me, Eric Nelson, the sales agent who sold my place, had represented the couple that bought it that day. It was still muted green and massive. I found it right away amid the other beach houses with cute names like Pelican Place, Del Sol, and Conch Out. The buyers of the house built to bribe the mayor had a sense of humor. They named it Kick Back.

Back toward town, a sign at a Gulf-front construction site caught my eye. JIM BROWN LLC, it said. The developer who'd bribed the mayor and then turned state's witness once he was caught was back to building colossal beach houses on spec.

There was one more house I wanted to see before I left. I wasn't sure I'd ever make it back to Alabama's beaches, so I decided to drive by my old place one last time. A few nights earlier, I had cruised the Audubon Place loop, but all I could really tell in the dark was that there wasn't a single FOR SALE sign in the neighborhood and that whoever lived in the house these days seemed to have made changes to the landscaping out front.

In daylight, I could see that the front door was still the same slate blue, but there had been changes enough that it no longer felt like mine at all.

The oleander was gone and so were the decorative garden stones, replaced by a little white plastic fence that obscured stubby pink flowers behind it. There were folding chairs on the front patio. A small tree near the sidewalk that flowered each spring was missing. The huge hedge along the driveway had been cut back to about half its old height and length, revealing an electrical transformer that I never realized was hidden in the bushes. Above the house where there used to be a verdant wall, the sky was empty. The cypress I'd planted twelve years earlier had been chopped down. So, too, had the two towering longleaf pine trees that caught my eye back in 2005.

On my way north to the interstate, I passed billboard after billboard advertising real estate. It was just like when I had arrived in 2003 as the market was beginning to boil.

An advertisement for one of Bob Shallow's condo projects was in rotation on a digital billboard just south of my old street. Nearby, another agent's sign assured, "Yes! You can afford the beach." One Realtor had rented several billboards and covered them with a picture of himself wearing a Hawaiian lei and a stern face. Another declared herself the Condo Queen.

The farther from the beach I got, the wackier the billboards became. One woman, "a Realtor you can trust," posed with a deer. I couldn't tell in passing whether the animal was dead and meant to show that she was a straight shooter or if it was alive and she was trying to convey compassion. Maybe she was an eccentric with a pet deer. Some guy whose name I didn't catch had two zany billboards. On the first he riffed on Superman, ripping open his dress shirt to reveal a red-and-blue T-shirt that said, "Sold." Up the road, he used a line from Dos Equis' beer commercials. He was "the most interesting agent in town," clad in a sport coat and imploring passersby, "Start investing, my friend."

It appeared that the condo game was back on. I was glad to be headed the other way.

# 27

## EPILOGUE

I'll probably pay for sitting out homeownership this time around. But I'm not alone. Rentership has skyrocketed since the crash. Between 2006 and 2016, when the homeownership rate fell to its lowest level in fifty years, the number of renters grew by about a quarter. The nearly 9.5 million new tenants aren't just the bottom-rung earners and subprime borrowers you'd expect. Rent rolls these days include a surprising number of upper-income professionals.

By 2018, about 19 percent of U.S. households with annual incomes of $100,000 or more were renters, up from 12 percent in 2006, according to U.S. Census Bureau data adjusted for inflation. That equates to about 3.4 million new renters that, given their incomes, probably would have been homeowners a generation ago. And they're not renting where you'd expect. Less than 20 percent of them are around New York City and San Francisco, where sky-high real estate values have long limited homeownership. Their ranks swelled in places such as Houston, Denver, and Nashville, as well as in Cincinnati, Seattle, and San Antonio.

The average tenant of both Invitation Homes and American Homes 4

Rent earns about $100,000. Bruce McNeilage's typical tenants are six-figure earners, too. "I can't think of anyone we've rented to recently who didn't make $100,000," he told me while we toured the houses he was building south of Nashville with well-heeled renters in mind.

Renting to the relatively well-to-do is an enticing proposition for a landlord. They can afford a lot more rent and they're usually more consistent in paying it than lower earners. A sick child or car troubles don't cost them hours at work and income. They also tend to stay put, willing to absorb regular rent hikes if it means not having to move their children to new schools.

"Very early in this business, we figured out that the cost to replace the HVAC unit is, for the most part, the same on a $1,200 or $1,300 rental as it is on an $1,800 or $1,900 rental," Dallas Tanner, Invitation Homes' CEO, told investors.

The bet on upmarket renters paid off big for Blackstone, which bankrolled Invitation Homes. By the time the investment firm sold the last of its Invitation shares in late 2019, it had reaped about $7 billion, more than twice what it had invested. Blackstone might have done even better had its business model not required it to sell in order to return cash to its own investors, whose money it locks up in funds for ten years at a time.

There are a lot of reasons for the surge in high-earning renters. Some aren't buying because they can't afford it. They have too much debt. They lack savings for a down payment. The houses in the booming cities where they can find good jobs might be too expensive even for people considered well-off. Others aren't buying by choice. They lack faith that their employment will last or don't believe that the run-up in home prices is sustainable. Some don't want to be tied down with a mortgage. I'm content to forgo homeownership if it means the flexibility to move whenever and wherever I wish, whether for whimsy or work.

That's a defining characteristic of my cohort, says John Burns, the real estate consultant and demographer. Burns has another name for us besides the Foreclosure Generation: Balancers is his alternate moniker for those born in the 1970s, who were settling down into houses right before the bust torpedoed their economic position. "Income alone does not define success for Balancers, unlike prior generations," Burns says. "A happy personal life is just as important."

That is very admirable and Zen of us, but contentment doesn't really pay the bills. Especially once we're no longer working. Far fewer people are due pensions these days than in earlier generations. Without a guaranteed stream of checks to cover living expenses during retirement, having home equity to tap or borrow against becomes even more important. Keeping up with the rent could become problematic as we age.

It's an old idea in economics that landlords have the most to gain over the long run. During economic expansion, production of most goods rises. Aside from the odd beach renourishment project to bolster Alabama's eroded beaches or the palm-shaped islands built off Dubai, there's not really any new land being created. Scarcity relative to other assets pushes up the price of property as well as the cost of renting it. The influential economist David Ricardo outlined this in 1817. His worry was that landlords would amass a growing share of income and wealth. Ricardo didn't have the data back then, but his assessment was prescient.

Between 1970 and 2010, housing wealth accounted for about two-thirds of the increase in the U.S. wealth-to-income ratio, according to economists Thomas Piketty and Gabriel Zucman. They found even greater proportions of wealth created by home-price appreciation in other developed countries, such as Canada and the United Kingdom. It was thanks to rising home prices that the U.S. middle class was able to hang on to its share of the country's overall wealth in the decades following World War II, despite losing major ground to the wealthiest Americans in terms of income, University of Bonn researchers Moritz Kuhn, Moritz Schularick, and Ulrike I. Steins wrote in a 2018 paper.

The wealth of the bottom half of wage earners doubled between 1971 and 2007 despite incomes that were stagnant once adjusted for inflation, they found. Wealth gains for the middle class also basically doubled even though inflation-adjusted wages rose by less than 40 percent. Most Americans weren't really making any more money at work. They were richer because they owned homes that rose in value.

"It is conceivable that these large wealth gains for the middle and lower middle class helped to dispel discontent about stagnant incomes for some time," the German researchers wrote.

The housing crash wiped away a lot of that wealth, though, and with it some social tranquility. A lot of people never regained their economic footing. The median household earning $63,179 in 2018 can't afford the median-priced home in very many American cities—even on the off chance they manage to save a 20 percent down payment while paying ever-rising rent. Yet the rich, whose wealth is concentrated in the stock market and corporate equity, rode the rebounding economy to new heights, producing what the Bonn researchers described as "the largest spike in wealth inequality in postwar American history."

The lack of home equity is already showing. At about $47,000, John Burns's 1970s Balancers have much lower inflation-adjusted median net worth than their elders, his firm found in a 2016 study. At the same age, those born in the fifties or sixties were worth about $79,000 and $86,000, respectively.

Younger people don't appear to be in a much better position to pursue homeownership. The median income of young adults, those aged twenty-five to thirty-four, declined at a rate of about 1 percent a year between 2000 and 2013, according to Burns. Nearly one in five people born in the 1980s lives below the poverty line, which is the highest percentage for any cohort since the people born in the 1930s amid the dust bowl and soup lines of the Great Depression. Burns's firm forecasts the homeownership rate falling to lows not seen since the mid-1950s, when the American housing machine was still cranking up.

The financial woes of younger adults could become a big problem for older Americans. About 55 percent of owner-occupied U.S. homes are owned by people who are fifty or older. They're going to be downsizing and dying in the coming decades. More than twenty million of their homes could swamp the market through the mid-2030s, according to Issi Romem, an economist at listings-giant-turned-house-flipper Zillow. His projections forecast a surge in FOR SALE signs not seen since the last housing bubble. That's an ominous sign for prices given how distant from and disinterested in homeownership younger generations have been.

According to a 2019 survey by Freddie Mac, just 24 percent of renters said it was "extremely likely" that they would ever own a home, down eleven percentage points from four years earlier.

Seven years after Jeff and Shannon McLaughlin lost their savings and good credit selling their underwater central Florida home for less than they owed, they decided to go house hunting.

Their credit scores had recovered. They had saved more than $80,000 for a down payment. Borrowing costs were historically low. The relatives' condo where they had lived since their short sale was getting cramped. They had five children now. What should have been an exciting search for a new family home turned into a year of frustration as they learned that they were priced out of many decent neighborhoods around Orlando.

They decided they needed at least $400,000 to buy in a neighborhood that they could be reasonably confident wouldn't degenerate like the one they fled during the foreclosure crisis. The family's income was well above the area's median, which the Census Bureau puts at about $54,000. Their $80,000 savings, robust as it may be, falls short of 20 percent of anything priced above $400,000, which means paying for default insurance and higher interest rates.

"The people that are buying these houses cannot be the middle class," he said.

They felt the familiar fear of missing out, of watching home prices climb beyond their means. It was the same anxiety that impelled them to make their ill-fated home purchase back in 2005, which ended in them abandoning their life savings to get away from the black bears and drug dens that plagued their neighborhood. Here they were again, rebuilt financially yet back in the same precarious position as in 2005.

The people from whom the McLaughlins bought their house back then made $45,000 on the sale after owning it less than a year.

The investor who paid $95,000 in 2013 as part of the McLaughlins' short sale bagged $51,000 when he sold three years later for $146,000.

The McLaughlins were after shelter and got soaked coming and going by people prowling the same market for quick profits.

They're not eager to line anyone else's pockets again. Do they stretch for the right house? Settle for one they might come to regret? Or stay on the sidelines and risk being renters forever?

In February, after several months of looking, they found a house that they adored and could afford. It wasn't yet three years old, had four bedrooms, two and a half bathrooms, blue shutters and a brick driveway. It sat in a subdivision with a neighborhood basketball court and a swimming pool. There were houses snug on each side, but nothing built behind, which was on their wish list.

The interior was finished with granite, glass-paned French doors, crown molding, and bright white wainscoting. "Exactly how we would have done it," he said.

Between their savings and some early inheritance, they mustered a $95,000 downpayment. They agreed to pay $433,000 and gave $5,000 in earnest money to the seller. They were to pay another $5,000 in ten days, after an inspection.

Before they got the keys, though, the coronavirus pandemic shut down much of the U.S. economy. Worried for his job as a church-affiliated marriage counselor, they decided not to make the second earnest payment. Days later he was furloughed. Their lender bailed.

The seller let the McLaughlins out of the deal for the $5,000 they'd already handed over and another $2,000 to settle the second, skipped payment. He said he'd credit them the $7,000 if Jeff got his job back and they found financing before the house sold to someone else.

They don't like their chances, though, especially if the price comes down. "I wonder," he said, "will investors come scoop it up?"

# NOTES

Much of the reporting for this book was undertaken by the author for newspaper articles published by the *Mobile Register,* which was renamed the *Press-Register* in late 2005, and *The Wall Street Journal.* Included in each chapter's notes are the relevant articles in the order in which the reporting first appears in the narrative, along with more specific citations for work that was not produced by the author.

## 1. THIS IS THE ONE

Ryan Dezember, "My 10-Year Odyssey Through America's Housing Crisis," *Wall Street Journal,* January 26, 2018.

**4 The collapse of the U.S. housing market wiped out** Financial Crisis Inquiry Commission, "The Financial Crisis Inquiry Report," New York: PublicAffairs, 2011, xv.

**5 At its depths, more than twelve million Americans** CoreLogic, "New CoreLogic Data Shows Second Consecutive Quarterly Decline in Negative Equity," news release, August 26, 2010.

**5 Some estimates put the number north of fifteen million** Zillow, "Underwater Homeowners Sink Deeper, Even as Home Values Rise," news release, March 20, 2015.

**5 People my age and a few years older were hit** John Burns and Chris Porter, *Big Shifts Ahead* (Charleston, SC: Advantage, 2016), 56.

**6 Today these firms** Invitation Homes, "Investor & Analyst Day Slide Deck," October 4, 2019.

**7 Home-price appreciation has historically** Moritz Kuhn, Moritz Schularick, and Ulrike I. Steins, "Income and Wealth Inequality in America, 1949–2016," Forthcoming, *Journal of Political Economy.*

## 2. THE CONDO GAME

Ryan Dezember, "Russians allege job mistreatment," *Press-Register,* July 16, 2006.

**10 In less than an hour** Kathy Jumper, "Island Tower's Units Presell in Under an Hour," *Mobile Register,* January 19, 2003.

**11 "I like to cut to the chase"** Kathy Jumper, "Shallow Again Top Agent," *Press-Register,* March 18, 2007.

**11 He cared more about** Kathy Jumper, "Making a Splash at the Gulf," *Mobile Register,* March 20, 2005.

**15 Shallow sold ninety units** Kathy Jumper, "FORECAST '97 Higher Home Prices, Attractive Interest Rates, More Commercial Activity," *Mobile Register,* January 5, 1997.

**15–16 The condos in the first Caribe tower** Kathy Jumper, "Longtime Plan to Come to Fruition at Caribe Resort," *Mobile Register,* June 25, 2000.

**16 By 2002, Shallow was** Kathy Jumper, "Bob Shallow: Work Smart, 'Sell from the Heart,'" *Mobile Register,* February 16, 2003.

Ryan Dezember, "The Condo Game," *Mobile Register,* July 4, 2004.

**18 One agent likened listing** Kathy Jumper, "Condo Values Soar," *Mobile Register,* May 4, 2003.

Ryan Dezember, "Older Condo Moved Off Beach to Make Way for High-Rise," *Mobile Register,* March 24, 2004.

———, "Wanted: Help Moving 55-Foot Lighthouse," *Mobile Register,* May 6, 2003.

**19 Sales agents bragged** Kathy Jumper, "Condo Values Soar," *Mobile Register,* May 4, 2003.

**19 Rick Phillips, one of the developers** Kathy Jumper, "Condominium Development," *Mobile Register,* June 20, 2004.

Ryan Dezember, "Developers Looking Up at the Gulf," *Mobile Register,* October 22, 2003.

## 3. "THEY NEVER SING SONGS ABOUT A PILE OF RENT RECEIPTS"

**24 "Why are these homes"** Clifford Edward Clark, Jr., *The American Family Home, 1800–1960* (Chapel Hill, NC: University of North Carolina Press, 1986), xi.

**24 Whereas Europeans of the time liked to escape their troubles** Alexis de Tocqueville, *Democracy in America: The Complete and Unabridged Volumes I and II* (New York: Random House, 2004), 353.

**25 In French, he wrote something** Kenneth T. Jackson, *Crabgrass Frontier* (New York: Oxford University Press, 1985), 50.

**25 Benjamin Franklin, a successful property investor** Matthew Edel, Elliott D. Sclar, and Daniel Luria, *Shaky Palaces* (New York: Columbia University Press, 1984), 22.

**25 Take Franklin's own father** Ibid., 24.

**25 Soon after Tocqueville's tour** Jackson, *Crabgrass Frontier,* 128.

**25 In colonial America, the English love** Ibid., 53.

**26 "A man is not a whole and complete man"** Walt Whitman, "New York Dissected," *Life Illustrated,* July 19, 1856, 93, Walt Whitman Archive, https://whitmanarchive.org/published/periodical/journalism/tei/per.00270.html.

**26 "The individual worker might be able to sell his house on occasion"** Karl Marx and Frederick Engels, *Collected Works* (New York: International Publishers, 1988), Volume 23: 344.

**26 Early feminists didn't see** Jackson, *Crabgrass Frontier,* 51.

**26 Willard Phillips, a nineteenth-century political economist** Willard Phillips, *A Manual of Political Economy with Particular Reference to the Institutions, Resources, and Condition of the United States* (Boston: Hilliard, Gray, Little and Wilkins, 1828), 186.

**27 "To possess one's own home is"** Jackson, *Crabgrass Frontier,* 172.

**27 About a year into World War II** Associated Press, "Home Owners Hailed in Roosevelt Note," *New York Times,* November 17, 1942.

**27 Thousands of people** David Halberstam, *The Fifties* (New York: Villard Books, 1993), 134.

**27–28 In North Dakota** Clark, *The American Family Home,* 196.

**28 Del Webb, whose eponymous** "A Place in the Sun," *Time,* August 3, 1962.

**28 "No man who owns his own house"** Halberstam, *The Fifties,* 132.

**30 While most retreated from the mortgage market** Michael Lewis, *Liar's Poker* (New York: W. W. Norton & Co., 1989), 125.

**30 At Ranieri's behest** Cezary Podkul, "The Regrets of Lewis Ranieri," *Wall Street Journal,* September 6, 2018.

**31 The personal savings rate** Josh Rosner, "Housing in the New Millenium: A Home Without Equity Is Just a Rental with Debt," Graham Fisher & Co., June 29, 2001.

**31 The debt-to-income ratio** Ibid.

**32 In 2000, $460 billion worth of refinance loans** Financial Crisis Inquiry Commission, "The Financial Crisis Inquiry Report," 5.

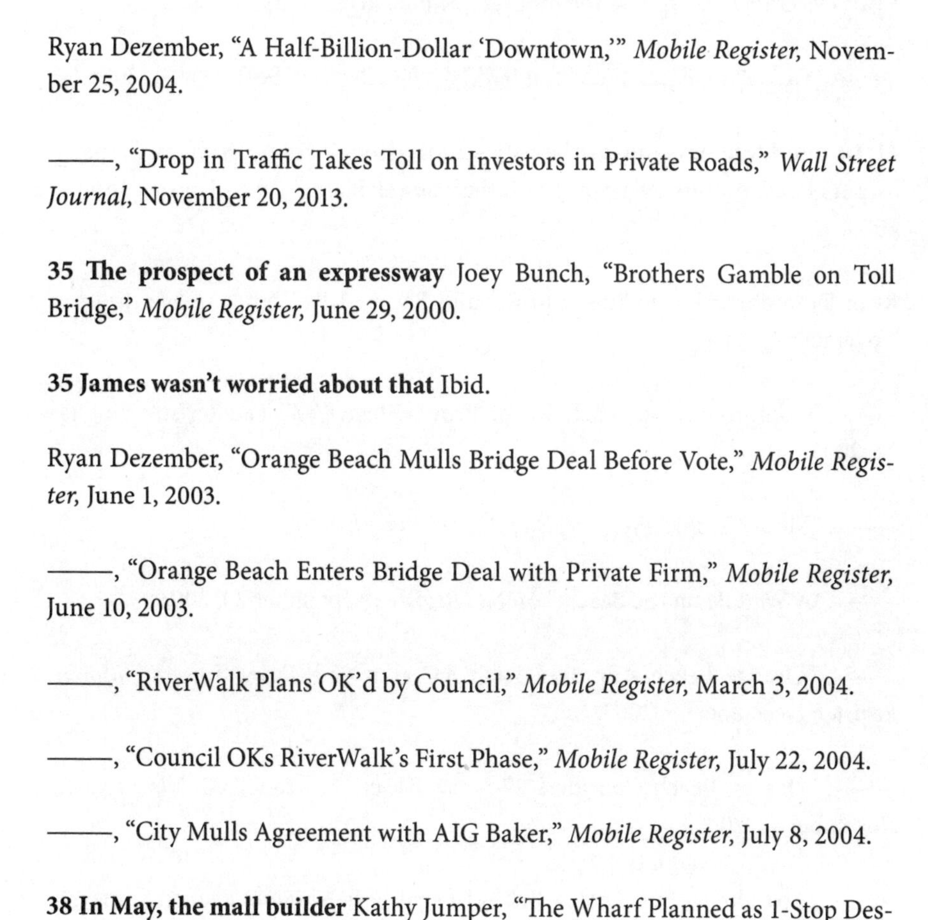

## 4. SWIM WITH THE DOLPHINS

Ryan Dezember, "A Half-Billion-Dollar 'Downtown,'" *Mobile Register,* November 25, 2004.

———, "Drop in Traffic Takes Toll on Investors in Private Roads," *Wall Street Journal,* November 20, 2013.

**35 The prospect of an expressway** Joey Bunch, "Brothers Gamble on Toll Bridge," *Mobile Register,* June 29, 2000.

**35 James wasn't worried about that** Ibid.

Ryan Dezember, "Orange Beach Mulls Bridge Deal Before Vote," *Mobile Register,* June 1, 2003.

———, "Orange Beach Enters Bridge Deal with Private Firm," *Mobile Register,* June 10, 2003.

———, "RiverWalk Plans OK'd by Council," *Mobile Register,* March 3, 2004.

———, "Council OKs RiverWalk's First Phase," *Mobile Register,* July 22, 2004.

———, "City Mulls Agreement with AIG Baker," *Mobile Register,* July 8, 2004.

**38 In May, the mall builder** Kathy Jumper, "The Wharf Planned as 1-Stop Destination," *Mobile Register,* May 23, 2004.

Ryan Dezember, “City Mulls Agreement with AIG Baker.”

———, “Boom Canal,” *Mobile Register,* November 25, 2004.

**39 Former Krispy Kreme Doughnuts chief executive Mac McAleer** George Talbot, “Family Capitalizes on Company Success,” *Mobile Register,* November 14, 2004.

## 5. THE BEACH PAC

Ryan Dezember, “Island on the Market,” *Mobile Register,* March 29, 2004.

———, “Gulf Place Faces Wrecking Ball,” *Mobile Register,* September 1, 2004.

**41 In one large and out-of-the-way subdivision** Virginia Bridges, “Homeowners File Lawsuits over Spills at Lillian Sewer Plant,” *Press-Register,* June 5, 2006.

Ryan Dezember, “Firm Chosen to Rebuild Battered Beaches,” *Mobile Register,* November 4, 2004.

———, “Compromise on Beach Mouse Proves Elusive,” *Mobile Register,* August 22, 2003.

———, “Mouse Trap!,” *Press-Register,* November 19, 2007.

———, “A Waddle on the Beach,” *Mobile Register,* September 20, 2003.

———, “Orange Beach Approves Twin 357-Foot Gulf-Front Towers,” *Mobile Register,* December 19, 2003.

———, “Orange Beach Considers 27-Story Towers in Trade,” *Mobile Register,* November 13, 2003.

———, “Abandoned Suit Leaves Behind Legal Fees,” *Mobile Register,* June 14, 2004.

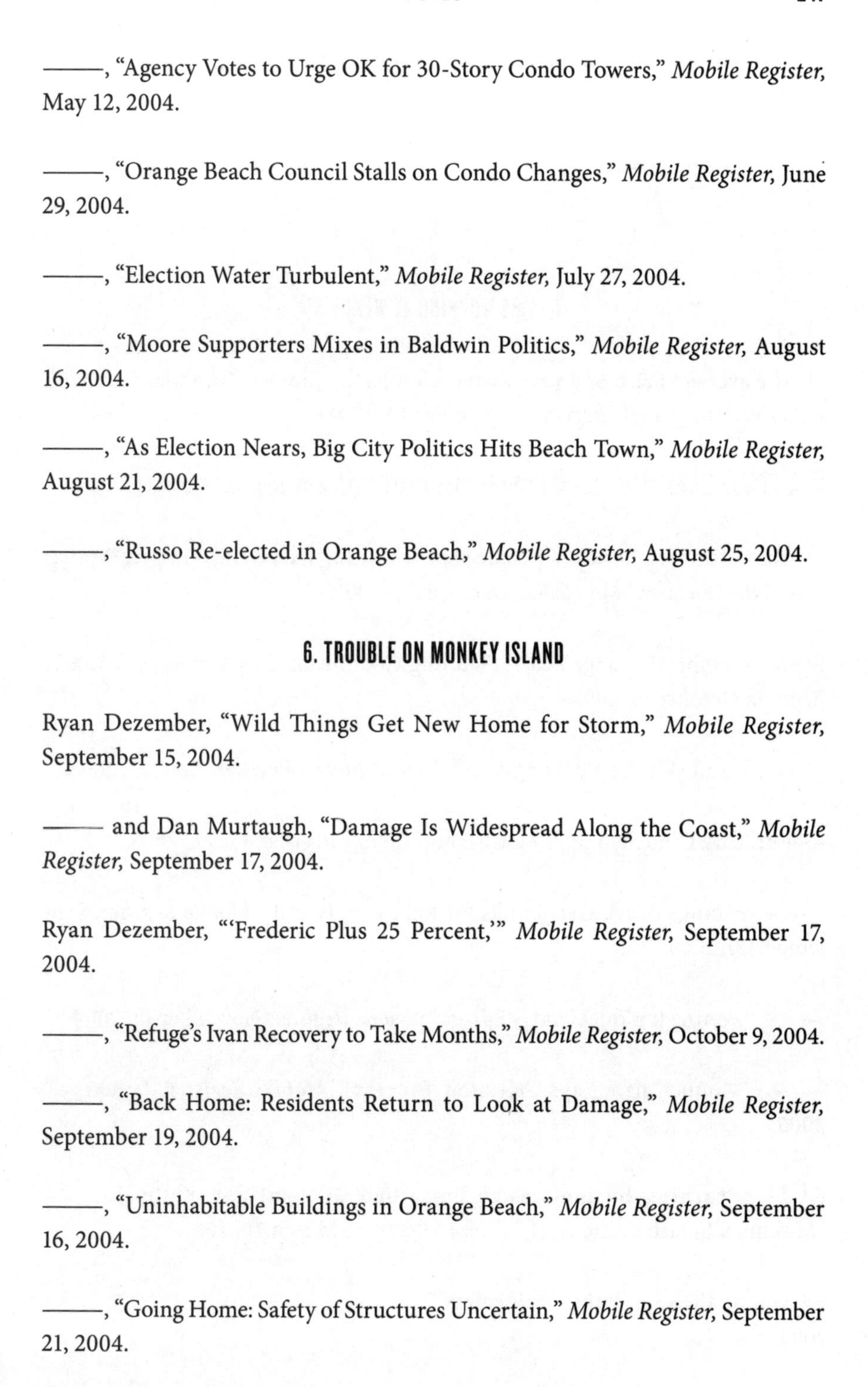

——, "Agency Votes to Urge OK for 30-Story Condo Towers," *Mobile Register,* May 12, 2004.

——, "Orange Beach Council Stalls on Condo Changes," *Mobile Register,* June 29, 2004.

——, "Election Water Turbulent," *Mobile Register,* July 27, 2004.

——, "Moore Supporters Mixes in Baldwin Politics," *Mobile Register,* August 16, 2004.

——, "As Election Nears, Big City Politics Hits Beach Town," *Mobile Register,* August 21, 2004.

——, "Russo Re-elected in Orange Beach," *Mobile Register,* August 25, 2004.

## 6. TROUBLE ON MONKEY ISLAND

Ryan Dezember, "Wild Things Get New Home for Storm," *Mobile Register,* September 15, 2004.

—— and Dan Murtaugh, "Damage Is Widespread Along the Coast," *Mobile Register,* September 17, 2004.

Ryan Dezember, "'Frederic Plus 25 Percent,'" *Mobile Register,* September 17, 2004.

——, "Refuge's Ivan Recovery to Take Months," *Mobile Register,* October 9, 2004.

——, "Back Home: Residents Return to Look at Damage," *Mobile Register,* September 19, 2004.

——, "Uninhabitable Buildings in Orange Beach," *Mobile Register,* September 16, 2004.

——, "Going Home: Safety of Structures Uncertain," *Mobile Register,* September 21, 2004.

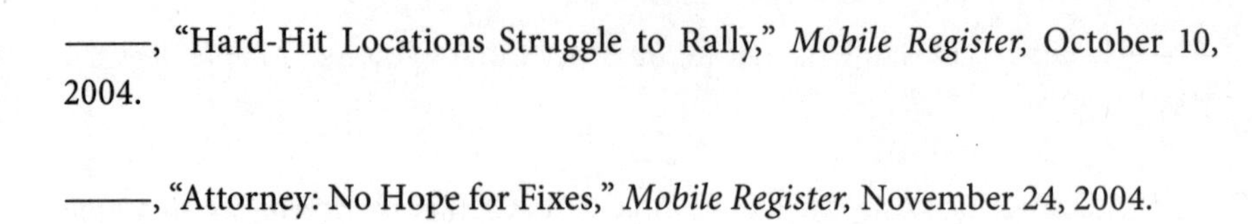

———, "Hard-Hit Locations Struggle to Rally," *Mobile Register,* October 10, 2004.

———, "Attorney: No Hope for Fixes," *Mobile Register,* November 24, 2004.

## 7. "LIKE WORKING AT WENDY'S"

**60 The average price of a preconstruction** Kathy Jumper, "Realtors Deal with Ivan's Wrath," *Mobile Register,* September 19, 2004.

Ryan Dezember, "Condos OK'd for Plant Site," *Mobile Register,* July 21, 2005.

**61 About thirteen hundred people signed waiting lists** Kathy Jumper, "Waterfront Life-Cheaper," *Mobile Register,* April 24, 2005.

Ryan Dezember, "Orange Beach Planning Commision Has New Look," *Mobile Register,* October 19, 2005.

———, "Land Deal Could Bring $3.5 Million," *Mobile Register,* April 27, 2005.

———, "City Land Sold to Pay for Island," *Mobile Register,* May 8, 2005.

———, "Orange Beach Gets Funds for Robinson Island," *Mobile Register,* September 20, 2005.

———, "Zoning for Tall Condos Passes," *Mobile Register,* November 10, 2004.

———, "Councilman Raps Selection Process," *Mobile Register,* January 7, 2005.

**63 Even turning business away he tallied $172 million** Kathy Jumper, "Making a Splash at the Gulf," *Mobile Register,* March 20, 2005.

**63 Among the superlative performers** Ibid.

## 8. FLIPPED

Ryan Dezember, "Prices Limiting Worker Housing," *Mobile Register,* April 10, 2005.

———, "Project Puts Focus on What Is 'Affordable,'" *Press-Register,* April 7, 2006.

**71 Countrywide Financial, which had recently eclipsed Wells Fargo** James R. Hagerty, "Countrywide Pulls on the Reins," *Wall Street Journal,* August 8, 2006.

**72 The agency created by Congress amid the Great Depression** Federal Deposit Insurance Corporation, "In Focus This Quarter: The U.S. Consumer Sector," December 7, 2004.

**73 In doing so, they were bucking thousands of years of habit** Cesare Marchetti, "Anthropological Invariants in Travel Behavior," *Technological Forecasting and Social Change* 47 (1994): 75–88.

## 9. WANNA BUY A BRIDGE?

**75 Bob Shallow wound up selling $173.3 million** Kathy Jumper, "Bob Shallow Is RE/MAX's Top Agent on Earth," *Press-Register,* March 26, 2006.

**75 He was making more than $20,000 a day** Ibid.

**75 By the end of 2005, more than twenty-six hundred condos** Kathy Jumper, "Developers Holding Back," *Press-Register,* February 19, 2006.

Ryan Dezember, "Through the Roof," *Press-Register,* July 16, 2006.

———, "Soaring Tax Bills Slam Ivan Victims," *Press-Register,* October 11, 2005.

**76 Rick Phillips and his partners were having** Kathy Jumper, "Condo Market: What's Sold, Selling, Stalling," *Press-Register,* November 13, 2005.

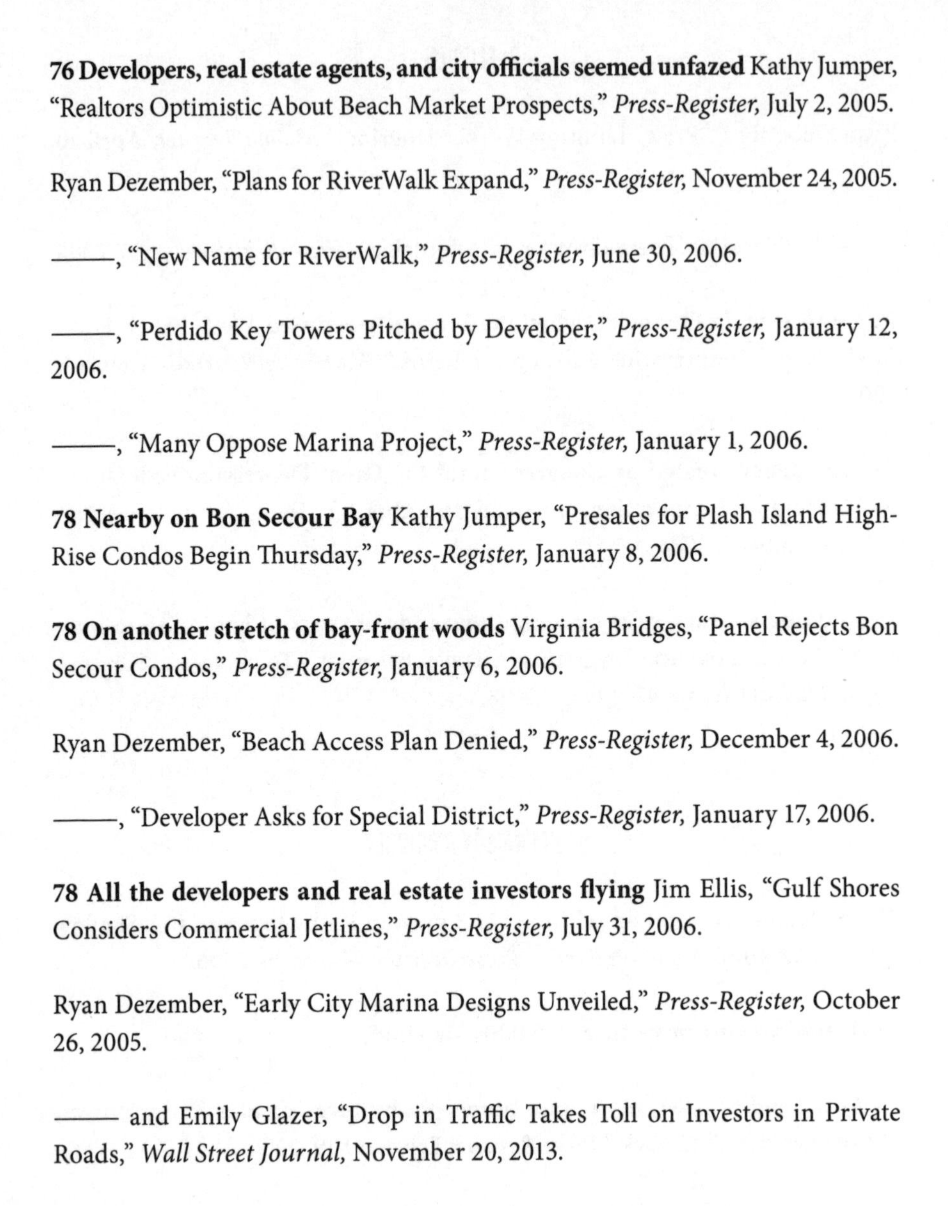

**76 Developers, real estate agents, and city officials seemed unfazed** Kathy Jumper, "Realtors Optimistic About Beach Market Prospects," *Press-Register,* July 2, 2005.

Ryan Dezember, "Plans for RiverWalk Expand," *Press-Register,* November 24, 2005.

——, "New Name for RiverWalk," *Press-Register,* June 30, 2006.

——, "Perdido Key Towers Pitched by Developer," *Press-Register,* January 12, 2006.

——, "Many Oppose Marina Project," *Press-Register,* January 1, 2006.

**78 Nearby on Bon Secour Bay** Kathy Jumper, "Presales for Plash Island High-Rise Condos Begin Thursday," *Press-Register,* January 8, 2006.

**78 On another stretch of bay-front woods** Virginia Bridges, "Panel Rejects Bon Secour Condos," *Press-Register,* January 6, 2006.

Ryan Dezember, "Beach Access Plan Denied," *Press-Register,* December 4, 2006.

——, "Developer Asks for Special District," *Press-Register,* January 17, 2006.

**78 All the developers and real estate investors flying** Jim Ellis, "Gulf Shores Considers Commercial Jetlines," *Press-Register,* July 31, 2006.

Ryan Dezember, "Early City Marina Designs Unveiled," *Press-Register,* October 26, 2005.

—— and Emily Glazer, "Drop in Traffic Takes Toll on Investors in Private Roads," *Wall Street Journal,* November 20, 2013.

## 10. "THERE'S A MILLION DOLLARS TO BE MADE HERE"

Testimony of James Madison Brown, *United States of America v. Steven Eugene Russo, Laurence Peter Sutley, and Kenneth David Wall,* U.S. Case No. 1:05-cr-00345, Docs. 302–303, August 21–22, 2006.

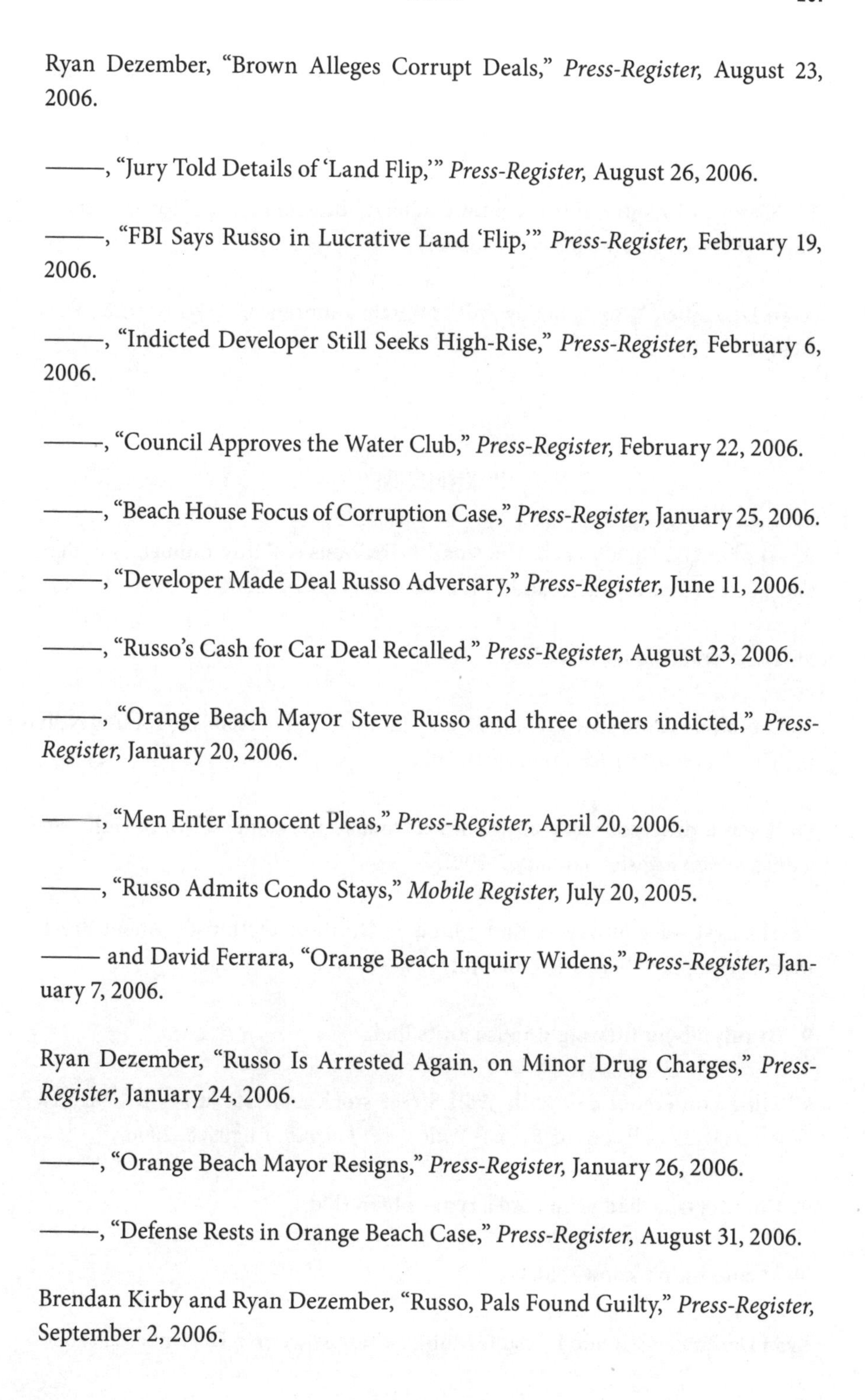

Ryan Dezember, "Brown Alleges Corrupt Deals," *Press-Register,* August 23, 2006.

———, "Jury Told Details of 'Land Flip,'" *Press-Register,* August 26, 2006.

———, "FBI Says Russo in Lucrative Land 'Flip,'" *Press-Register,* February 19, 2006.

———, "Indicted Developer Still Seeks High-Rise," *Press-Register,* February 6, 2006.

———, "Council Approves the Water Club," *Press-Register,* February 22, 2006.

———, "Beach House Focus of Corruption Case," *Press-Register,* January 25, 2006.

———, "Developer Made Deal Russo Adversary," *Press-Register,* June 11, 2006.

———, "Russo's Cash for Car Deal Recalled," *Press-Register,* August 23, 2006.

———, "Orange Beach Mayor Steve Russo and three others indicted," *Press-Register,* January 20, 2006.

———, "Men Enter Innocent Pleas," *Press-Register,* April 20, 2006.

———, "Russo Admits Condo Stays," *Mobile Register,* July 20, 2005.

——— and David Ferrara, "Orange Beach Inquiry Widens," *Press-Register,* January 7, 2006.

Ryan Dezember, "Russo Is Arrested Again, on Minor Drug Charges," *Press-Register,* January 24, 2006.

———, "Orange Beach Mayor Resigns," *Press-Register,* January 26, 2006.

———, "Defense Rests in Orange Beach Case," *Press-Register,* August 31, 2006.

Brendan Kirby and Ryan Dezember, "Russo, Pals Found Guilty," *Press-Register,* September 2, 2006.

Ryan Dezember, "'It's Been a Long Two Weeks,'" *Press-Register,* September 3, 2006.

———, "Water Club Fails to Win Approval," *Press-Register,* December 6, 2006.

**91 "Can you imagine if every public official"** Brendan Kirby, "Russo Gets 10 Years," *Press-Register,* February 24, 2007.

Ryan Dezember, "Russo, Sutley Still Maintain Innocence," *Press-Register,* February 24, 2007.

## II. INTERESTONLY™

**95 At about $250,000 each, the small brick houses** Kathy Jumper, "Builders and Buyers Are Moving Inland," *Press-Register,* April 2, 2006.

**96 The average house price** Ibid.

**96 Lots alone could cost $225,000** Kathy Jumper, "Subdivisions Sprouting Near the Gulf," *Press-Register,* January 21, 2007.

**96 It was a different story on the waterfront** Kathy Jumper, "More Gulf Bargains?," *Press-Register,* January 7, 2007.

**96 The first wave of buyers** Kathy Jumper, "Realtors Optimistic About Beach Market Prospects," *Press-Register,* July 2, 2005.

**97 By July, about fifty Lighthouse units** Ibid.

**97 On a conference call with Wall Street stock analysts** James R. Hagerty, "Countrywide Pulls on the Reins," *Wall Street Journal,* August 8, 2006.

**97 Countrywide had promoted a type of loan** Ibid.

**98 Mozilo didn't know** Ibid.

Ryan Dezember, "Condo Lawsuits Multiply," *Press-Register,* December 23, 2006.

## 12. OVER THE HEDGE

**102 In June 2007, a dozen anxious creditors** Kate Kelly and Serena Ng, "Bear Stearns Bails Out Fund with Big Loan," *Wall Street Journal,* June 23, 2007.

**102 The more leveraged fund managed less than $700 million** Ibid.

**104 Timothy Geithner, the soon-to-be Treasury Department secretary** Financial Crisis Inquiry Commission, "The Financial Crisis Inquiry Report," 115–17.

**104 Consider CMLTI 2006-NC2** Ibid., 8.

**104 There were loans to house flippers** Financial Crisis Inquiry Commission, "Story of a Mortgage Security: Inside CMLTI 2006-NC2," accessed June 16, 2019, https://fcic.law.stanford.edu/resource/staff-data-projects/story-of-a-security.

**105 Not even Lewis Ranieri** James R. Hagerty, "Mortgage-Bond Pioneer Dislikes What He Sees," *Wall Street Journal,* February 24, 2007.

## 13. "WE'VE HAD QUITE A FEW PEOPLE WALK AWAY"

Ryan Dezember, "Russo Beach House Sold," *Press-Register,* October 31, 2007.

———, "Judge: Marshals to Handle Beach House Sale," *Press-Register,* May 13, 2007.

———, "Wharf Condo Buyers Balking," *Press-Register,* July 7, 2007.

———, "Condo Collapse," *Press-Register,* November 11, 2007.

## 14. SYSTEM ERROR

**112 Thain replaced Stan O'Neal** Randall Smith and Aaron Lucchetti, "Merrill Taps NYSE's Thain as CEO," *Wall Street Journal,* November 15, 2007.

**112 It amounted to something like an eighth** Randall Smith and Jed Horowitz, "Merrill Takes $8.4 Billion Credit Hit," *Wall Street Journal,* November 15, 2007.

**113 That security was just one of** Kate Kelly, Serena Ng, and David Reilly, "Two Big Funds at Bear Stearns Face Shutdown," *Wall Street Journal,* June 20, 2007.

**113 CDOs were already difficult to value** Financial Crisis Inquiry Commission, "The Financial Crisis Inquiry Report,"128–55.

**114 A year earlier, the wobbling mortgage lender's market value** Valerie Bauerlein and James R. Hagerty, "Behind Bank of America's Big Gamble," *Wall Street Journal,* January 12, 2008.

**114–115 The mortgage giants had eased their standards** Financial Crisis Inquiry Commission, "The Financial Crisis Inquiry Report," 122–25.

**115 Washington Mutual, with $307 billion in assets** Robin Sidel, David Enrich, and Dan Fitzpatrick, "WaMu Is Seized, Sold Off to J.P. Morgan, in Largest Failure in U.S. Banking History," *Wall Street Journal,* September 26, 2008.

**115 A septuagenarian husband and wife** Dennis K. Berman, Carrick Mollenkamp, and Valerie Bauerlein, "Wachovia Strikes $26 billion Deal for Golden West," *Wall Street Journal,* May 8, 2006.

**115 In April, Wachovia disclosed a $350 million loss** Financial Crisis Inquiry Commission, "The Financial Crisis Inquiry Report," 304–5.

**115 There was turmoil in Europe** Matthew Karnitschnig, Carrick Mollenkamp, Robin Sidel, and Dana Cimilluca, "Wells Fargo Eyes Wachovia; Crisis Hits European Banks," *Wall Street Journal,* September 29, 2008.

**116 Thain took a lot of heat** Rachel Louise Ensign and Peter Rudegeair, "John Thain to Retire as CIT CEO," *Wall Street Journal,* October 21, 2015.

**116 The biggest infusions went to Wall Street institutions** Paul Kiel and Dan Nguyen, "Bailout Tracker," ProPublica, April 15, 2019, accessed December 21, 2019, https://projects.propublica.org/bailout.

## 15. "THE WHOLE CAPER WAS OVER"

Ryan Dezember, "Bankrupt at the Beach," *Press-Register,* June 8, 2008.

———, "Settlement Reached in Orange Beach Foreclosure Suit," *Press-Register,* April 3, 2008.

Kathy Jumper and Ryan Dezember, "Mandalay Developers Now Facing Foreclosure," *Press-Register,* January 13, 2008.

Ryan Dezember, "Council Gives New Life to Mandolay Beach Project," *Press-Register,* January 14, 2009.

**120 A launch party they hosted at the Birmingham Museum of Art** Kaija Wilkenson, "Bon Secour Village Seeks Tax Deal," *Birmingham Business Journal,* July 29, 2005.

Ryan Dezember, "Money Troubles Muddy Future," *Press-Register,* June 8, 2008.

———, "Court Asked to Lift Deed Restrictions," *Press-Register,* December 20, 2005.

———, "No Ruling Yet in Turquoise Place Trial," *Press-Register,* December 21, 2005.

———, "Ruling Removes High-Rise Obstacle," *Press-Register,* October 27, 2006.

———, "High Court Upholds Turquoise Ruling," *Press-Register,* January 19, 2008.

———, "High-End High-Rise," *Press-Register,* June 29, 2008.

———, "Condo Buyers Change Minds," *Press-Register,* May 22, 2008.

———, "Owner's 'Plan B' Working at the Gulf," *Press-Register,* January 24, 2010.

**124 Shallow had repeated as the world's top-selling** Kathy Jumper, "Shallow Again Top Agent," *Press-Register,* March 18, 2007.

**124 His sales dropped to $77 million** Kathy Jumper, "Shallow Does It Again," *Press-Register,* April 13, 2008.

## 16. STREETS WHERE NOBODY LIVES

Ryan Dezember, "Orange Beach Pinches Pennies," *Press-Register,* May 11, 2008.

———, "City Could Break Even This Year," *Press-Register,* August 30, 2009.

———, "Gulf Shores to Cut Jobs," *Press-Register,* December 11, 2008.

**129 The child's young mother** David Ferrara, "Mother May Be Charged in Death of 11-Month-Old Son," *Press-Register,* November 6, 2007.

Ryan Dezember, "Bama Bayou Goes Bust," *Press-Register,* April 12, 2009.

———, "No Return on That Investment," *Press-Register,* April 12, 2009.

———, "Foley's Empty Subdivisions," *Press-Register,* May 3, 2009.

———, "Streets Where Nobody Lives," *Press-Register,* May 3, 2009.

———, "Can Subdivisions Come Back to Life?" *Press-Register,* May 3, 2009.

———, "Condo Opening Set for 2011," *Press-Register,* July 4, 2009.

———, "Regions Bank Sues BP," *Press-Register,* September 1, 2010.

**134 In Gulf Shores, the auction of sixty-two units** Kathy Jumper, "Homes of Gulf Sell for Steep Discount," *Press-Register,* February 8, 2009.

Ryan Dezember, "Failed Property in Lonely Auction," *Press-Register,* September 16, 2009.

## 17. BUYER'S REMORSE

Ryan Dezember, "They Lost—Condos and Big Money," *Press-Register,* February 22, 2010.

**137 In an expensive area northeast of Atlanta** Christopher Quinn, "Potential Fix for Forsyth Landfill Leaking Dangerous Amounts of Methane," *Atlanta Journal-Constitution,* April 22, 2010.

Ryan Dezember, "Turquoise Place Developer Wins Ruling, Keeps Deposits," *Press-Register,* October 19, 2009.

———, "Turquoise Place Condo Rulings Mixed," *Press-Register,* November 16, 2009.

———, "Condo Buyers Wield RICO," *Press-Register,* February 9, 2009.

———, "Island Villas Condo Saga," *Press-Register,* February 8, 2009.

———, "Condo Lawsuits Closed," *Press-Register,* November 5, 2009.

## 18. THE SPILL

Ryan Dezember, "Beach Hit in Baldwin," *Press-Register,* June 5, 2010.

———, "Hangout Festival Goes on Despite Threat of Oil Slick," *Press-Register,* May 7, 2010.

———, "Festival Organizer, Gulf Shores Mayor Hope for Hangout 2011," *Press-Register,* May 23, 2010.

———, "The View from Home," *Plain Dealer,* July 18, 2010.

———, "Vendors Show Oil-Fighting Products at Spill 'Summit,'" *Press-Register,* June 18, 2010.

———, "Firm Pitches Miracle Fix for Gulf," *Press-Register,* June 17, 2010.

——, "Order Against Firm Selling 'Miracle' Cure," *Press-Register,* July 9, 2010.

——, "Frustration in Baldwin," *Press-Register,* May 27, 2010.

——, "Slick Slips into Perdido Pass," *Press-Register,* June 10, 2010.

Guy Busby, Jeff Dute, and Ryan Dezember, "Authorities Say Charter Boat Captain Took Own Life," *Press-Register,* June 24, 2010.

Ryan Dezember, "Letters Missing Check," *Press-Register,* August 18, 2010.

## 19. FOR RENT

Ryan Dezember and Peter Rudegeair, "The Future of Housing Rises in Phoenix," *Wall Street Journal,* June 19, 2019.

**158 Homeownership, long upheld as the American dream** Oliver Chang, Vishwanath Tirupattur, and James Egan, "Housing Market Insights: A Rentership Society," Morgan Stanley, July 20, 2011.

**159 They estimated that even in the worst-case scenario** Oliver Chang, Vishwanath Tirupattur, Paul Morgan, Swaroop Yalla, Adam Parker, and Betsy Graseck, "Housing 2.0: The New Rental Paradigm," Morgan Stanley, October 27, 2011.

**159 The phones at Morgan Stanley were flooded** Oliver Chang, Vishwanath Tirupattur, James Egan, and Jose Cambronero, "Housing Market Insights: An Investor's Guide for Buy-to-Rent," Morgan Stanley, April 11, 2012.

**159 By then, more than $1 billion had been raised** Oliver Chang, Vishwanath Tirupattur, James Egan, and Jose Cambronero, "Housing Market Insights: Buy-to-Rent," Morgan Stanley, February 16, 2012.

**160 The firm's first find was a bunch of garden apartments** Stephen A. Schwarzman, *What It Takes: Lessons in the Pursuit of Excellence* (New York: Avid Reader Press, 2019), 137–39.

**160 He engineered the firm's $25 billion takeover** Miriam Gottfried, "Blackstone to Check Out of Hilton Investment," *Wall Street Journal,* May 18, 2018. Peter Grant, "Blackstone Sells Last of Record Office Purchase, Books a $7 Billion Profit," *Wall Street Journal,* October 8, 2019.

Ryan Dezember, "Blackstone Gains from Banks' Financial-Crisis Pain," *Wall Street Journal,* January 21, 2016.

**161 Blackstone's leaders had also been spooked** Schwarzman, *What It Takes,* 205–7.

Ryan Dezember, "'This Could Be Huge,' Blackstone CEO Said of Foreclosure Opportunity," *Wall Street Journal,* December 6, 2016.

**163 Hughes had risen from a *Grapes of Wrath* upbringing** Public Storage, "Public Storage's History: Two Friends and an Idea," October 23, 2014, https://www.publicstorage.com/blog/public-storage/public-storages-history-two-friends-and-an-idea.

Ryan Dezember, "Got Junk? Self-Storage Investors Hope So," *Wall Street Journal,* December 21, 2018.

———, "As Crude Collapsed, Alaska Capitalized on the U.S. Housing Bust," *Wall Street Journal,* November 13, 2016.

## 20. MEET YOUR NEW LANDLORD

Matt Jarzemsky, Dana Mattioli, and Ryan Dezember, "Blackstone Group's Invitation Homes Files Confidentially for an IPO," *Wall Street Journal,* November 30, 2016.

**171 One of the big stories I had followed in the *Register*** Brendan Kirby, "Nine Face Criminal Charges in Alleged Gulf Shores Retirement Real Estate Fraud," *Press-Register,* April 24, 2011. Bruce Sims, "Real Estate Business Is About More Than Just Making a Sale," *Press-Register,* July 20, 2006.

**171 In a September 2011 auction** Kathy Jumper, "Huge Auction to Sell Condos, Homes on Gulf Coast," *Press-Register,* September 11, 2011.

**171 A few weeks later, Park National held another** Kathy Jumper, "Bank Sells $7 Million in Properties at Auction," *Press-Register,* October 19, 2011.

Ryan Dezember, "Bayou Seeks Light," *Press-Register,* March 7, 2010.

**172 Across the toll bridge from Bama Bayou** Kathy Jumper, "Bank-Owned Projects Wait for Buyers on Intracoastal Waterway," *Press-Register,* October 17, 2010.

**172 Those same investors paid $4.5 million** Kathy Jumper, "Bon Secour Village Bought by Point Clear Investors," *Press-Register,* April 24, 2011.

## 21. JOANIE

**179–180 Even Ben Bernanke, who was rolling in six-figure** Nick Timiraos, "Tight Credit? Why Ben Bernanke Couldn't Refinance His Mortgage," *Wall Street Journal,* October 2, 2014.

Ryan Dezember, "Big Landlords to Merge, Betting on Rising Rents," *Wall Street Journal,* September 21, 2015.

**180 In 2013, though, Blackstone and investment bankers** Al Yoon, "Blackstone Tries Bond Backed by Home-Rental Income," *Wall Street Journal,* October 31, 2013.

Ryan Dezember, "Wall Street as Landlord: Blackstone Going Public with a $10 Billion Bet on Foreclosed Homes," *Wall Street Journal,* December 6, 2016.

———, "A Onetime Housing Skeptic Plans $1 Billion Bet on Homes," *Wall Street Journal,* October 5, 2016.

———, "Blackstone Wins Fannie's Backing for Rental Home Debt," *Wall Street Journal,* January 24, 2017.

## 22. FOR SALE

**184 Phillips was offering preconstruction condo units** Marc D. Anderson, "New High-Rise Condos in Works in Gulf Shores and Orange Beach," *Press-Register,* June 13, 2014.

**184 With the blemishes gone from their credit reports** AnnaMaria Andriotis, Laura Kusisto, and Joe Light, "After Foreclosures, Home Buyers Are Back," *Wall Street Journal,* April 8, 2015.

## 23. WALKING AWAY

Ryan Dezember, "A Hedge Fund Makes Billions Off Americans' Underwater Mortgages," *Wall Street Journal,* December 25, 2018.

**194 He argued that lenders, the government, and other institutions** Brent T. White, "Underwater and Not Walking Away: Shame, Fear and the Social Management of the Housing Crisis," *Wake Forest Law Review,* vol. 45 (2010): 971–1023.

**194 White used an example from 2009** Brent T. White, "The Morality of Strategic Default," *UCLA Law Review Discourse* (2010): 155–64.

**194 In a 2010 paper** Brent T. White, "Take This House and Shove It: The Emotional Drivers of Strategic Default," *SMU Law Review,* vol. 63. (2010): 1279–1316.

**195 Other economic researchers who disagreed** Luigi Zingales, "The Menace of Strategic Default," *City Journal,* spring 2010.

**195 A group of them surveyed two thousand Americans** Luigi Guiso, Paola Sapienza, and Luigi Zingales, "Moral and Social Constraints of Default on Mortgages," Working Paper 15145, National Bureau of Economic Research, July 2009.

**196 In 2011, White, the University of Arizona professor** Brent T. White, *Underwater Home: What Should You Do If You Owe More on Your Home Than It's Worth* (Lexington, KY: self-published, 2010).

## 24. FROM THREE HOUSES TO FOUR

**201 A few years later, the National Bureau of Economic Research** Stefania Albanesi, Giacomo De Giorgi, and Jaromir Nosal, "Credit Growth and the Financial Crisis: A New Narrative," Working Papers 23740, National Bureau of Economic Research, August 2017.

**202 She was working on a follow-up to the 2017 paper** Stefania Albanesi, "Investors in the 2007–2009 Housing Crisis: An Anatomy," University of Pittsburgh, National Bureau of Economic Research, and Center for Economic and Policy Research, September 17, 2018.

**203 The surge of people going from two first mortgages to three** Stefania Albanesi and Domonkos F. Vamossy, "Predicting Consumer Default: A Deep Learning Approach," Working Papers 26165, National Bureau of Economic Research, August 20, 2019.

**204 "The great misnomer of the 2008 crisis"** Manuel Adelino, Antoinette Schoar, and Felipe Severino, "The Role of Housing and Mortgage Markets in the Financial Crisis," *Annual Review of Financial Economics* 10 (2018): 25–41.

## 25. COMPANY TOWN

Ryan Dezember and Laura Kusisto, "Meet Your New Landlord: Wall Street," *Wall Street Journal,* July 21, 2017.

Ryan Dezember, "How to Buy a House the Wall Street Way," *Wall Street Journal,* September 16, 2018.

——— and Laura Kusisto, "House Money: Wall Street Is Raising More Money Than Ever for Its Rental-Home Gambit," *Wall Street Journal,* July 9, 2018.

Ryan Dezember, "Blackstone, Starwood to Merge Rental-Home Businesses in Bet to Be America's Biggest Home Landlord," *Wall Street Journal,* August 6, 2018.

**214 Goldman Sachs analysts crunched the numbers** Arjun Menon, David J. Kostin, Ben Snider, Ryan Hammond, Cole Hunter, Nicholas Mulford, and Jamie Yang, "Wealth and Equity Flows: How the Top 1% of Households Compares with the Rest," Goldman Sachs, January 29, 2020.

Ryan Dezember, "Wall Street's Big Landlords Are So Hungry for Houses They're Building Them," *Wall Street Journal,* January 2, 2019.

## 26. CUT DOWN

**229 Alabama even got spill money** Mike Cason, "Alabama Lawmakers Prop Up Medicaid with Another Short-Term Fix," *Birmingham News,* September 9, 2016.

**229 renovate the gubernatorial beach mansion** Associated Press, "Alabama's Abandoned Governor's Mansion Getting Facelift from BP," AL.com, December 2, 2015.

**229 Condo developer Brett/Robinson coaxed** Hare Wynn Newell & Newton LLP, "Client Brett/Robinson Reaches Settlement with BP," news release, November 30, 2010.

**229 Larry Wireman, the rival developer** Kathy Jumper, "Orange Beach Developers Want BP Funds for Turquoise Condo Project," *Press-Register,* April 29, 2012.

## 27. EPILOGUE

Ryan Dezember, Laura Kusisto, and Shane Shifflett, "So You Make $100,000? It Still Might Not Be Enough to Buy a Home," *Wall Street Journal,* October 15, 2019.

Ryan Dezember, "Blackstone Moves Out of Rental-Home Wager with a Big Gain," *Wall Street Journal,* November 21, 2019.

**236 Between 1970 and 2010** Thomas Piketty and Gabriel Zucman, "Capital Is Back: Wealth-Income Ratios in Rich Countries 1700–2010," *Quarterly Journal of Economics* (2014): 1255–310.

**236 It was thanks to rising home prices** Moritz Kuhn, Moritz Schularick, and Olrike I. Steins, "Income and Wealth Inequality in America, 1949–2016."

**237 At about $47,000** John Burns and Chris Porter, *Big Shifts Ahead,* 57.

**237 Nearly one in five people born in the 1980s** Ibid., 199.

**237 More than twenty million of their homes** Issi Romem, "The Silver Tsunami: Which Areas Will Be Flooded with Homes Once Boomers Start Leaving Them?," *Zillow Research,* November 22, 2019, https://www.zillow.com/research/silver-tsunami-inventory-boomers-24933/?mod=article_inline.

# INDEX


ACLU. *See* American Civil Liberties Union
adjustable-rate mortgage, 98
affordability, 66
AIG. *See* American International Group
Alabama's Gulf Coast, 40–45, 83, 88
  beach reporter for, 52
  real estate on, 5, 33, 75–76
  sand flows on, 9
  Zoo, 52–54, 228
Alaska Permanent Fund, 164
Albanesi, Stefania, 200–204
algorithms, 211
Alinda Capital Partners, 80, 173
Alt-A loans, 31
American Civil Liberties Union (ACLU), 47
American Homes 4 Rent, 206–8, 220
  auction buyers for, 216
  Heck joining, 163, 168–71
  IPO offered for, 180
  rentals bought by, 177
  in Spring Hill, 215
American Hot LLC, 83, 107–9
American International Group (AIG), 38, 110, 115
American Roads, 173
Amherst Residential, 211–12
Anderson, Pam, 105–6
Andhurst Walk, 132
animal rescue groups, 128
apartment buildings, 44–45
arbitration proceedings, 99–100
artificial intelligence, 211
asking prices, 99
Atlanta, foreclosures in, 177–78
auctions, 142–43, 149, 168–70, 216
Audubon Place, 186–89, 219, 232
  description of, 69–70
  foreclosures in, 128, 148–49, 185, 202
  landlording in, 183–85

baby boomers, 37
Bair, Brian, 220
Baker, Alex, 38
balancers, 235–36
Baldridge, Kevin, 217–19
balloon-frame homes, 25
Bama Bayou, 131–32, 172–73
Bank of America, 114, 116, 178, 205
bankruptcies, 197
  American Roads, 173
  Bon Secour Village and, 119–21, 228
  Chapter 7 bankruptcy, 117–18, 193
  Chrysler, 169
  of condominiums, 120–21
  General Motors, 177
  from hedge funds, 102–3, 201
  Lehman Brothers, 115
  Phillips, R., and, 184
  Riverbrooke Capital Partners, 136–37
  Russo and, 231
  Villages of Creekstone, 132
Barrack, Tom, 169, 180, 208
Beach Club resort, 15, 18
beach highway, 56, 65
beach houses, 21, 45–46, 81–83, 88, 231
beach mouse, 41–42
Beach PAC, 47–48, 50–51
beach renourishment, 41
Bear Point, 67–68
Bear Stearns, 5, 102–3, 114, 201
Bella Luna, 97
Bernanke, Ben, 159, 179
Blackstone Group, 159–61, 174, 180, 220, 235
Bon Secour National Wildlife Refuge, 55
Bon Secour Village, 33–34, 66
  bankruptcy and, 119–21, 228
  condo towers in, 78
  partnership of, 120
bonds, 180–81, 192–94
borrowers, good-credit, 205
Brackin, Buddy, 109, 142
Brackin, Julian, 99
Brett, Gene, 133–34
Brett/Robinson, 134–35, 229
Brown, Jim, 81–84, 88–90, 110
  Federal indictment of, 85–87
  house built by, 107–8
  land deal with, 142
bubble, in housing costs, 74, 202–3
Buffett, Lucy, 147
Buffett, Warren, 169
bulk home buying, 170
burger joint, 47
Burns, John, 6, 216, 235–37
Burry, Michael, 158
Bush, George W., 62, 116
Butler, Steven, 91

Caribe Resort, 15–18, 21–22, 97, 122–23
Carlyle Group, 160
Carrey, Jim, 34

CDOs. *See* collateralized debt obligations
Cerberus Capital Management, 169
Chang, Oliver, 169
Chapter 7 bankruptcy, 117–18, 193
charter fishing, 78
Christian Family Association PAC, 47
Chrysler bankruptcy, 169
Citigroup, 116
Clark, Clifford Edward, Jr., 24
Clinton, Bill, 31
CMLTI 2006-NC2 security, 104–5, 113
collateralized debt obligations (CDOs), 102–5
colonial America, 25–26
Colonial Properties, 110, 119
Colonnades, 97
commissions, on real estate, 126
computer programs, 210–11
Concerned Citizens of Orange Beach Inc., 49–50
condominiums, 10–11, 40
  bankruptcies of, 120–21
  Beach Club prices of, 18
  in Bon Secour Village, 78
  flipping of, 21, 72, 79
  foreclosures influencing, 13–14
  James, T., taking deposits on, 78–79
  Lighthouse, 19, 96–97
  preconstruction sales of, 17, 20–21, 60–61
  real estate crash and, 124–25
  sales contracts for, 141
  Shallow, B., selling, 14–15, 63–64, 232–33
  stock prices compared to, 20
  subdivision development over for, 117–18
  Sunset Bay's auctioning off, 142–43
Connors, Cristie, 197
conservation, 62
conspiracy theories, 147
CoreLogic, 216
corporate buyout firm (KKR), 169
corruption charges, 87–88
Countrywide Financial, 71, 97–98, 114, 178
courthouse auctions, 149
credit default swaps, 103
credit scores, 202
credit-rating firms, 114
Cypress Village, 110–11

data science, 211
Davidson, Jerry, 36, 84, 86–87
debt, 7, 158, 171
debt-to-income ratio, 31
deed filings, 71
Deepwater Horizon oil spill, 144–46, 229
DeLawder, C. Daniel, 132

demand growth, 181
destruction, from hurricane, 54–55, 58
developers, litigious buyers and, 140
development projects, 77, 227
Dolphin Club, 17, 19, 72, 125
down payments, 28, 196
drug charges, 87
drug overdose, 129
DuBose, Kristi, 91
Dudley, William, 200

easy money, 21
ecology, 41
economy, 4–5, 177, 236
emergency management bunker, 54
Empire Group, 156
endangered species, 41
Engels, Friedrich, 26
English, Dewey, 43, 148, 230
Entera Technology, 209–11
Environmental Protection Agency (EPA), 146
Envision Gulf Shores, 123
EPA. *See* Environmental Protection Agency
equity, from homeownership, 126, 158, 214
eviction process, 218–19

Fannie Mae, 28, 114–15, 182
FBI. *See* Federal Bureau of Investigation
FDIC. *See* Federal Deposit Insurance Corporation
Federal Bureau of Investigation (FBI), 84–85
Federal Deposit Insurance Corporation (FDIC), 72–74
Federal Home Loan Mortgage Corporation (Freddie Mac), 30, 114–15, 182
Federal Housing Finance Agency, 182
federal indictments, 85–87
federal program, 150–51
financial documents, 71–72
Fir Tree, 191–93
first-lien mortgages, 201–2
First-time Homebuyer Affordability Act (1999), 30–31
Fish & Wildlife Service, 55, 77
fishing, for-hire crews, 146
fitness center, 139
Florida, 15–18, 33–34, 37–39, 120–21
Foley Beach Express toll bridge, 34–36, 172–73
Ford, Rich, 160
Foreclosure Generation, 6
foreclosures, 116
  in Atlanta, 177–78
  auctions of, 168–70
  in Audubon Place, 128, 148–49, 185, 202
  on Bama Bayou, 131

condominiums influenced by, 13–14
investments and, 203–4
in mortgage industry, 5
on oceanfront property, 118–19
in Phoenix, 157
rental properties from, 159
of San Carlos, 134–35
Shallow, B., selling, 14
short sales and, 169–70
subprime mortgages with, 200–201, 204–5
*Wall Street Journal* stories on, 184
Franklin, Benjamin, 25
Franklin, Josiah, 25
Freddie Mac. *See* Federal Home Loan Mortgage Corporation
Fulton Place, 132

Gaines, Chip, 226
Gaines, Joanna, 226
Geithner, Timothy, 104
General Motors, 208
Ginnie Mae. *See* Government National Mortgage Association
Golden West Financial, 115
Goldman Sachs, 116
Goodman, George Jerome Waldo, 72
Government National Mortgage Association (Ginnie Mae), 30
Gray, Jonathan, 160–61
Great Depression, 27
guilty verdicts, 90
Gulf Shores, 126–27, 144–46
Gulf Shores City Council, 123
Gulf World Marine Park, 37

Hall, Patti, 53
Hangout Music Festival, 145, 229
Heck, Ryan, 162–63, 168–71, 216
hedge funds, 102–3, 201
Heller, Jamie, 190
HELOCs. *See* home-equity lines of credit
highways, 28, 56, 65
Hilton Worldwide, 160
Holiday, Tracy, 128
Holk, Brett, 49–51
home construction, 25, 176
home loans, 97, 113, 158
home prices
demand growth influencing, 181
falling, 102, 196
increases in, 7–8, 32, 95–96, 131
mortgages and, 235
in Phoenix, 156
real estate agents influenced by, 183
rent increases and, 23–24
retirement funded from, 214–15
home-equity lines of credit (HELOCs), 73
homeowner's association, 187, 218–19

homeownership. *See also* houses; real estate property
boom in, 28
debt soaring in, 31
declining, 179, 213
equity from, 126, 158, 214
first home in, 4
government boosting, 30–31
home-price appreciation in, 7–8
housing market rates of, 72–73
investments in, 215
neighborhood association and, 173–74
normalization of, 27
price ranges in, 68
renting compared to, 213–15, 234–35
standard deductions influencing, 217
underwater mortgages in, 195–96
U.S. goal of, 24–25
views on, 26–27
wealth built through, 214, 236–37
Hoover, Herbert, 27
Horton, D. R., 162
hot-air balloons, 12
house flippers, 19–20, 104, 162–63, 220
households, lower-income, 205
house-hunting technology, 212–13
houses, 45, 156–57, 176–78
Audubon Place money lost on, 189
bubble costs of, 74, 202–3
bulk buying of, 170
Orange Beach costs of, 67
real estate agents hunt for, 70–71
repairs for, 186–88
housing market
Alabama's Gulf Coast collapse in, 5
crisis in, 7, 101, 200–201
economic disaster in, 4–5
homeownership rates in, 72–73
meltdown of, 123
price collapse of, 13–14
property value collapsed in, 4
Shallow, B., and stagnant, 227–28
speculative mania in, 72
in Spring Hill, 206–7
subprime mortgages in, 7, 101, 200–201
undercapitalized speculators in, 76
value lower in, 102
Hughes, B. Wayne, 163–65, 168, 180, 207
Hull, Bruce, 209
Hurricane Ivan, 52, 54–55, 58
Hurricane Katrina, 65, 134
hurricanes, in U.S., 76

Icahn, Carl, 160
income, wealth ratios to, 236

Industrial Revolution, 26
insurance costs, 76
interest-only mortgages, 73–74, 97–98
Interstate Land Sales Full Disclosure Act, 138
inventory control, 63
investments, 211–13
  first-lien mortgages and, 201–2
  foreclosures and, 203–4
  home density for, 170–71
  in homeownership, 215
  private-equity, 161, 181
  properties for, 6, 10
  in real estate, 81–82, 161
  second-lien mortgage bonds in, 192–93
  in toll roads, 35, 79
Invitation Homes, 157, 162, 170, 182, 213, 220
Island Tower, 18
*It's a Wonderful Life* (film), 28

Jacobs, Geoff, 156–57, 169, 227
James, Fob, 34
James, Tim, 38–39, 60–61, 67, 80
  condo deposits taken by, 78–79
  Foley Beach toll bridge and, 35–36
  sentencing speech of, 91
Joe Raley Builders, 36–37, 132, 172
JPMorgan Chase & Co, 103, 114

Kavana, Jordan, 212, 215
Kay, Martin, 210, 216
Kennon, Tony, 131
Kinloch Partners, 178
KKR (corporate buyout firm), 169
Kleros Real Estate CDO III, 105
Kuhn, Moritz, 236

land purchase, 118
landlords, 167, 183–85, 216
Leatherbury, Greg, 67
Lehman Brothers Holdings, 5, 115
Levin's Bend, 109
Levitt, William, 28
Lewis, Michael, 29
Lighthouse condominiums, 19, 96–97
loans
  Alt-A, 31
  home, 97, 113, 158
  NINA, 104
  piggyback, 73–74
  refinance, 32, 183
lower-income households, 205

Macquarie Group, 79–80
Mandalay Beach, 62, 118
Marchetti Constant, 28
margin calls, 102–3
Martinez, Ruben, 178–79
Marx, Karl, 26
material costs, 88
Mattei, Jim, 118, 228
McAleer, Mac, 39, 147
McCarron, Joe, 85
McLaughlin, Jeff, 195–96, 238–39

McLaughlin, Shannon, 195–96, 238–39
McNeilage, Bruce, 175–76
 houses sold by, 177–78
 *Mr. Bruce Needs His Money* made by, 221–23
 neighbors as leads to, 179
 promotional borrowing rates to, 212
 rental properties of, 179–80, 207–8, 224–25
 tenants of, 235
mega-developments, 49
Merrill Lynch, 5, 112, 114–16
middle-class, 181–82
Million Dollar Club, 17
Mobile Bay, 77
*Mobile Register*, 11
money
 borrowing, 180–81
 easy, 21
*The Money Game* (Goodman), 72
Moon, Jeff, 67, 198
Moore, Roy, 47–48
Morgan Stanley, 116, 157–59, 194
Mortgage Forgiveness Debt Relief Act (2007), 197
mortgage-backed securities, 30–32, 112–14
mortgage-interest tax deduction, 197–98
mortgages, 71–74, 170. *See also* subprime mortgages
 adjustable-rate, 98
 broker for, 184–85
 down payments on, 196
 first-lien, 201–2
 foreclosures in, 5
 home prices and, 235
 interest-only, 97–98
 Phoenix borrowers for, 155–56
 rates, 116
 refinancing in, 150–51
 rental properties compared to, 175–77
 renting instead of, 7
 savings and loan associations and, 29–30
 second, 191–92
 strategic default on, 197–98
 tax breaks from, 27
 underwater, 5, 98, 190–99
move-in-ready, 188
Mozilo, Angelo, 97–98
*Mr. Bruce Needs His Money* (promo show), 221–23
Mullen, Donald, 169, 181–82, 211

National Bureau of Economic Research, 201
National Partners in Homeownership, 31
National Rental Home Council, 216–19
National Shrimp Festival, 119
neighborhood association, 173–74, 218
neighbors, as leads, 179
Nelson, Eric, 185, 187–88, 231
newspaper reporters, 91–92

newspapers, 127, 130, 148, 166
NINA loans, 104
Nugent, Don, 206–7

Obama, Barack, 130
oceanfront property, 118–19
Offerpad, 216, 220–21
oil revenue, 164
oil spill, 144–46, 229
O'Neal, Stan, 112
Ono Island, 141
open house, 134
Opendoor, 216, 220
opioids, 128
Orange Beach, 10, 34–35, 61–63, 118
  beach mice of, 41–42
  City Council meeting of, 87
  housing costs in, 67
  insurance costs in, 76
  mansion vanished on, 56
  oil-absorbent boom in, 146
  properties in, 85
  real estate investments in, 81–82
  Riverwalk, 36–37, 77
  sewer system of, 4
  shortfall faced by, 126
  waterfront condos on, 55
  Young, C., in, 57
  Zislin building restaurants in, 229

PAC. *See* political action committees
Park National, 108–9, 116, 171–72
Parton, Dolly, 141
Paulson, John, 158
Perdido Key, 44–45, 57, 63, 77, 96–97
Perdido Pass, 44–45, 118, 126, 134, 229
personal savings, 214
Phillips, Rick, 19, 61–62, 184, 229
  Chapter 7 bankruptcy of, 117–18
  Lighthouse units and, 97
  property taxes influenced by, 76
  San Carlos and, 98
Phillips, Willard, 26–27
Phoenix, AZ, 155–57, 221
Phoenix West II, 133–34, 229
piggyback loans, 73–74
Piketty, Thomas, 236
Pilot Town, 77
Pleasure Island, 10, 134
political action committees (PAC), 47–48, 50–51
preconstruction sales, 17–21, 60–61, 172, 184
predictive models, 211
prices. *See also* home prices
  asking, 99
  collapse in, 13–14
  ranges in, 68
  stock, 7–8, 20
prison time, 91, 230–31
private-equity investments, 161, 181
Progress Residential, 181, 220

promotional borrowing rates, 212
property investors, 6
property taxes, 76
property value, 4
public beach access, 46
Public Storage, 163
purchase contracts, 17, 138–40
purchase price, of Vision Bank, 172

Quonset huts, 27

Racketeer Influenced and Corrupt Organizations Act, 142
Raley, Scott, 37, 172
Ranieri, Lewis, 29–30, 32, 105, 169
real estate agents, 105
  home prices influencing, 183
  house hunt with, 70–71
  oil spill influencing, 229
  Shallow, B., as top-selling, 124
real estate crash, 124–25, 130, 166, 204
real estate property
  Alabama's Gulf Coast, 5, 33, 75–76
  Blackstone Group investing in, 159–60
  commissions on, 126
  investment business in, 161
  Orange Beach investments in, 81–82
  prices rising of, 19
  selling of, 16–17
  Shallow, B., selling, 16, 75
  speculation in, 25, 138, 155
  waterfront, 55
Realty, Joan T., 61
redevelopment pact, 137
redlining, 28
refinance loans, 32, 183
refinancing, 150–51
Regions bank, 71, 134, 184, 191
*Register,* 55, 127, 184, 202, 230
  English editor of, 43
  full-page ad in, 50
  layoffs at, 147
  as reporter for, 49
regulatory response, 204
RE/MAX franchise, 15–16, 63, 124
rental properties, 157, 167, 182
  from foreclosures, 159
  home prices and increases in, 23–24
  Kay's software scanning, 210–11
  of McNeilage, 179–80, 207–8, 224–25
  mortgage-interest tax deduction and, 197–98
  mortgages compared to, 175–77
rental-home business, 6
rent-backed bonds, 180–81
rentership society, 158
"A Rentership Society" (report), 157
renting
  costs of, 209
  homeownership compared to, 213–15, 234–35

mortgages changing to, 7
in Spring Hill, 209
upmarket, 235
for well-to-do, 235
repossessed houses, 156–57
residential construction, 28
retirement, 214–15
retirement homes, 187
rezoning request, 90
Ricardo, David, 236
RICO Act, 142
Riley, Bob, 52
Riverbrooke Capital Partners, 136–37
road construction, 35
Romem, Issi, 237
Roosevelt, Franklin D., 27
Russo, Steve, 49–51, 61, 230–31
arrest of, 86
Brown known by, 81–82
corruption charges against, 87–88
drug charges against, 87
FBI investigating, 84–85
Federal indictment of, 85–87
guilty verdict against, 90
as mayor, 36
sentencing defense of, 91

sales agents, 11–12, 19
sales contracts, 141
Salomon Brothers, 29–30
San Carlos, 98–100, 134–35
Sandler, Herb, 115
Sandler, Marion, 115
Sandy Cove, 58
Sapphire Beach, 136–37
savings and loan associations, 13, 21, 29–30
Schoar, Antoinette, 205
Schularick, Moritz, 236
Schwarzman, Stephen, 161, 174
SE Properties Holdings, 172, 231
sea turtles, 42
second mortgages, 191–92
second-lien mortgage bonds, 192–93
securities, 103–4
securities fraud investigators, 147
self-storage industry, 163
shale drilling, 167
Shallow, Bob, 10–13, 17–20, 57–59
in Alabama's Gulf Shore, 40–41
Beach Club resort units sold by, 15
Beach PAC donation of, 48
burger joint threat from, 47
Caribe Resort units sold by, 15–16
condominiums sold by, 14–15, 63–64, 232–33
development projects of, 227
foreclosures sold by, 14
inventory control by, 63
real estate crash foresight of, 124–25
real estate sold by, 16, 75
real estate stagnant and, 227–28

Shallow (*continued*)
San Carlos foreclosures with, 134–35
Sunset Bay condo's bought by, 142–43
as top-selling agent, 124
Zislin meeting with, 123–24
Shallow, Susan, 12, 57
short sales, 169–70, 197
Singelyn, David, 164, 208, 217, 219
Sizemore, Daniel, 48, 89, 109, 141–42
skyscraper proposal, 45
songbirds, 42
South Florida, 203
special zoning, 45–46
speculation, in real estate, 25, 72, 76, 138, 155
Spring Hill
American Homes in, 215
economy in, 177
General Motors locating to, 208
houses built in, 176
housing market in, 206–7
renters in, 209
subdivisions in, 224–25
standard deductions, 217
Starck, Philippe, 122
Starwood Waypoint Homes, 180, 208, 213
Steins, Ulrike I., 236
Sternlicht, Barry, 169, 180, 208
stock prices, 7–8, 20
strategic default, 194–95, 197–98
student debt, 7, 158
subdivisions, 28, 117–18, 132
subprime mortgages, 31, 158–59
with foreclosures, 200–201, 204–5
in housing crisis, 7, 101, 200–201
securities backed by, 103–4
suburban communities, 25–26
Sunset Bay, 140–43
Super Tuesday, 169
Sutley, Larry, 83, 85, 90–91, 231
Syncora Guarantee, 173

Tanner, Dallas, 159, 161, 213, 217, 235
TARP. *See* Troubled Asset Relief Program
tax breaks, 27
tax returns, 86
Ten Commandments monument, 48
Thain, John, 112, 114, 116, 205
Tocqueville, Alexis de, 24–25
toll roads, 25, 34–36, 79
tourism, 145
Treehouse Group, 159–62
Tricon Capital Group, 212, 217–18
Troubled Asset Relief Program (TARP), 116
*The Truman Show* (film), 34
turnpikes, 79
Turquoise Place, 22, 45, 230
burger joint next to, 47
buyer purchase contracts on, 138–39

Caribe owners buying in, 122–23
city council vote on, 46–47
grievances against, 138–39
sales brochure deviations of, 137–38
splendor of, 122
Wireman's troubles in, 121–22, 139–40

undercapitalized speculators, 76
underwater mortgages, 5, 98, 190–99
underwriting, mortgage, 73–74
unemployment, 130
United States (U.S.), 24–26, 76
upmarket renters, 235
U.S. *See* United States

Villages of Creekstone, 132, 137
Vision Bank, 131–32, 141, 171–72
Volcker, Paul, 29

Wachovia, 115, 135
Waldie, Aaron, 213
walking away, 155, 191–92, 194–99
Wall, Ken, 83, 89–91, 110
*The Wall Street Journal*, 190, 207–8, 215
Bama Bayou photos for, 173
foreclosure stories in, 184
job offer at, 149–50
New York City office of, 171, 174
Water Club, 83, 90–91
water parks, 77
waterfront properties, 55, 96
Watson, Gregor, 169–70, 208
wealth, 214, 236–37
Webb, Del, 28
wetlands, 41
White, Brent, 193–97
Whitman, Walt, 26, 215
Willoughby, Jay, 164–65
Wireman, Larry, 15, 45–51, 229–30
Caribe Resort of, 21–22, 97
indictment mentioning, 86–87
property taxes influenced by, 76
Turquoise Place troubles of, 121–22, 139–40
Wojtowicz, Al, 198–99
Wolf Bay lots, 82, 85

Young, Cecil, 57
Young, Dean, 47–51, 131–32

Zachary, Chris, 177, 222
Zell, Sam, 160
Zillow Group, 220
Zislin, Shaul, 48, 58–59, 123–24, 145, 229
Zucman, Gabriel, 236